surfaced.
the formation of twisted structures

the work of SYSTEMarchitects

The City College of New York

This book is made partially possible by the generous funding from The City College of New York, Bernard and Anne Spitzer School of Architecture

surfaced.
the formation of twisted structures

the work of SYSTEMarchitects

contributions by
Chee Pearlman
Carolina Miranda
Paul Chatterton

edited by
Oscar Riera Ojeda

OSCAR RIERA OJEDA
PUBLISHERS

contents

acknowledgements.

This book looks particularly at the design activities of SYSTEM over the past six years, none of which would have been possible without the 12 years that came before. We have limited the projects of those years to BURST*003 and 008, Wellfleet, and fulcrumSTAIR in an attempt to contextualise the ideas that influence the current activities.

This book would not have been possible without the support and counsel of the dean of architecture of the great City College of New York, George Ranalli, who gave me the idea for the book, the space to write it, and the belief that I could pull it off.

Making the book took enormous effort for many. It would not have happened without the guidance, wordsmith skills, and countless hours of my wife, Belinda Luscombe. Not only did she agree to upend our family schedule but she organised the space we needed to think clearly about the book. I must thank our children Spike and Ginger for their patience while our minds were elsewhere.

Jamie Edindjiklian, Alanna Lauter, Florian Gjoka, Nick Napoli, Helen Levin, and Robert Baker from SYSTEM's office were invaluable and I'm profoundly grateful to them.

I thank the interviewers who engaged with the work during their busy schedules, Vladimir Belogolovsky for the idea, the design guru Chee Pearlman and journalist Carolina Miranda, and the environmental activist Paul Chatterton.

The work at SYSTEM is always a labor of love and devotion and the hours people have put in reflect that. Douglas Gauthier and I worked side by side for many hard but fun years. Henry Grosman devoted years of his life to the making of the BURST* projects, and Chris Knapp, Sarkis Arakelyan, Barry Bergdoll, Peter Christensen, Cristobal Correa, Katherine Keltner, and John Fuller gave us such important support. I remain deeply indebted to Stacey Greenwald and Martin Cook, true friends who have helped us out at key moments. Robert Baker (again), Charles Kwan, and Jesse Lee Wilson have given their time, energy, and talent in a way that is humbling and inspiring.

My colleague at the Mercer Street studio, Maggie Mahboubian told me early on in the practice to find great makers and design for them. The great makers we have found and continue to design for include Sue Wantz at Paul C. Steck, Armando Saca at Millennium Steel, Corey Akers at Precision Metals, Laserfab, Perry Randazzo, and Art Kozyr, Bill Young, Robert Bridges at eFab Local, and the guys on site with the awe-inspiring hands: Tommy Kozlowski and Richard Wilson.

Supportive clients are the lifeblood of any architecture practice, most crucially because they engage with the thinking of the projects and improve them. Without the faith and loyalty of clients, all buildings are just dreams. I am honoured to have worked with Andrew Katay and Catriona Grant, Douglas and Michelle Monticciolo, Caroline McFadden, Jeff and Susan Rubenstein, Michel Gainet, Dalton Conley, Natalie Jeremijenko, Milind Sojwal and All Angels Church, Michelle deMilly and Andy Breslau, Ross Whelan and Mark Cooper. They have each taught me so much.

Jeremy Edmiston
SYSTEMarchitects

preface.

Things were pretty much at a fever pitch in the last few weeks before the opening of the Home Delivery Exhibition at New York City's Museum of Modern Art (MoMA). Douglas Gauthier and I hadn't slept much and neither had the dedicated students and workers who were putting together BURST*008, a full scale home built in MoMA's parking lot, and our contribution to this groundbreaking exhibition. Right at one particularly stressful point (there were many, as can be imagined when building a house in one of the prime tourist destinations of Midtown Manhattan), Max Risselada a European curator helping out at MoMA came up to us and said he found it remarkable how the project looked beautiful in all its phases of construction. We'd been so busy that we hadn't really noticed, but his kind remark stopped me. It made me realise that not only were we constructing a building we'd designed, but it was being built using a method of construction we had designed as well.

Design and construction are not a linear process; the design of the construction method has an influence on the design of the project. Many of the details of a project come from an idea for how to construct something, and many of the ideas about how to construct come from the intentions of a project. I wanted to articulate this in a book, and we thought it would be helpful if we organised the projects by the kinds of drawings and models we make to work through the ideas of a project. This book looks at a number of works that have come through the studio in the past six years as well as two important precedents from when I was working with a former partner, Douglas Gauthier: a guest house at Wellfleet, Massachusetts, and the BURST* projects in North Haven, Australia, and at MoMA.

Answering the right question.

A conversation with Chee Pearlman

What was the problem you were asked to solve with the aA SHELTER?

This space is in the bottom of a church, and the church occupies one of the buildings that was originally a parish house. And someone came to me and said, 'which colour linoleum should we choose when we redo the floor?' I didn't want to be involved in linoleum choosing but they kept pursuing me. So I offered them a deal that we would donate our time for something bigger, but we wouldn't go to meetings and they would have to build whatever we came up with if it came under budget. And I thought they wouldn't take that deal, but they did.

So in other words you were asked the wrong question about the linoleum, but you gave the right answer: 'we'll make something that you maybe didn't realise you would really benefit from?'

Because I felt that we could talk to the folk who used the space, who used the shelter, used the church.

When you were presented with this, how familiar with the end-user were you, and what did you learn about them?

I knew of the activities that happened in the space because I'd helped out with the meals that were served to the homeless every week. I knew that they slept in the space at least one night a week, sometimes more. I knew that there were medical services, psychiatric services, social services that were run out of that space.

But I didn't really know the people who were using it at the time. So we started talking and interviewing, and watching what was going on. The space has been kind of a multi-purpose space. All sorts of groups use it.

So you had to make sure everyone could use it; it has multiple programmes.

It does. And the church members who are paying for it have a view of what the space is, which is quite different from how it's used perhaps in the evening or during the meals.

But what we felt was that you can't really design a multi-purpose space unless you have something quite specific that you want to achieve. We felt that the shelter aspect of the space was the most fundamental, and that it tied the building to kind of a network of homeless services in the city. The church's other activities are more insular.

There's a regular constituency that shows up there for meals, for a place to sleep. I would imagine that design wasn't their top priority in terms of what they needed to receive. How did you feel design could help them?

In my experience working with the meals, and serving them, what's really striking to me is that, like all people, they don't only have physical needs, they have preferences, they have opinions. I'm not sure architecture is about meeting physical needs. It's perhaps best meeting the needs of the mind, of imagination, of hope. We'd done some work earlier in the practice with emergency housing. You know, it struck me that architects as a whole are probably terrible at providing emergency housing; there are engineers and builders that do that stuff really fast, and well.

Architecture is doing something else. It's offering a culture to that solution, to that issue of emergency housing after a natural crisis. It's thinking about the terrain in that country that is still intact, it's thinking about the whole landscape and what it might contribute to the environment in the long term.

Chee Pearlman is the director of the editorial and design consultancy Chee Company, the curator of the Curry Stone Design Prize and the former editor in chief of *I.D. Magazine*.

And to have some insight into the cultural needs and the traditions of the people who might be in that condition. A need for emergency housing can happen to anyone, but you don't just necessarily throw all into the same generic kind of situation.

Right. I think needs can also be emotional, and cultural, and of the mind. It's not just a bench to sit on. And engaging those ideas is more specific to a place, a moment, an action, perhaps even a material.

This client came and said, 'should we have pink or blue linoleum,' and you said, 'I think we want to take this a lot further. But you have to let me solve this problem the way I want to'. Typically that's where designers and architects can end up doing their best work—with the constraints being defined only by the end-user.

Right. I enjoyed the very direct relationship with the end-user. And taking that idea back into the studio, and thinking about it in that way. I asked for a budget and we took the budget quite seriously. We'd just finished the MoMA show, and what I noticed about that process was that those who donate their time or material or money are really invested in the project. You're not just paying them for something, they're giving it. So they take a lot more care, and they pay a lot more attention. And that's really helpful when you're trying to do something quite particular. A lot of people helped out, a lot of the homeless community came and helped us on the construction as well as regular people from the church.

In a way this really was a design-build community project. It sounds like you went far beyond being the architect here, you were also the driver of the vision, and of making it viable. They didn't just hand you a blank check.

I think all designers do that extra. If anything is to be produced, then somebody has to fill all of those roles.

What is the concept here, what's the over-arching design and aesthetic?

Broadly, the idea is that there's a flow to the way we observe the homeless navigate the city. They find the leftover spaces, they find alternate routes through the city, they aren't as wedded to the avenues and streets as we, the non-homeless, may be. We have a catalogue of known addresses that we navigate the city by. There's the addresses for the kids' schools, there's home, there's the office, university. These are coordinates that we schedule our lives around, a matrix that we build our lives on. And it seems that the homeless have a more fluid matrix. We wanted to express that in the space. So you couldn't use the grid. Instead, the idea became a continuous flowing three-dimensional ordering system.

What does that mean?

The space is three-dimensional and you have to make interventions into this space for it to work, so those interventions have a structure, they have coordinates, they have measurements. For this project, the measuring system wanted to be other than a grid or a vertical measurement or a horizontal measurement or an 'x-y-z'. So it became this system of lines, and the lines track through the floor and up the wall that we have to put in, and on to the ceiling. And these lines start at 90 degrees to the wall and parallel with each other at the entrance, and that's the last time they ever are.

This free, open-flowing interior, not made with right angles, not built, necessarily on math and geometries, do you think that gives comfort to people who also live in that same construct?

The hope is that it makes a connection. And the hope is that it provided a way for them to connect with the rest of the church.

What do you remember about when it was first revealed and opened?

I remember that the homeless guys who were helping out were very intrigued by carrying in these really strangely shaped pieces that were going to be part of the space. And that set a huge buzz through the space. And of course they thought it was fantastic because it was painted and clean. If we provide something that the church thinks is fantastic, they have more desire to keep it clean and tidy, and that did happen.

That's an interesting point because you've given them a sense of dignity by saying, you deserve a place that's clean and well lit, and even beyond that, has an an architectural higher communication than what you might find in an institution. I think it is an interesting response from people to start to respect the place, and perhaps even themselves because this dignity has been kind of bestowed on them.

You see that in the guys who run the front door of the church, who have come through the programes and now have a job there. They're the boss of the space, and keep these rules about how the panels we installed open and close. And there's a pride to that, and I love that. They sort of take that ownership.

I'd say that there's a large percentage of the folk who use the space who are really just there to get off the street, and need a place, and that's what the space is for. But the space is part of some folks' lives who've been going there for decades, and they hang out, and they want to know what the lines are what the numbers mean what the surface is about. To this day, we get questions about that.

How do you answer them?

I'm reluctant to say much about it because I think it's for them to invent. We do what we do, and then it has to be occupied by them, not us.

Exactly. You're not imposing that narrative on them. Let's talk a little bit about some of the functional uses, and some of the ways in which you invented storage and ways for the room to be multipurpose, for it to transform.

It's basically a large room with very, very little natural light, and it needs a big cupboard for tables and chairs and stuff that is used in the room. It seemed to us that the active part of the scheduled use of the room is the closet. All these guys come down from church and they have to pull out the tables and set them up, and get all the chairs—there's this kind of ritual, to setting up the meal, and then packing the meal away.

So we sort of made an event of that setting up and putting away. The wall that becomes the closet is up to 18 inches thick, freestanding, and pivots. Each of these panels is 600 to 1,000 lbs, and there are several locked positions, so there's a physical play that happens around it. It was quite tricky to plan spatially because of the layout of the windows and doors and exits. So the wall had to do some sort of curvature and we took that as an opportunity to create a kind of contoured surface.

Do you find people touching it and wanting to explore it?

Sure, sure, particularly kids. They jump all over it, which is fun. And I always enjoy seeing people kind of leaning up against it, trying to prop themselves up. You know, people tend to congregate around it a little bit.

I can imagine this was one of the more rewarding kinds of projects in that it's not expected that any real design, or big-thinking design would appear in a space that is used in such a practical way. Perhaps the users are not typically invited into a place that has an elevated design sensibility.

I also think the churchgoers with homes have no advantage when they go into that space because it's not something they've ever experienced before either. It's highly designed but it's not polished, it's not orthogonal, it's not about a particular finish or sensibility. It throws them. I think that's the really interesting part, it doesn't have a hierarchy, it's not this wonderful space which was provided and funded by and only enjoyed by rich folk going to church.

They maybe have a bigger problem with it than the street folk, who come in for shelter.

I'm just curious to think about this as a strategy —an architect going far beyond the boundaries of his or her scope to realise something that was not considered even feasible. I think this is becoming an interesting new role for the architect: not to just wait for permission from a client, but to get ahead of that and to take a vision and figure out how it can be realised.

When you've invested so much time and so much of your life into thinking about the environment, the built environment, the places we inhabit, why wait for the money to come before you start that engagement? A huge tradition of designers and architects is making drawings of dreams. That's our role, right? To show what could be possible and find a way of working on it. Certainly, it's a more active engagement with the world, to become part of the discussion of what we actually should be doing.

Form isn't the only parameter.
An interview with Carolina Miranda

How do you approach interiors in buildings that come from different eras of history? How much do you want to respect them?

As a place to build, the city is already occupied. And very few layers get completely erased over time. Some of the older ideas and influences start to diminish, but they're always there. So the site is always a highly layered, textural place. And there's a freedom in that because you're inserting a contemporary layer. We've come to realise it works better if our interventions touch the existing infrastructure quite lightly. So they become not free-standing, but connected at specific points. Another tactic we use with existing spaces is to pare them back, almost trying to reveal some of their hidden layers, by almost scraping them.

You have worked quite a bit in New York City, is there an era of architecture that you find particularly interesting to penetrate and adapt?

Not at all: it's all architecture. It's always interesting to see how different minds have approached a particular space and a particular project. So, for example, Pied-à-Terre was originally a commercial building. It was the building where the Manhattan Project was housed in the Second World War. But it was renovated by a developer who was only interested in the picture that he could sell. The floor was literally half an inch thick, but it looked like an old wooden floor. The client said, 'I can't live here. It has no individual character.' And I think what he meant by that was it hadn't been studied in a way.

You've worked a lot with plywood, which is not a material that a lot of people use to create an interior. Why?

I think it's fascinating how designers have found plywood to be a material that they can experiment with; Buckminster Fuller, Charles and Ray Eames, and Harry Bertoia all messed with plywood, because it's inexpensive and seems to do a lot. It's a board, so you can think of it as a flat sheet material. It's very strong structurally, strong in different ways.

In your work you've also found a way of making it kind of space age. You're taking this material that is so common and you're making it feel a little *2001: Space Odyssey.*

We're highly invested in geometrically complex forms, but the form isn't the only parameter. When you build a complex shape or a form, the form becomes subdivided into lots of elements. And those subdivisions give you an opportunity to create a pattern over the surface; these kind of secondary lines that help you see and help you define what that shape is. And then the pattern of the plywood adds another surface, another texture. And that patterning is just quite unpredictable, it adds to the instability of the form in a way.

Has it been a challenge to convince clients that plywood is a viable construction and interior material?

Some people have actually asked us for plywood. The clients for the 2E project were very interested in that kind of mid-century wood, so they wanted this kind of interior. It's also a very warm colour, the pine that we've used. Also, I like the idea that you can just hammer into it anywhere so that the life that comes into the space once we, the architects, leave, adds a whole other layer and texture.

Two of your early plywood projects were 2N and 2E: the boats. In what context were these inserted? How did you arrive at this design concept specifically for those spaces?

These two projects were neighbouring apartments in a 1927 light manufacturing building. They have 12-foot ceilings made from steel and concrete. And families live there. They like the idea of open loft living, but the kids need rooms and those rooms need windows. The spaces were quite narrow and we

Carolina Miranda is the editor of the Culture: High & Low blog at the *Los Angeles Times*. She has also written for *Time*, *ARTnews*, *Art in America*, *Fast Company*, *NPR's All Things Considered* and *PRI's Studio 360*.

had to fit two bedrooms in. So we ended up with a division between the spaces that was the boat.

The boat conceals—or reveals, whichever way you look at it—a mezzanine space. We used the height to give the bedroom a little more floor area. So either the kids throw all their junk in the mezzanine or sleep up there, or use it as a play space. And it has transformed as the kids have aged, and they use it in different ways.

So out of a single space, you're able to create two layers of space that people can use in different ways. But how did you arrive at the boat shape?

The wall comes to a vertical edge where the window is, and as you move away from the window, the mezzanine emerges, to maximise the light and the air and then at the back of the room, you have the full mezzanine. The form is really about negotiating these elements in a smooth surface, bringing together the folds and the curves and the twists. Being a fairly small space, that geometry gets quite complex. That's where we had to test and play with the plywood to see whether we could bend it to the degree that we wanted to.

As it turned out to be a boat shape, we had to investigate how they built boats to see whether we could actually put this thing together. We had to test how much we could twist the plywood. We ended up writing a computer script that etched the back of the plywood so that it would bend for us in the way that we wanted to make those forms.

What aspect of it has inspired some of your work since?

Well, we used those projects to figure out a couple of things: the degree to which a curved surface works within a space. We've always felt that when you start to curve or fold the surface, you're introducing a very foreign element into the life of a place. And it can very quickly get too heavy. With the boats, it was important that you could read the form, that you could see the lines through it. It wasn't just some bizarre folly. And then of course we developed a more sophisticated kit of parts.

Those projects had to be built with two weeks of construction for them to be affordable. So to build that complex of a geometry, the original kit of parts that we developed for BURST* had to become very sophisticated with multiple pieces that would hold the kind of curved surfaces.

What kind of existing architecture were you dealing with in Pied-à-Terre? Did you have to completely redo the interior?

It was an interesting proposition; the architecture is almost invisible in the plan, but the space is just radically different. We put a steel scrim on the ceiling to hide the cheap lights. And rather than use those tiny holes so you get an even light, we perforated with much larger holes in a pattern that changes based on where the windows are. So the windows bring in natural light and the light of the city at night. And as you move back into the room, the holes kind of begin to open up.

And they cast these shadows over the walls and over the floor that make it almost like the dappled light through the forest, these shadows of high light and low light. The client loved the red that he saw in Japanese temples, so we had a friend take a scraping off some temples in Japan and send it over to us. We tried to match that red within the lip-like curved bookcase in the entrance space. It was an interesting experience to work with that colour and the surface of our form.

I think the success of Pied a Terre has to do with the subtlety of that lip-like form. It's quite the opposite of the boats. It is probably the most complex form that we've made, but it's also quite subtle. So when you stand next to it, when you're up against it, it's moving towards you and moving away from you. But it's doing it in a way that you can feel, that you can touch, that feels modeled to the scale of who we are, I think.

The Pied-à-Terre had a metal ceiling. So how does that compare to 3N, which has a metal screen?

The screen in 3N has to do with privacy and translucency. You have a big loft space with a moving screen that separates a guest bedroom or an office from the main space. The screen opens up if you want a large entertaining space, and it closes off if you need privacy. When it's closed, it's all about the suggestion of something beyond. And that beyond is framed by the pattern in the surface, which is again quite active and based on where the windows are. So there's this kind of pull towards the window of that pattern that's the digital invention that we're able to laser cut.

So what exactly inspires a pattern such as this? These are geometric shapes I don't think I can even describe.

It's sheet metal that's laser cut, and then formed over structural ribs that hold the geometry. The folded and twisted surface is welded to these ribs, and the perforations in the metal are also notched out of the ribs so each hole is almost like a three-dimensional form. It's in the negative as it's cut out of the material. Again it's that idea that the connection point to the existing structure is quite minimal, and then the intervention is quite complex and intricate.

Also, I think for us the grid is toxic or at least very static. There's something that feels false about the grid, as if everything is that determined, is that well understood. These patterns have a very, very strict order. But the ordering is based on another set of values than those you would find in the grid.

When I saw it, I almost got this sense of a fabric being pulled and it's being pulled tighter in some places than in others.

It's a pattern that I guess has a life to it. It has a direction. It's suggesting things are moving. It's suggesting that your eye has to move or your body has to move.

There's slackness, and there's tautness.

Right. Which to us rings more true to the way that we are and the way we live. You know, we are attracted to things or we're not attracted to things. It's not so absolute. And so that tension of becoming tighter or becoming looser feels to us like a more necessary way to order a space or describe a space, or write into a space. Forces like natural light on the windows give a direction to the pattern. Elements like where the door is, where the bathrooms are, they also have a pull on the pattern. And so those kind of tensions within the space shape the type of translucency. They shape the privacy between the a two rooms. And then of course those panels move, so you can mess it up. You can create your own pattern. You can apply your own force on it to change it up.

You have the texture of the pattern shifts over the panels, but why the physical texture of the fold in the metal plate?

What that does is bounce the light off the surface of the screen differently. So if it were vertical you would have the light maybe at the top that gradually dapples to the bottom. But with folds, you get one surface that's reflecting the light and another surface that's in the shade. So that wall has a number of readings to it. And one of those tensions points in the pattern occurs right around a fold.

And 3N also has a plywood screen?

The plywood screen is in the master bedroom. So it's a very, very warm, lush, tactile screen. You just want to go up and touch it and rub it when you see it. And we kept to the plywood and we oiled it. It conceals his walk-in closet and his bathroom.

We tried to reinforce the structural grid and keep the tough bones of the loft. The screens allow the client to occupy it as a private space.

You've done a lot of work in plywood and sheet metal. Is there anything else you're looking at?

What we've discovered is that the surface of architecture is fundamental to the way people perceive the space and the way people feel in the space. I love the abstract nature of movement within a space and the form within the space. But until that form has a materiality to it, has a texture, I'm not sure you feel it.

We're always very interested in finding a way for the material to become part of the forms we use. So, whether or not you even see the form or understand it, there's a connection and the connection comes through the surface of the material.

Recently, we've found it really exciting to work with brick because it lends itself to the shapes of the geometries we're using. We have to reinvent the way that we build it, and that's been exciting to work with, too.

In terms of its shape, or how it's used?

It's really about finding a way to design something that gives bricklayers the ability to lay these shapes.

So the design isn't just the surface or the object, but it's also about how you make it. Part of the design is giving a set of instructions for the production of that design. So we came up with this digitally fabricated, full-size permanent template that the bricklayers use and just follow. They don't have to measure, they don't have to cut, they just have to lay their bricks. And it's interesting to find ways of making these micro spaces within a larger space that's used for the domestic activities: the place where you pull up a chair, open a book and read with the sunlight coming on you. Those kind of moments of domesticity are written into the shape of the architecture and the materiality of the architecture. Also, when we're thinking about materials now, we're thinking about the whole cycle of the material: how it's made, where it comes from, how it's reused, how long it lasts, the energy package of the material.

And how it will decay...

Yeah, exactly. Which is part of that experience of the surface. That's very important to us as we work and live in these environments. At the moment, we're into brick and stainless steel.

When we think about where our materials come from and the impact they have, the brick is actually quite an ingenious invention. Are you trying to give it new relevancy by twisting it?

Building technology is not as intuitive as we like to think. When we design something, it may be five years before it's built, and then it will be used hopefully for another 20 years . So it's in the future. A future that deals with the changing character of energy usage and energy production. And that takes you to unpredictable places like old-school masonry. Who knew that would be one of the most useful materials to think about future building?

All of these ideas aren't coming from nostalgia for an older time, but they're coming from a place of research into the longevity of the material, the amount, and the type of energy you need for the production of the material. So the natural gas fired kiln starts to look pretty good after a while when you look at the life cycle and the energy production of something. In our building we can achieve incredible insulation, noise reduction, waterproofing just from using this material.

But I think it means nothing unless you're able to make a contemporary connection with the cultural values.

A hierarchy of surfaces.

A conversation with Paul Chatterton

One of the key questions we environmental advocates have is how do we look after our land, wherever it is. But also how do we respect each other as cultures across that land? And how do we have an economy that does both? So how do you actually make good intentions work in reality, in a very different world to the one that most climate or environment bureaucrats are used to?

It's exactly the same challenge for you with your school in Kokoda: spatially, you're bringing a whole set of ideas that are very foreign to the New Guineans. And they have a very complex set of knowledge and understanding and skills for managing their environment spatially as well. How do you constructively put those together? How did you run that dialogue?

We're very lucky that there was a local family, the head of a tribe who really buys into this idea of high school education. The village elders see that there are a number of opportunities for primary school, and the kids learn to read and write and speak English up to a particular level, but that level isn't high enough for them to be useful in Western culture. So it actually creates problems because these kids are not happy going back to live village life and they have no place in the city. And they see all of this mining coming into the country and they feel powerless to engage with it. And so the idea behind high school education is that more of their kids get into college and can be more actively part of the Western interests.

I've seen just how much difference a primary school can make in a set of villages. We sponsor six primary schools, have been receiving reports and the difference that made in just a couple of years was amazing. But secondary school is just orders of magnitude more powerful.

I lived in New Guinea for six years, and went back and forth for about 15 years before that. And your school has a remarkable feel for the layout of the village. The way put that school together looks very much like the way a village is organised, a set of huts that individual families would have within a larger village structure.

One of the questions for us about the school was to what extent the Western influence should come into that village culture and that wilderness context.

We had the idea of organising the school in a familiar way. So we planned it around small pavilions and social areas. But of course the articulation of those pavilions was important.

The normal village school is classrooms in rows, and all of those rows are lined up. It's a bit foreign and regulated; villages tend to flow a lot more. It will be interesting to have children respond to the space you've created, as opposed to the more linear path that kids would get used to elsewhere.

You're right; it seemed to me that there were a number of developments in the area based almost on barracks. The police headquarters has those kind of rows of buildings. The way that we set up the design and construction for the school was that we would sit down with the elders on the site and have their input in the sketching of the pavilions, so that there was an engagement there. And then we would take that sketch and produce it as a kit of parts which they could put together.

The local way of building is to close everything and have very few openings but have a very good air flow, through the roof and through the floor, which is exactly what you've done. Is that what you were thinking?

One of the things I noticed on the several hour 4WD journey from Popondetta to Kokoda was how many ruins there were...

Paul Chatterton is the deputy leader of the Forest and Climate division of the World Wildlife Fund and was formerly its conservation director in New Guinea. He is a lifelong environmental activist.

The skeletons of previous aid projects.

Right, exactly. So it seemed that you didn't want to bring in much technology, or you wanted to be very careful with the technology you imported. And the walls and the sides of the buildings they make help to narrow the opening and promote higher airflow. If everything's open it's very difficult to get the air moving at all.

I stayed in a village house one night, which was just beautiful. Then I stayed in one of the guest houses at the hospital, which was made in a more Western way. And you notice that the windows were just full of cobwebs. There's no continuous flow of air.

I think at some point you have to question what you're doing there. The traditional buildings are really quite beautiful. And they work very well. Obviously they've worked for a long time but there is a robustness issue. A lot of people will be using the school. The local buildings tend to fall down in the large weather events. The wind or the floods take them out. And so if you have that many people, it seemed to us they wouldn't rebuild it. Or it would take so long to rebuild, that the structure of the school might collapse. The organisation of the school may not come back. So, we had to make something that would withstand the weather events. The thatched roof, which while quite beautiful and ingenious, needs a lot of maintenance. And when you have a development as large as the school, would that ever really happen?

That maintenance is usually taken up by the village. But it's often contested, and buildings fall apart even faster because everyone's arguing about who should maintain it. The more long-lasting you could make the school, the better. The sago palm thatching is beautiful, it's much better for heat resistance than a tin roof. But you only have to replace a tin roof once every 10 to 20 years whereas the thatching, you have to do it every 3 to 5 years, and you've got insects falling out of it all the time. Plus, you can assume there's always a lot more money to build something than there is to maintain it. So it's a wise decision to focus on durability.

We also lifted the buildings up off the ground like the local buildings; it rained every day I was there. And that ground water really needs to be unencumbered. All the buildings we saw that were in the ground had serious mold and maintenance issues.

You have the airflow from the side, from the floor, the bottom of the floor up the wall, which is very interesting because most traditional houses right across New Guinea have slatted floor made of palm bark and so the air comes up automatically through the floor and it creates the circulation, plus you don't have to have trash cans because you just drop everything through the floor to the pigs underneath. But this is the first time I've seen circulation up from the floor in a modern building.

The shade of the building creates slightly cooler air under the building. So a natural convection happens. And we worked with engineers in New York on this idea of micro climate and control, where you don't try to make the entire interior a comfortable temperature, but you promote a workable temperature, or a comfortable temperature, around your desk.

One question I have is, as you strive to protect these vast areas of rain forest and natural environments, to what degree do you have to change that natural environment so that it can fulfill its new orders its contemporary agenda?

There's this very strange relationship that's developing where the world wants to pay rain forest owners for not doing anything to their rain forest. 'Don't touch it and we'll pay you.'

Which is completely incomprehensible to most people anywhere in the world, let alone people in a village in the middle of the Peruvian Amazon. So that's pretty weird.

But long-term protection of biodiversity in the environment will only work if it's done by the local people. And in New Guinea, there's this real, very different understanding of what nature is. To mix nature with village culture is very foreign to them. People see the immediate environment as the human environment. That's where you live in this village, and then the human-managed environment, which is where you have your gardens, and then the mixed zone between humans and nature, which is where you have your forests, but you take your timber trees or your canoe trees or you collect things. Then you have the deep dark forest which is where all of the other nonhuman things live; there's a whole set of nature spirits that live out there and it's dangerous to go there.

When you go, you speak quietly, you move softly, and you sometimes use different language because you don't want those spirits to hear you because they can bring sickness back into your village. And so there's this real, very different understanding of what nature is. To mix nature with your village culture is actually a very modern idea. It doesn't mean they don't respect nature. They have a very high respect for nature, but a very different way of thinking about it.

Right, the boundaries are different. I guess what you're describing is a hierarchy of surfaces. It's interesting this kind of urban sensibility is informing our view of nature and our view of occupying that particular territory. What we were trying to articulate was an idea that we saw there where some surfaces get more attention than others. It's extraordinary the way they keep the landscape. The forest grows back so quickly, and yet there are these areas, these almost quadrangle-like spaces in the dirt that I guess get swept every day. And the order and the arrangement is chopped and kept in a very neat border or line, and then there's the grass area and more decorative elements happen within that grassed terrain. And then there's the forest beyond. It's interesting, because we're looking for something between landscaped grassy area and the forest. I guess we didn't really find it because that's not the way that they relate to the wilderness.

There's a garden where you have your yams and your pineapples and your bananas, and then there's the garden forest which will look like a forest, but it's actually fruit trees and timber trees and various other things, that will be left to grow back. And then we could get further out into the forest, you've got a much wilder forest. What you're planning may be quite workable because you've got your main ceremony area, and your empty space. Then your ornamental garden, then your production garden.

And then you've got your productive forest which to a Westerner looks like a wild rain forest but it's actually quite different to a New Guinean.

In terms of technology and wilderness, what do you think of our plan of importing digitally driven milling machines onto the site and having folks teach the locals how to use them?

I think the question is, is it a technology that works and will it continue to work? It's a new technology. New Guineans have been incredibly able to accommodate newness over the last 100 years, since they've been contacted by the outside world. So novelty is not something that's dangerous to them. It's how much do you give the power to them, and if you're training them to use it, you're doing that. And then how much can they keep it going? Can you get the spare parts and does it do the job as well or better than an axe?

This sort of honeycombing gives the building significantly more strength than a normal stick frame or weatherboard building does. You're making, say, 400 connections with steel angle and some bolts as opposed to 10 or 20 connections. So when the force of a cyclone or flood or earthquake hits it, there's so many more points of connection to distribute that force through its system. It's like a basket. It'll move but it'll come back to its shape. There's no point where all the stresses come to, and break. I think that's the pay off for the technology.

When New Guinea has cyclones, there's not much protection for people. And if you've got something that would survive through a cyclone, or at least very large storms, that'll be valuable.

How has all your work in the forest, the wilderness, changed the way you live and operate in the urban environment?

I spent a lot of the time in the wilderness, absolutely in love with it. But there was always a feeling that there was something missing. In the environmental campaigns, it was always just us against the loggers. What I realised after a while is that you need a wilderness that has people in it, for it to be truly alive. Maybe it's less wild, but it's truly alive. And the revelation for me in New Guinea was to try and find what looked like completely wild places that had people right through or had the marks of people right through them.

There was no such thing as wilderness in that sense. Vienna, where I now live, is an extremely cultured city. The core of it has an enormous history and culture. We live on the edge of it, at the beginning of the forests of the Alps, and those forests look wild but in fact they are plantations. They're planted forests, with vineyards in between them, and in some ways they remind me of New Guinea. You've got a very cultured centre of a village with your gardens, leading into your vineyards and your agricultural land. And then your forests. So I sometimes wonder if we have we forgotten where we came from and that wilderness was once not wild It was peopled. And can we create a landscape, a new understanding for landscape that draws from some of these old understandings.

It sounds to me like you're advocating a position that in order to fully comprehend our civilisation, one needs an engagement with the civilisation that exists in the wilderness. In our work, we're invested in creating environments. And in New York, I've noticed that we're constantly trying to make that sort of connection with the idea of the outside. How do you render the interior of a place so that you understand the light as it changes in the city? Or the weather? Or what happens around you? New York is still the city which weather can bring to a standstill.

I think there's a fundamental power to that question that has to do with our desire to know what is going on out there. And so, I guess in our work we'd like to explore this tension between the inside world, the world that's cultivated by the mind, and that connection with an outside that is unruly but occupied, or occupiable. The physical character of architecture defines that connection.

1

form + use

form + use

In the studio at SYSTEM, form is never really talked about directly. Each project requires a multiplicity of actions as the project grows and is influenced by a deeper understanding of the programme, the site conditions, the owner stipulations, the needs of the user, and the many agencies that have jurisdiction over the project. What everyone wants to know, however, is what the project looks like, and try as we might to explain that one needs to understand how the project came to be in order to 'read' how it looks, very few folks ever really grasp the relationship between how the building works and how it appears. Nevertheless, everyone has a connection to the visual. It's a necessary function of architecture to show ideas for building in the environment through form. The built work documents a moment when ideas for space made a coherent argument in a form in a place.

The relationship between form and use is more complex than it initially appears. Obviously, the uses of a project fit within the shape of the project and its appendages, and in cities or highly built environs, once this is achieved there is often little extra space around to 'add' additional formal gestures. The form in this instance is very tightly connected to the use. But while working through this tightly woven connection, architects might discover there are often loopholes within the ordinances of a place. For example, in New York City, architectural elements may project from the building into the space of the street, balconies may also project into the street, setbacks might enable a building to be taller, or the thickness of a wall might affect the permissible height of a building. We used a combination of these in making the form for the UNhistoric townHOUSE project (see p. 182) shown in a later chapter.

The usefulness of a project may be thought of not only in terms of the layout of rooms and closets and corridors, but also as the creation of an interior environment, and as the creation of the relationship that environment has with the outside. This suggests not only a social arrangement of spaces and elements, but also how the users feel inside. The view, the light, the movement of air around a space influences the way a place is used, and these play out in the form of a project.

For form to be an agent of communication within the environment, it must have a provisional character—a sense that change is a part of the terrain in which it operates. From the outside, this change may best be characterised by movement, as in a form that is moving around the corner or moving across the horizon. This form is not interested in bringing the eye to rest, but quite the opposite, in carrying the eye across or around an object and out into the environment in which it sits. This positions the object as just one of many elements within the environment, playing its role within the ecology of that place. From the inside, this change may be described as transition. A space that is defined as much by its connection or transition to another as by the elements that contain the space. For example, a room may be made of pieces or elements that continue into other places within the interior.

In the projects that follow, form is developed at a number of scales. There is the form that responds to a zoning diagram, to the flow of a room, to the constraints of a site and the necessities of a programme and then there is the scale of a human moment within the project—leaning against a wall, having a place to put your keys, sitting and reading a book in a slice of sunlight. All these moments are suggestions within the manipulation of the form. In this chapter, five projects will illustrate the relationships that come into focus during the making of a project.

1.1 Burst*003

Jeremy Edmiston & Douglas Gauthier partners

This project was to be used by a family of five for their summer vacations, on a coastal site about a five hours drive from Sydney, Australia. North Haven is a small beachside town of retirees, young families, and vacationers. The beach is a five minute walk from the project site, which is surrounded by one- or two-storey brick veneered homes on a cul-de-sac without beach views.

My then partner at SYSTEM, Douglas Gauthier, and I found out that the local council had recently mandated that new houses needed to be elevated more than 1.5 metres (4.5 feet) above the ground because of flooding. The owners neither wanted air conditioning nor heating. So we focused on using natural ventilation, shading and solar heating. In that area, a cooling breeze comes off the ocean at 2:00 p.m. every day during the summer. We consulted a local architect on the maximum width of the interior space that would allow this breeze to be useful; too deep and the airflow would not be strong enough. We also lifted the building a little higher than mandated, so the undercroft would be a useful space, and to further take advantage of the prevailing air currents.

The breeze could adequately cool a space that was between 3.2 metres (10.5 feet) and 3.6 metres (12 feet) deep. With our narrow site we created a public bar, for living and dining, facing the garden, and a more private zone, with bedrooms and bathrooms, behind. The two areas were separated by a wall of storage serving both the bedrooms and the public room. Because we needed the sun in winter and it faced the garden side of the building, we used the windows to bring the cooling summer breezes through the house with a clerestory window above the roof of the public space and vents at the base of the stairs to the private spaces. For winter warmth, we maximised the glass area facing the sun. All these devices are operable so the family can 'trim' the house in summer and close it up in winter.

These were the natural and technical systems that our design was predicated on, but we also wanted to understand the social system and get a feel for the interior. As can be seen on the section, a ceiling is raised to contain the space in the living area, and lowered and angled toward the outside to define the dining area. These are boundaries that encourage flow; just as the wind is not obstructed by walls, and a familial disagreement is not limited to the kitchen, so too the shape of the space must flow from one place to another. The defining moments written into the space are connected with each other causing the initial profiles to leave only a trace within the rooms of the interior.

1 TEXPLODED perspective — structure + skin
2 DIAGRAM — folded and flattened skin

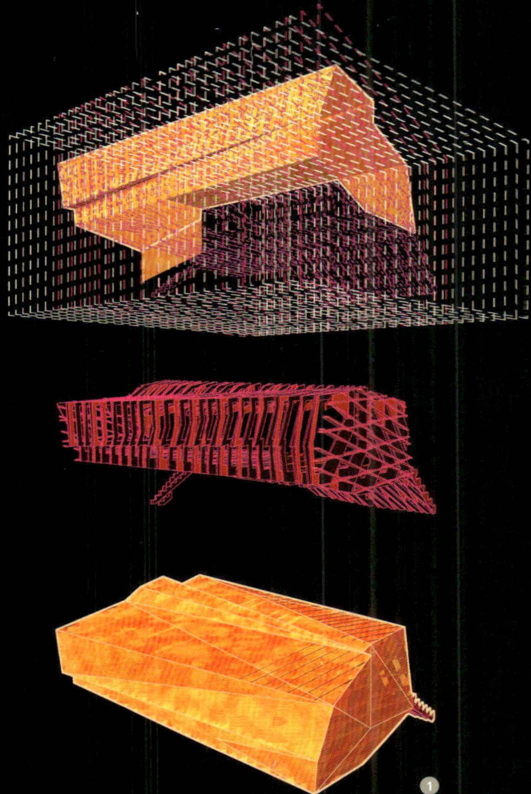

1

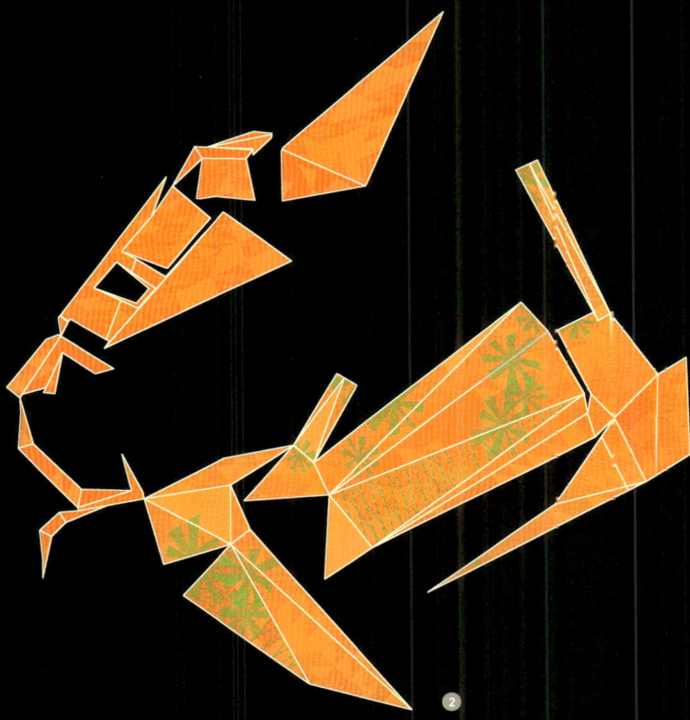

2

The form then may be read as an arrangement of space, a mechanism for cross ventilation, or a viewing platform for mixing sun with recreation. But there are also moments in the project that were unexpected, or could be written into the design process retro-actively. There's the way the wind stirs the hair, the sounds and smells of beach and salt that are carried on the breezes, the green light in the bedrooms as the sun bounces off the grass and through the ventilators onto the wall in the late afternoon, and the view of stars and grass through the clerestory and the ventilators. Sometimes the summers are very wet, and the rain falls in sheets. The undercroft was designed to be a space to park the car in the shade and to store beach gear. It has also become a place to hang out during one of those summer storms, undercover and out of the weather. From the start of construction, there has always been a steady stream of 'tourists' driving slowly around the cul-de-sac to look at the form. The owners have been able to connect with the locals as they hang out under the bleachers and become part of the community in the area.

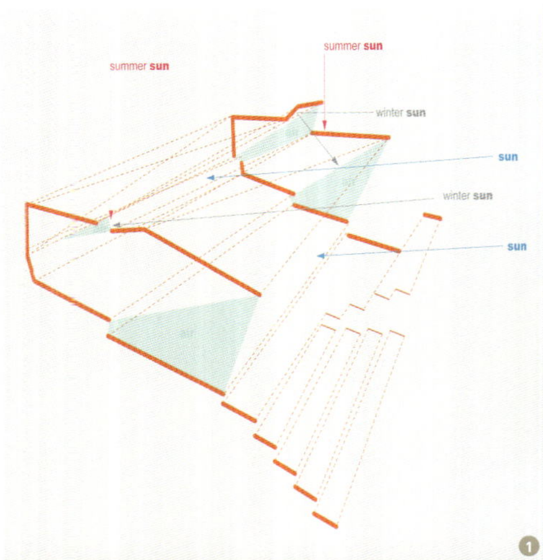

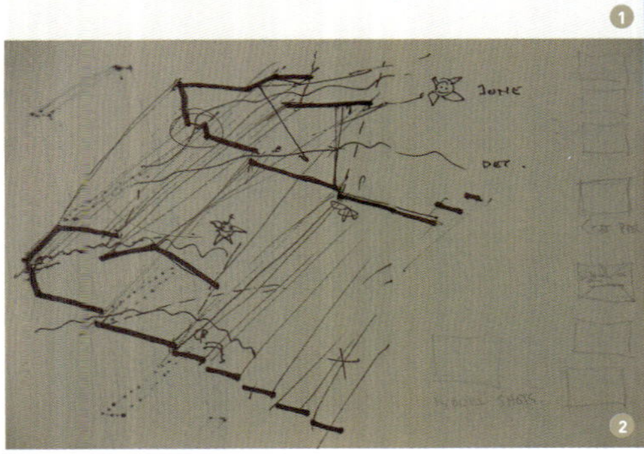

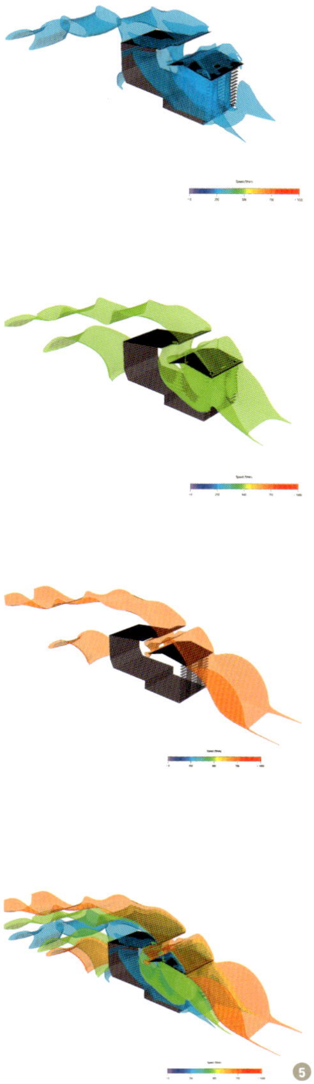

5

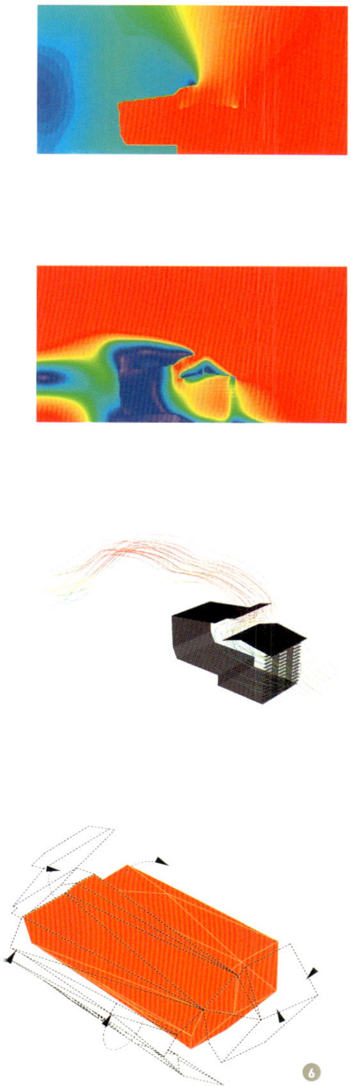

6

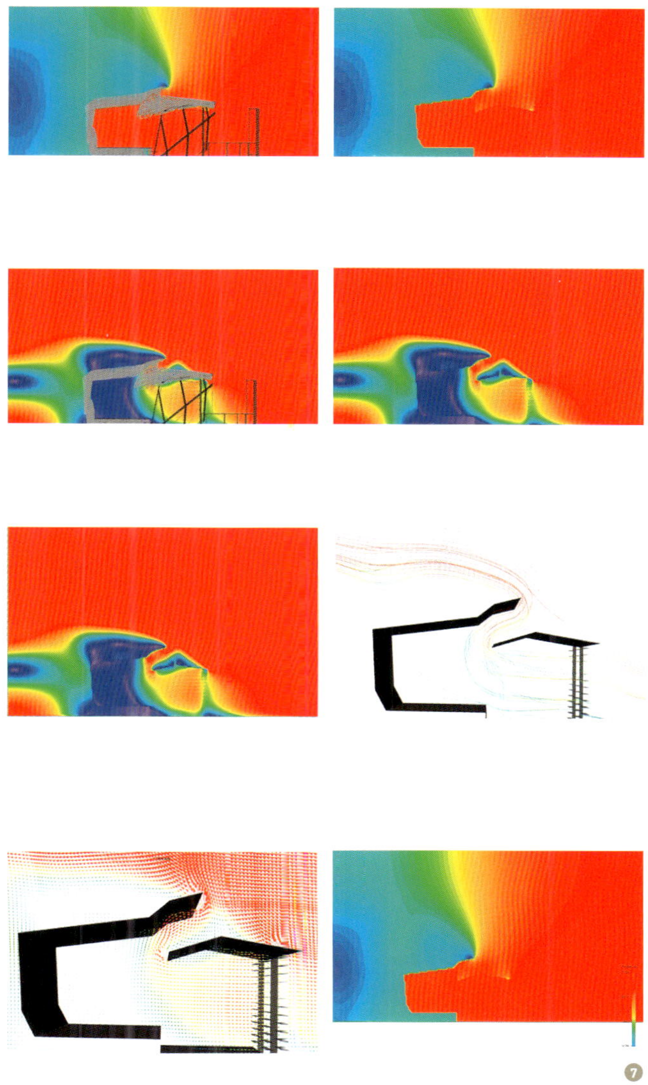

7

1 PASSIVE design sun diagram
2 SKETCH design strategies with defined profiles
3 VIEW North Haven beach
4 VIEW site
5 ANALYSIS wind dynamics
6 FORM unfolded surface
7 ANALYSIS computational fluid dynam cs: Buro Happold

1 VIEW Burst* in the neighbourhood
2 VIEW southwest
3 AERIAL perspective
4 Photo DIAGRAM showing BURST* patterns

2

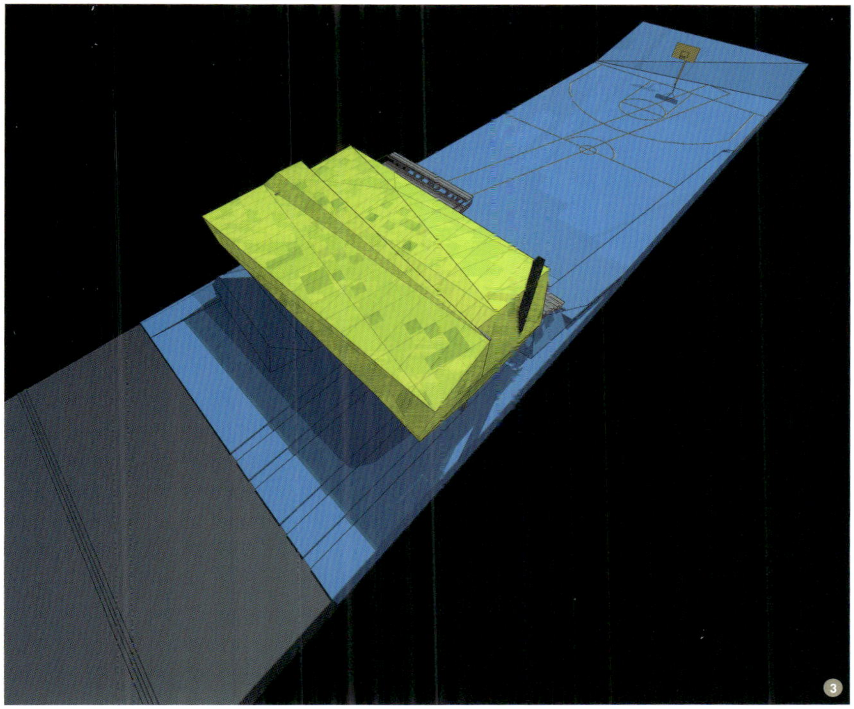

3

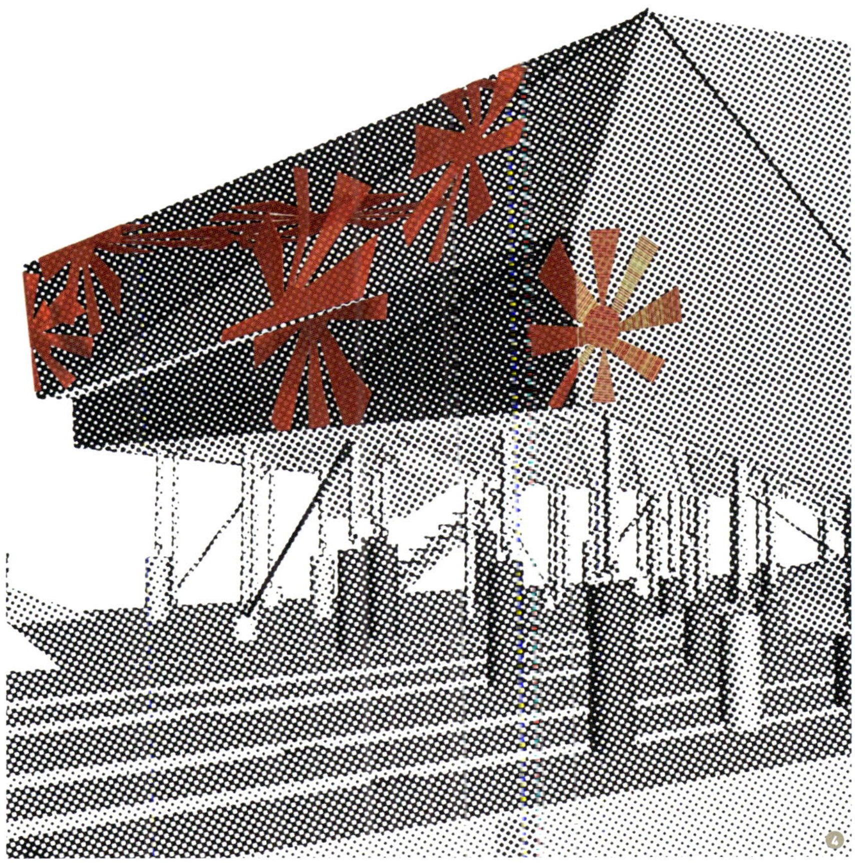

4

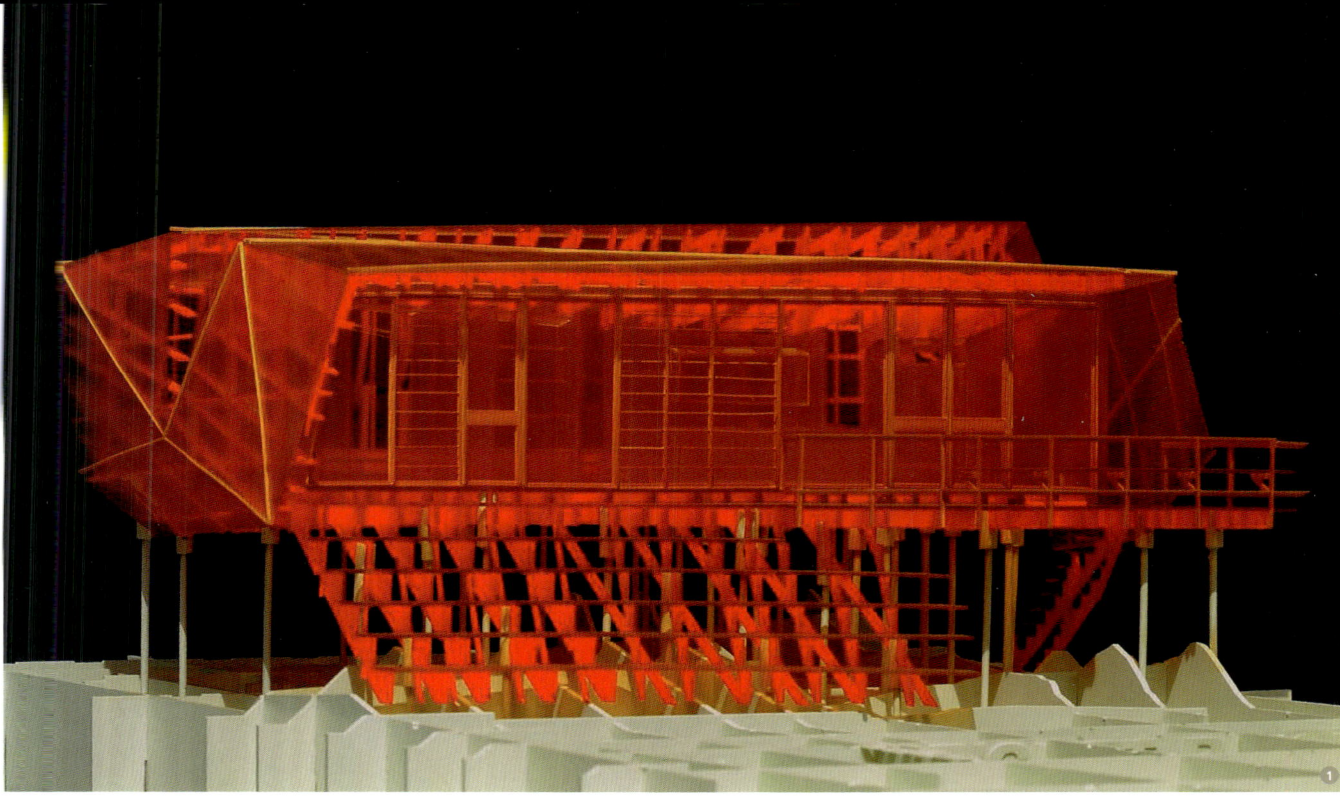

1

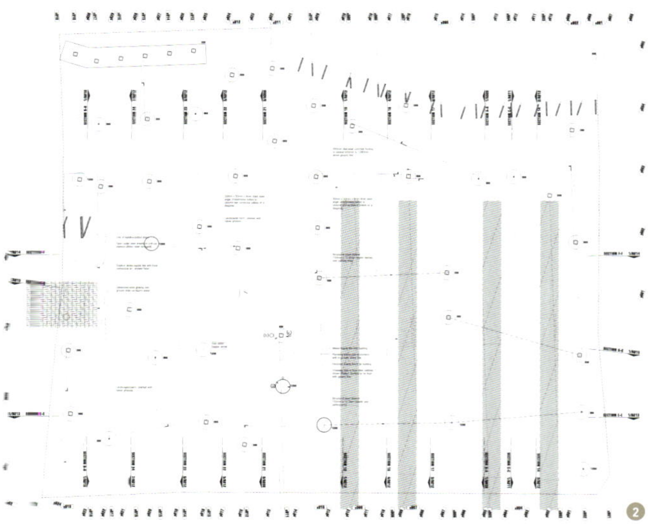

2

1 MODEL — northeast elevation
2 PLAN — ground level
3 MODEL — south elevation
4 PLAN — first level
5 PLAN — roof

3

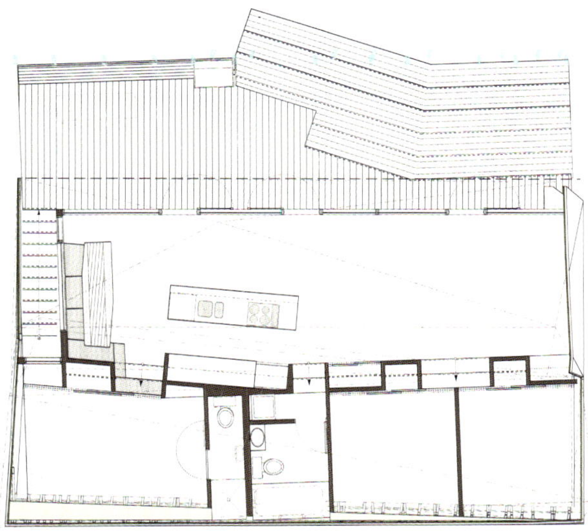

4

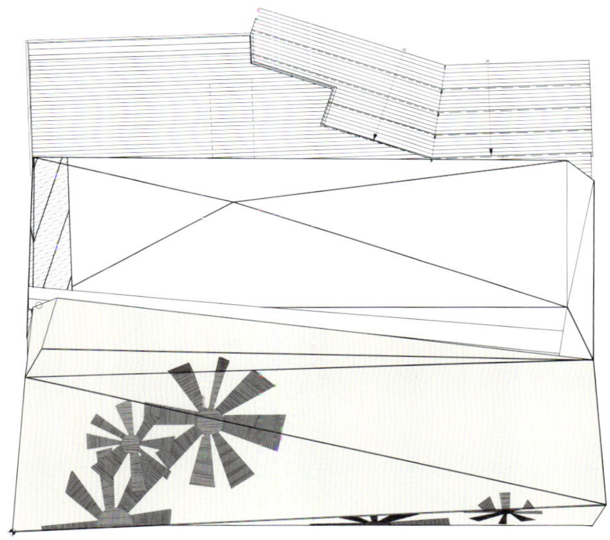

5

1 ELEVATION north
2 VIEW from the garden

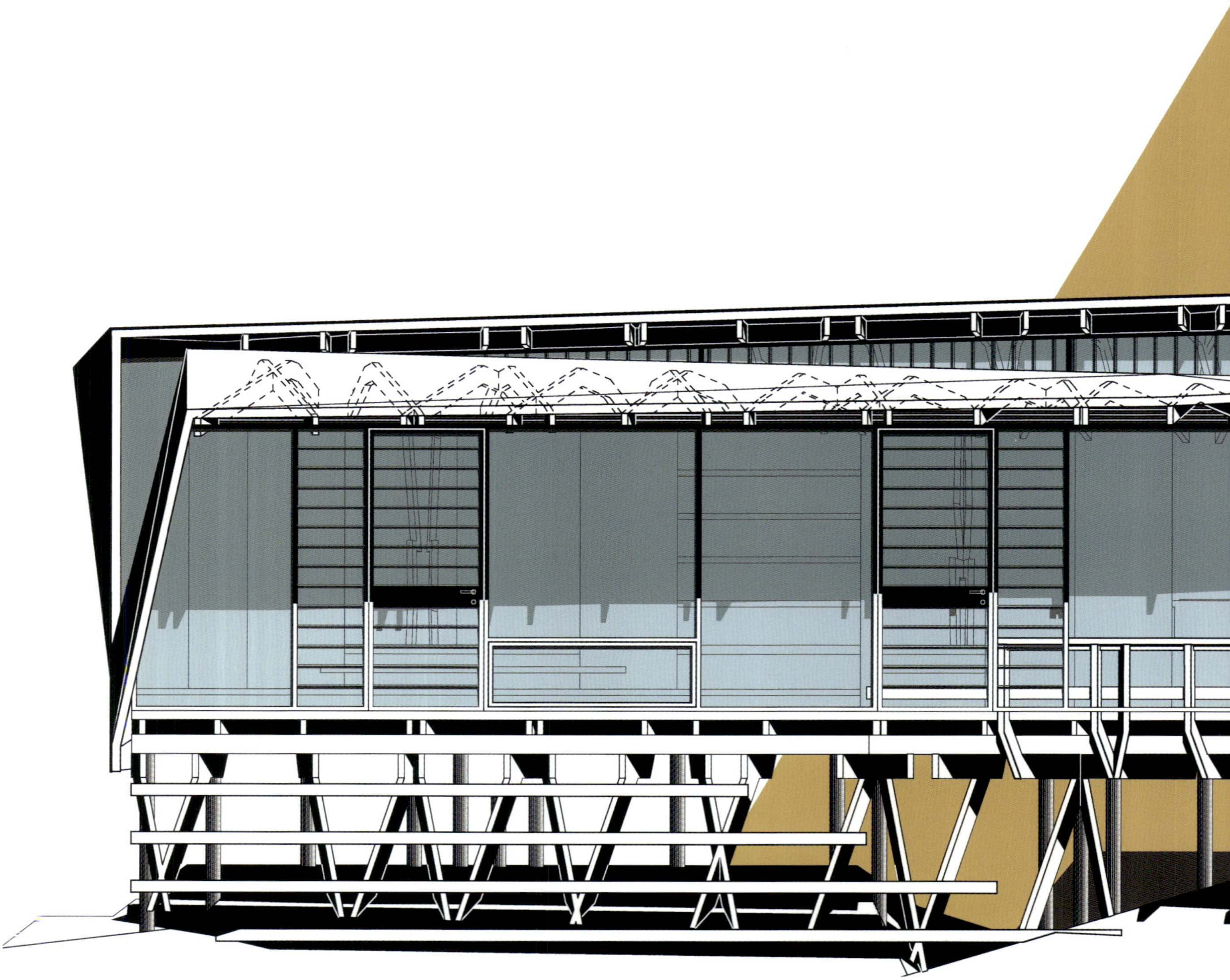

1

2

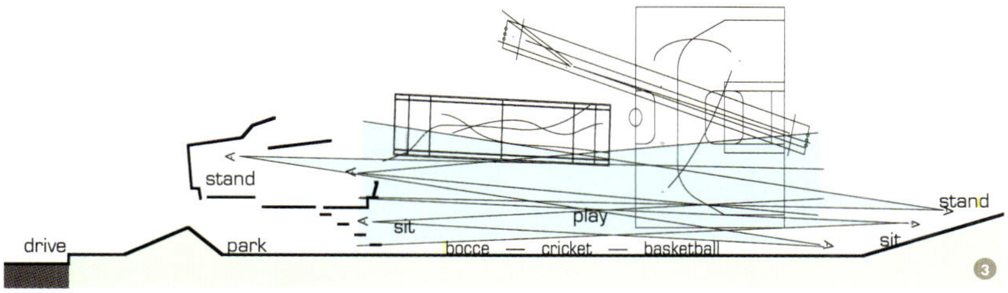

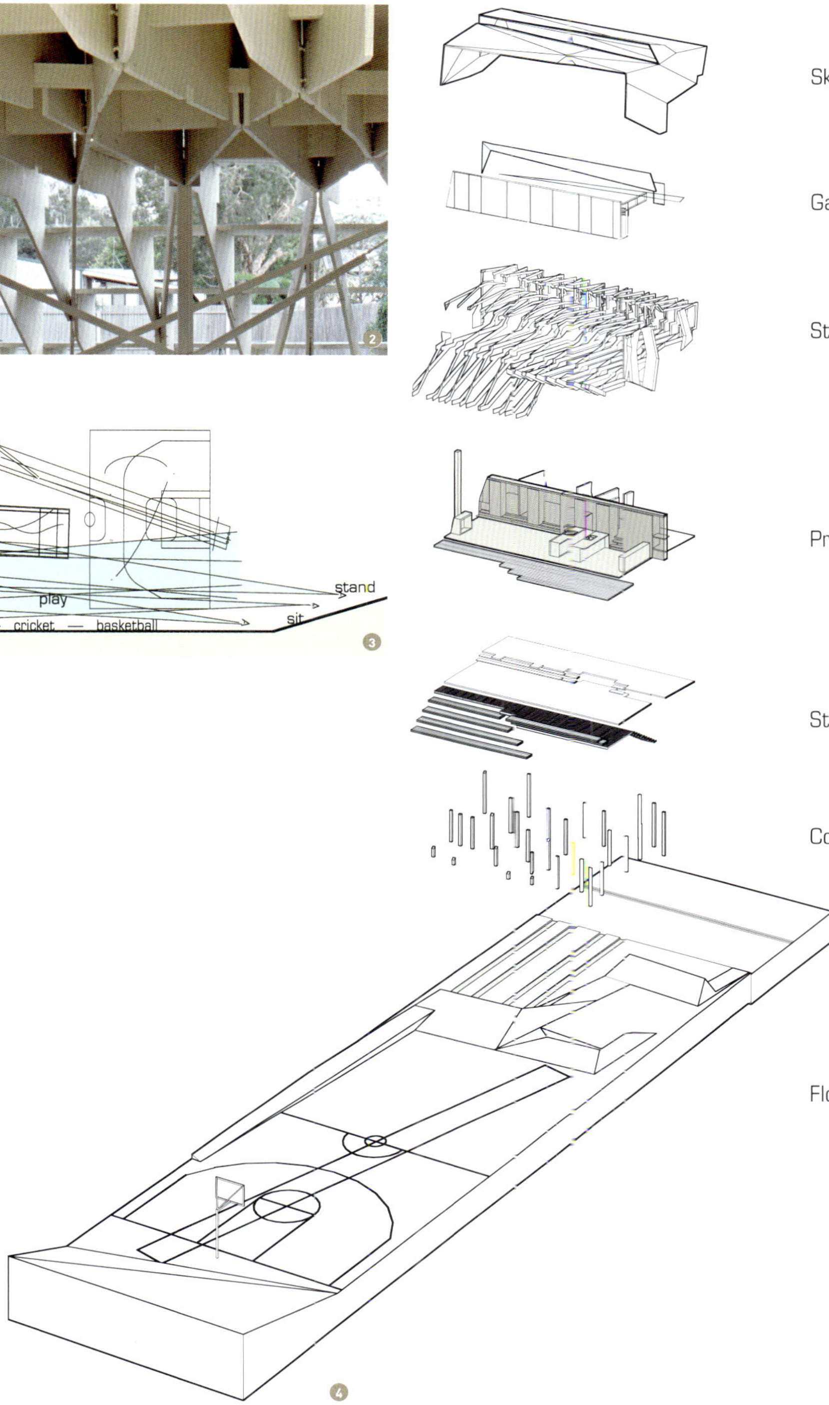

1-2 VIEW under croft
3 programmatic section DIAGRAM of the garden
4 exploded AXONOMETRIC

1 VIEW under croft looking towards entrance stair
2 VIEW from exterior entrance stair
3 VIEW entrance cowling
4 VIEW looking across deck
5 VIEW living room + exterior stair
6 VIEW dining room + entrance stair

1

2

5

6

10

1-4 VIEW public loft space
5-9 VIEW private bedroom spaces
10-13 VIEW bedroom ventilators

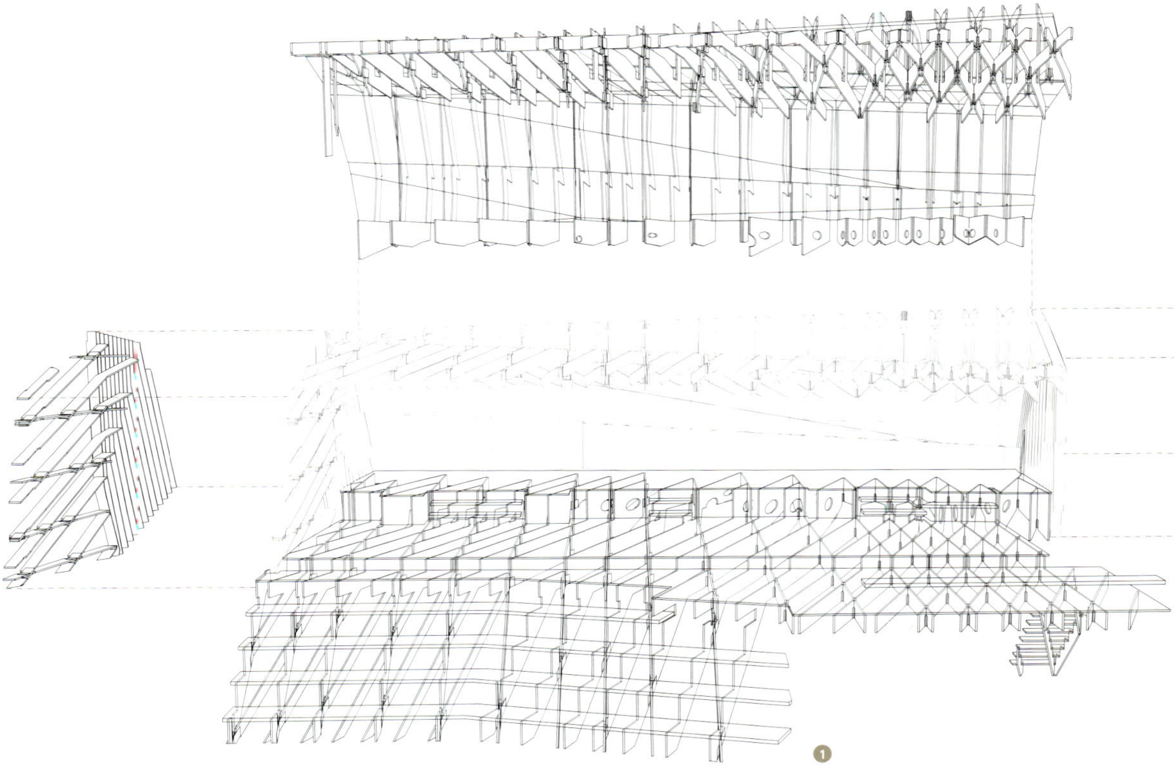

1

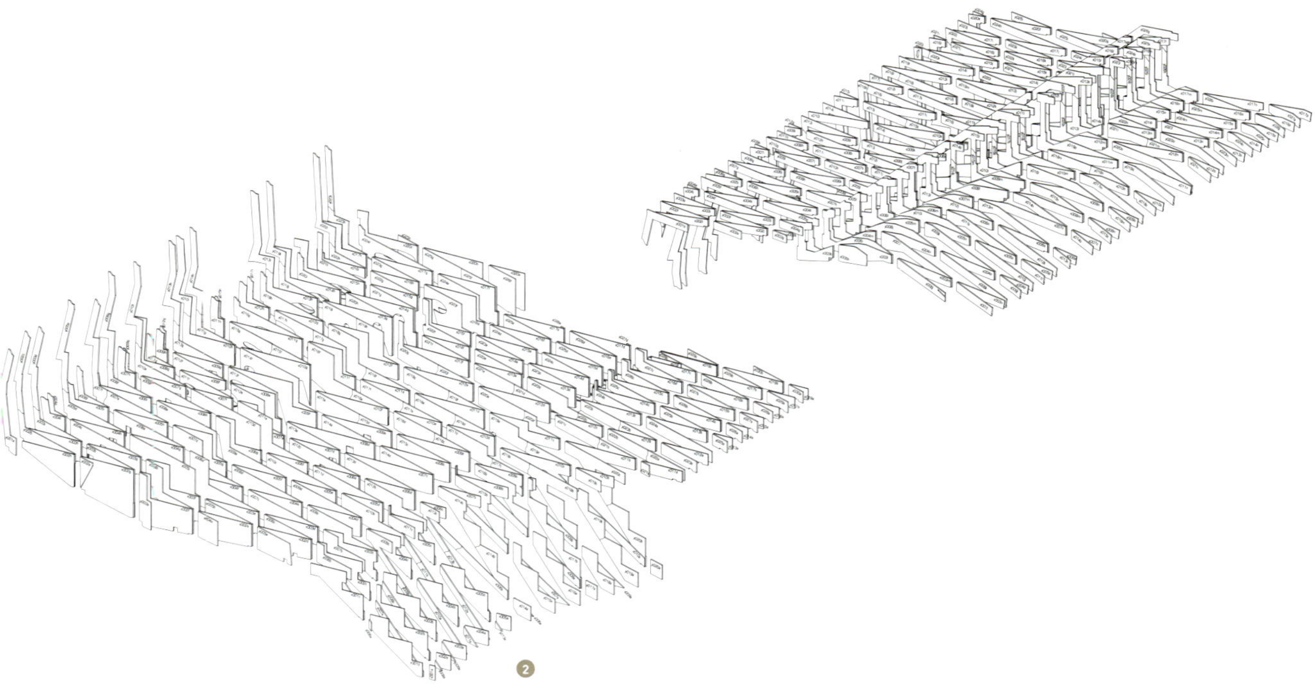

2

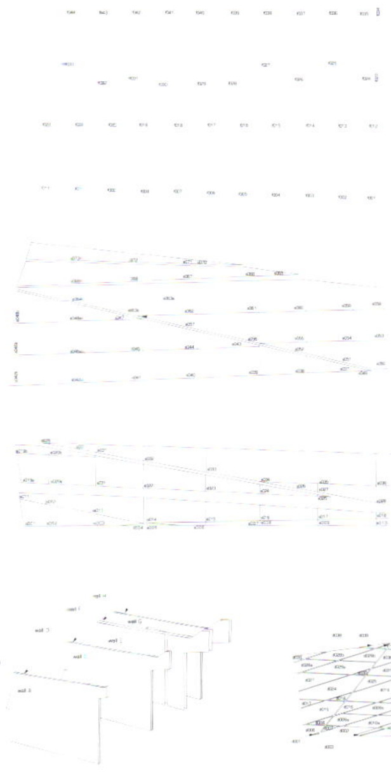

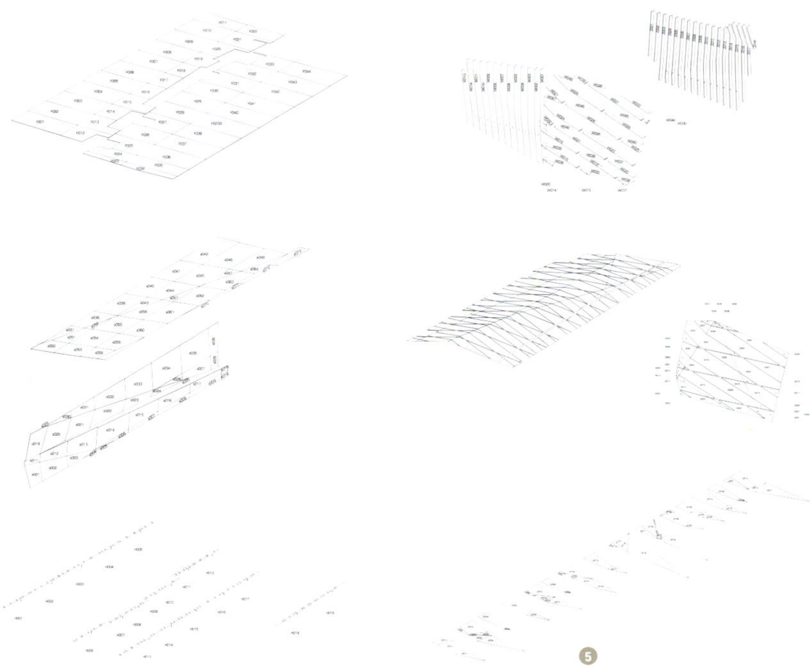

1 exploded PERSPECTIVE structural ribs
2 exploded AXONOMETRIC structural ribs
3 reflected ceiling PLAN — public space
4 ELEVATION — interior walls
5 Surface parts
6 LASER etch showing connection at the ribs
7 VIEW laser cutter

1 VIEW precut fabricated panel delivery
2 VIEW laser cut building components
3 foreground VIEW shipping waste
4 VIEW compost
5 SECTION — Y grid lines showing rib parts
6 CUT sheets ribs + surfaces

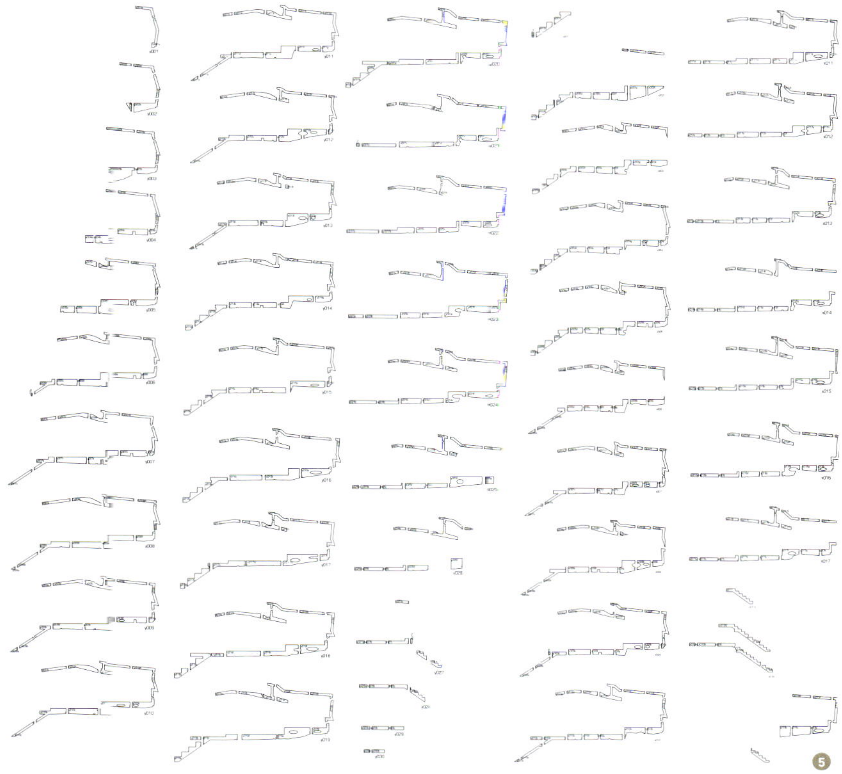

5

6

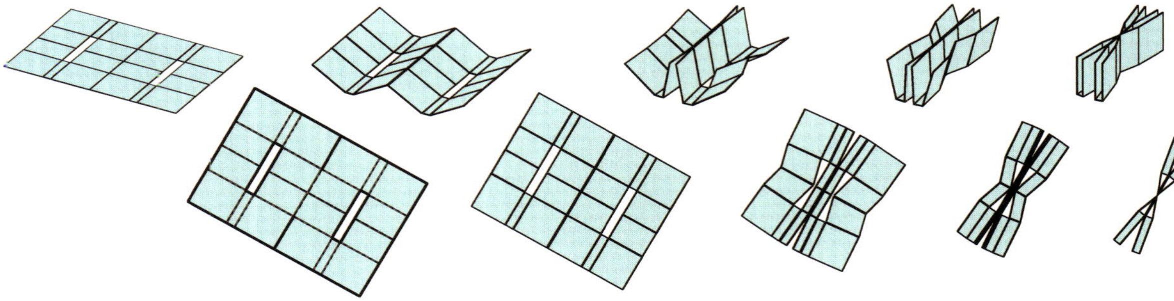

1

2

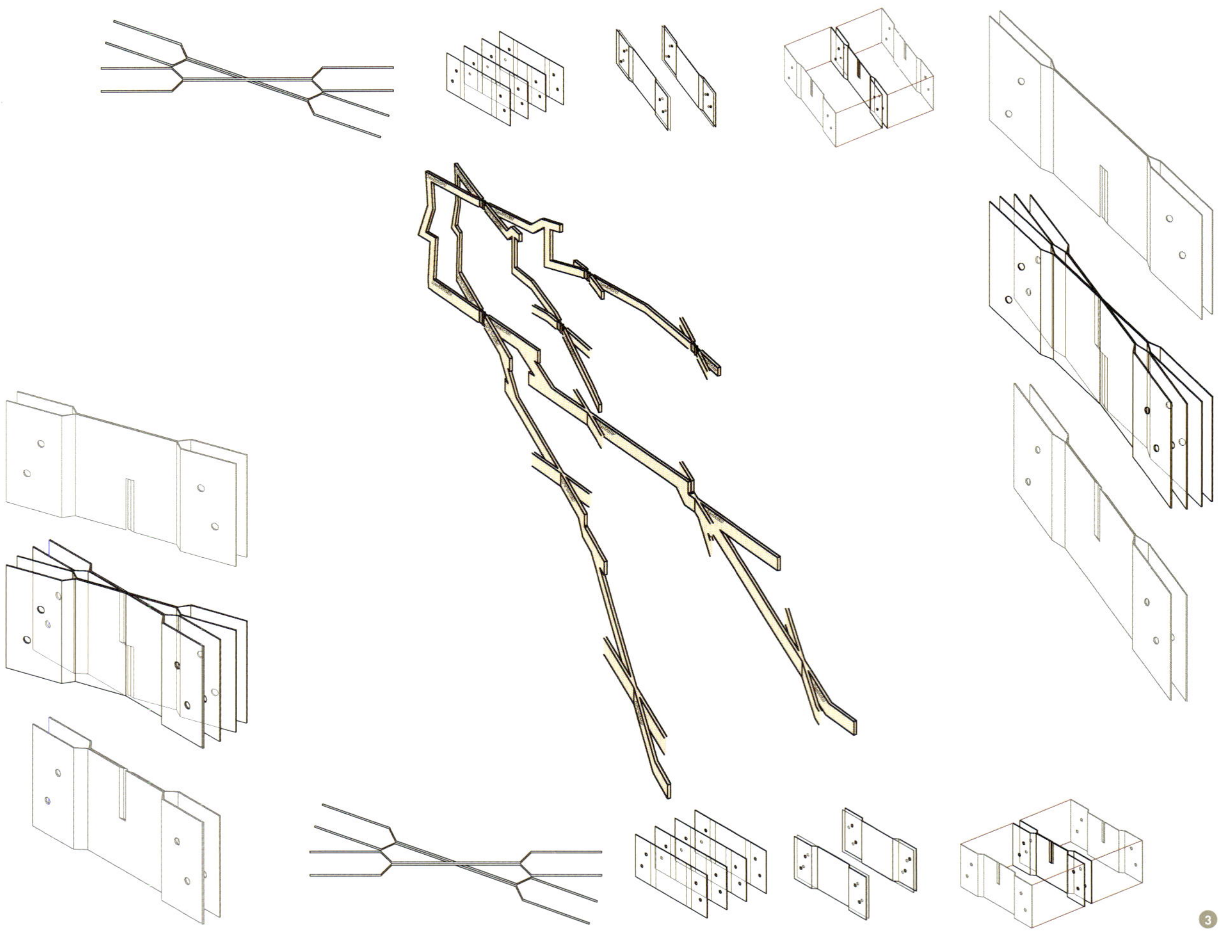

3

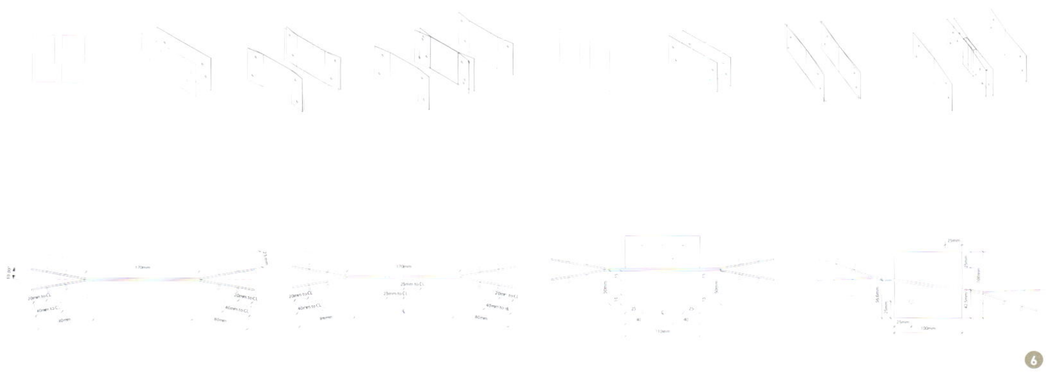

1 DIAGRAM folded clip prototype
2 TAXONOMY of steel clips
3 SKETCH clip design
4 VIEW structural clip
5 CONSTRUCTION roof ribs
6 ASSEMBLY clips
7 VIEW structural ribs for deck
8 VIEW structural steel clip connectors on floor surfaces

1 CONSTRUCTION floor
2 CONSTRUCTION rib connections
3 ASSEMBLY rib to column to floor steel clip
4 CONSTRUCTION under croft
5 CONSTRUCTION columns in place awaiting footing
6 VIEW construction south elevation

6

1 VIEW southeast: undercroft
2 VIEW nighttime from the garden

1.2 wellFLEET

Jeremy Edmiston & Douglas Gauthier partners

1 SITEPLAN
2-3 MODEL — ¾ view
4 MODEL — elevation looking into forest
5-6 MASSING — sketch models

The project at Wellfleet was a guesthouse in the National Seashore, in which very minimal building is allowed. The view to the Atlantic Ocean is clear and close above the treeline, and we wanted the forest to be very present surrounding the house. The guesthouse was to be used primarily as a sleeping pavilion that could accommodate nine people, but with a minimal footprint. All of this suggested it should be organised like a switchback stair; the pavilion became a journey to the rooftop with sleeping spaces along the way.

This form, while sculptural, and elevated like a tree house, needed to be challenged by the active use of the guests. In the studio, Douglas and I talked about lying in bed listening to the forest, the birds and the ocean, reading a book and having a drink. Some of these moments would happen on the edge of the form, and by extending its surface to accommodate such moments, the geometry of the surface changed and resulted in something more complex, made from folding planes that wrapped the switchback. The idea was that a useful but small moment in the life of a—house might have large consequences that would reverberate through the form and design of the project.

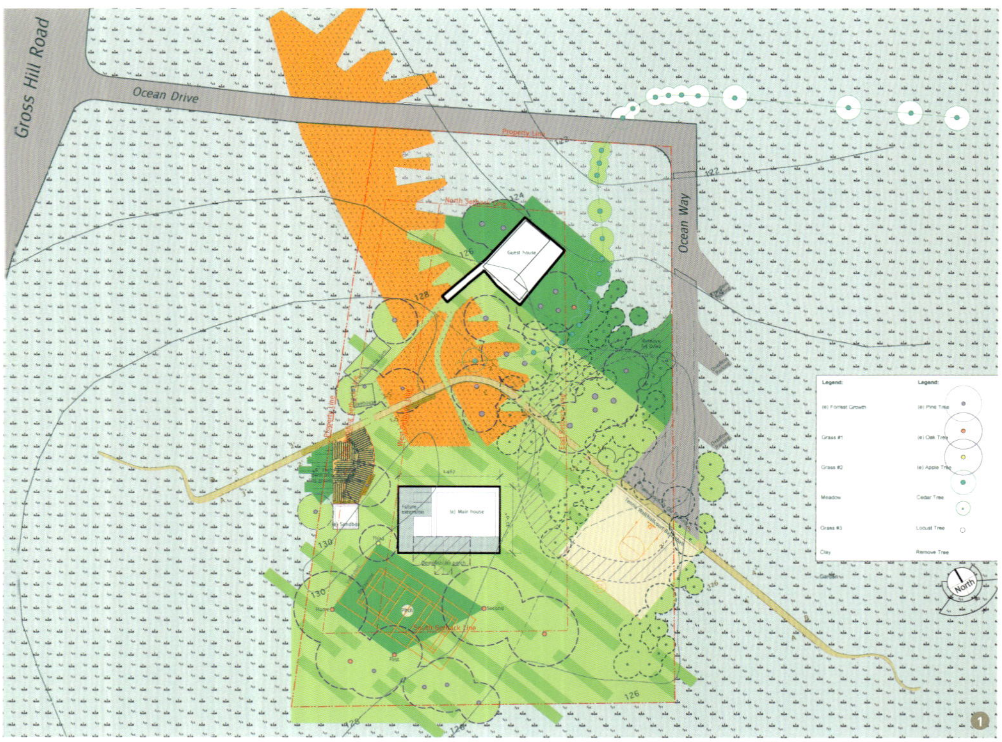

2

3

4

5

6

1

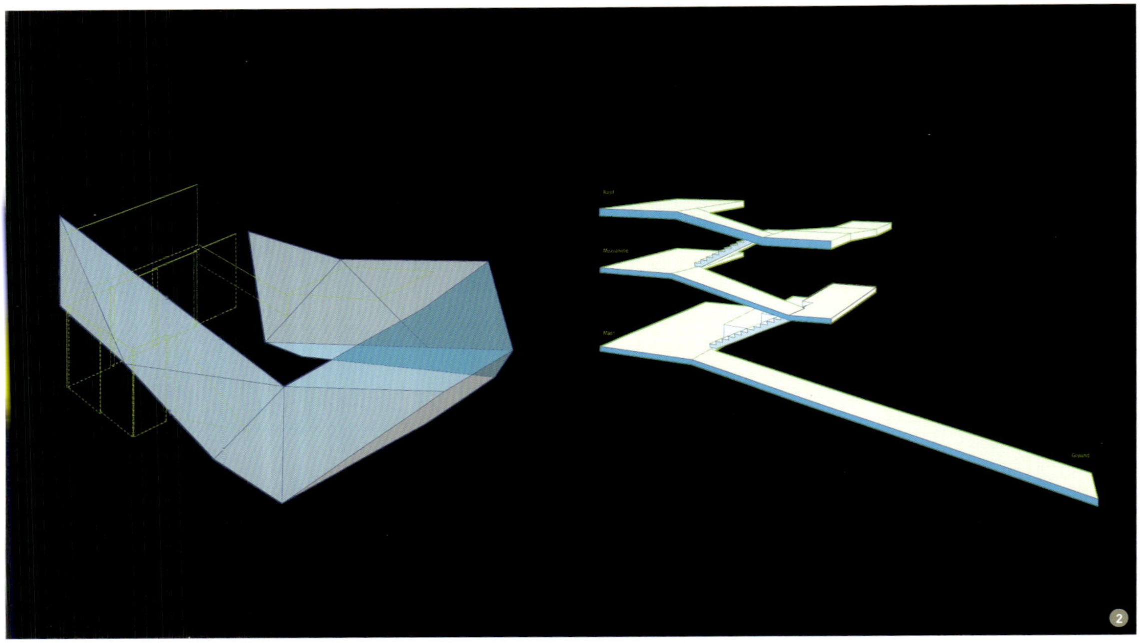

2

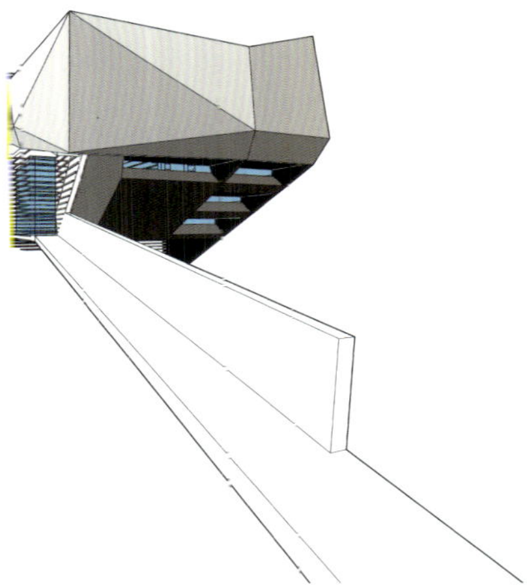

3

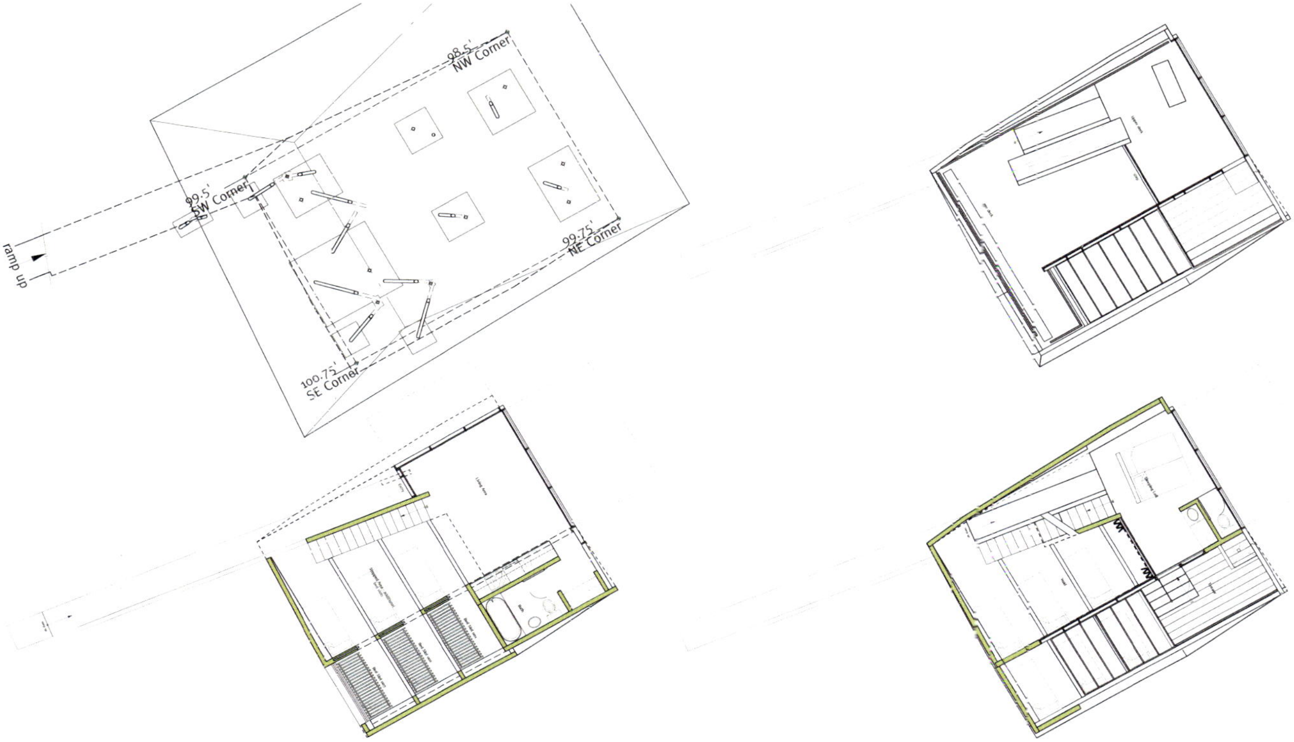

4

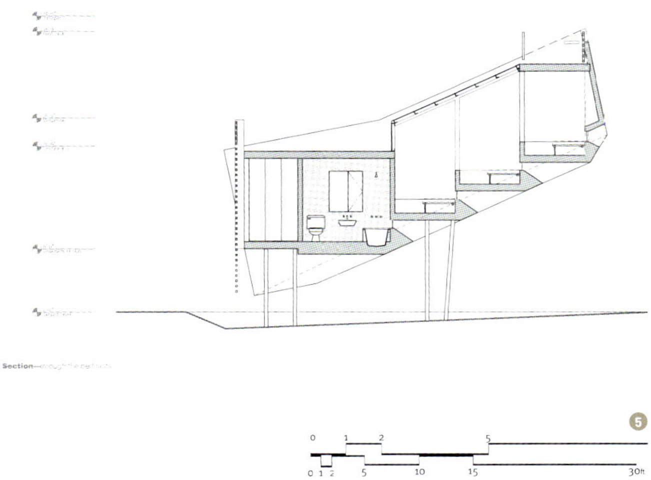

5

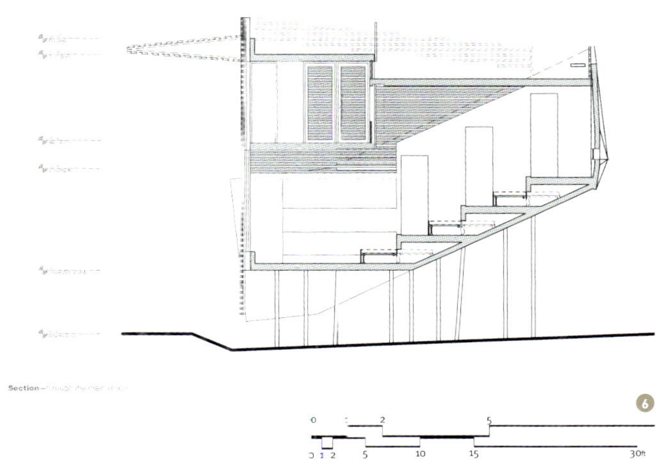

6

1 side ELEVATION
2 DIAGRAM — switchback circulation + surface
3 PERSPECTIVE of entrance ramp
4 ELEVATION — looking towards the main house
5 PLANS — ground level to roof level
6 SECTION — through bedroom spaces

1.3 USS (Urban Space Station)

With Natalie Jeremijenko

USS is a design for an urban garden on the rooftops of city buildings, a research project with New York University fine art professor Natalie Jeremijenko. The idea was to make a stand-alone space that could be supported by the roof of an existing building so that the experience of growing could be integrated into the life of the city. Freed from the constraints of the Cartesian grid below, the rooftop is a space that is underutilised in many urban centres even though it has some of the best access to sunlight in the city. These roofs are often occupied by the 'plant' of the building—the utilities and machinery that keep a building running—and it was thought that this usually forgotten space might provide a service for the building's users.

The USSpod is a lightweight structure with supporting legs that may be positioned to wherever the strongest parts of the roof. It is made from a kit of parts that can be brought to the top of the building by freight elevator, access stair, or crane and assembled onsite. It may be used as a greenhouse, extending the growing period in colder climates, or it could be fitted with hydroponics that maximise the production of plant growth. We believed that providing urban dwellers with a place on the roof with a view, where they could actually feel the weather while they participated in a key part of the food cycle, might be a way to broaden the environment they live in.

The form deflects wind flow and maximises sunlight penetration by exaggerating the south-facing façade. It looks as if the natural elements have formed it from the machinery that surrounds it. This is a place that's outside the traditional use of the building below, and outside the traditional city limits, and brings an industry that's usually outside the city—agriculture—into the building. The geometry of the form enhances that outsider status, working against the typical constraints of an urban environment where structures must fit up against one another. The twisting surfaces of the object are wrapped in a fabric (ETFE pillows) accentuating the idea that this place belongs outside the flat planes of masonry, concrete, steel, and glass that proliferate below.

While directed by the programme and materials however, the form also brings some of the imagery of the farm and of contemporary life, of sustainability. There's a nod to the embryonic nature of the growing process. This is an acknowledgment that form has to cater to the imagination as much as to anything.

It's important in the city not to neglect the desire for an engagement with the wilderness, with the outside and its inherent chaos. The urban farm may not yet be a viable economic model, but as a cultural idea, it's critical.

1 ANALYSIS wind studies — east — west closed system
2-3 PERSPECTIVE interiors
4-5 PERSPECTIVE exterior

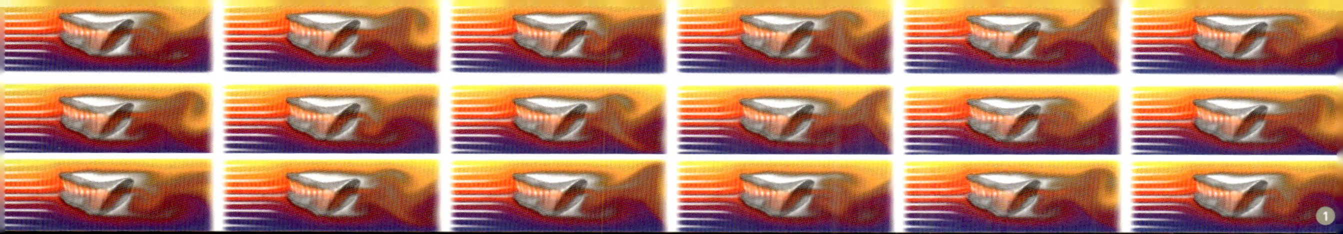
1

2

3

4

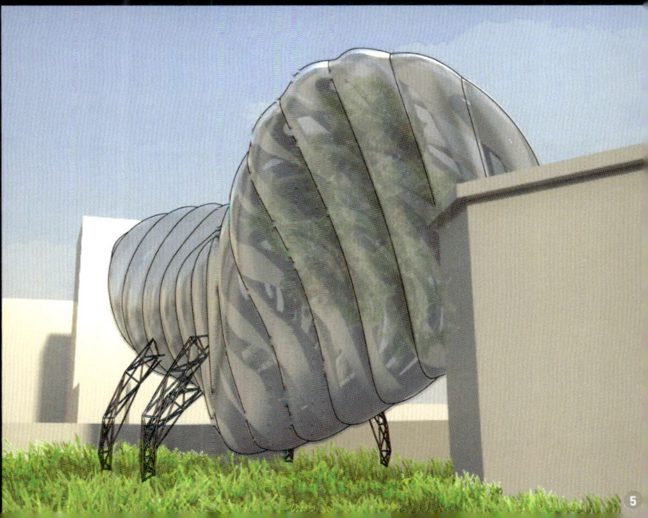
5

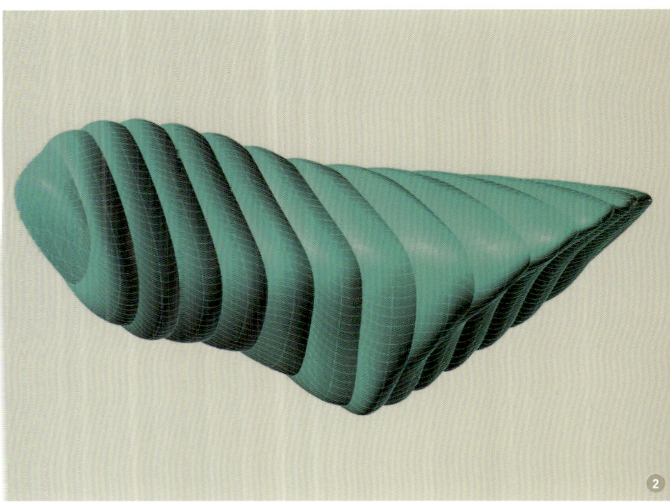

RENDERING rooftop view
MASSING of form
MASSING of forms with spiked air vents
exploded AXONOMETRIC
URBAN space station — Biodiver City Exhibition

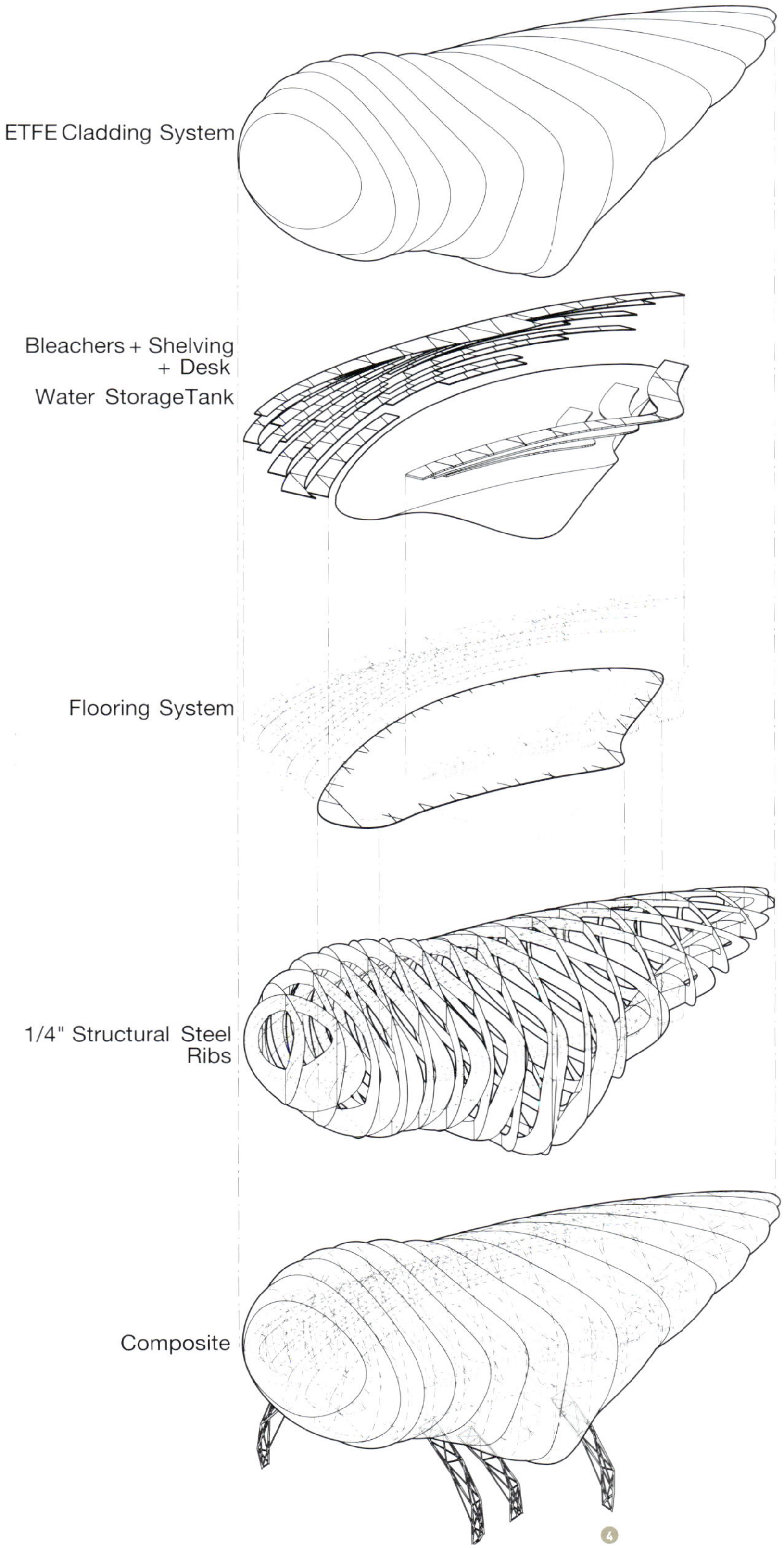
ETFE Cladding System
Bleachers + Shelving + Desk
Water StorageTank
Flooring System
1/4" Structural Steel Ribs
Composite

4

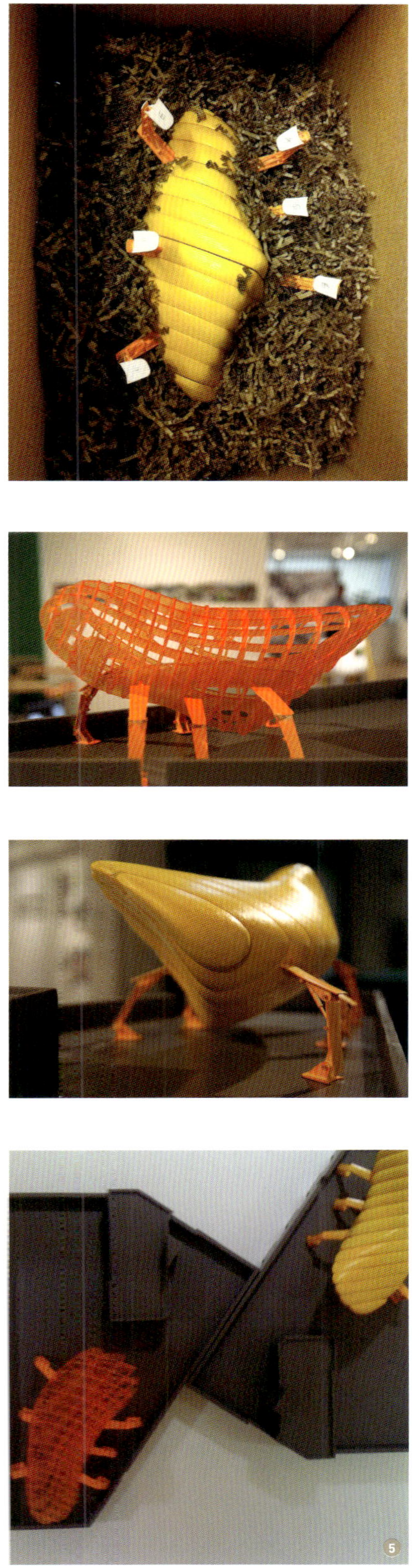

5

1.4 bulkhead 2E

When construction is no longer burdened by having to use only horizontal and vertical planes, form moves. Literally, metaphorically, or as the eye follows the lines. Diagonally or along curved lines, form influences the users and they become aware that the space is suggesting the force of movement on them.

The bulkhead is on the roof of a two-storey building surrounded by 16-storey buildings on three sides. It is seen from all those sides. On the outside the form folds along diagonal lines like creases in paper, shedding the water off the roof onto the deck below and away from the structure. This form obviates the necessity for drains or down pipes, which has the added benefit that the sound of the rain is amplified as it pours onto the decking surface.

Inside the bulkhead, there is a staircase and landing that leads to the roof. The stair wraps around a bookcase that is open on both sides. Desks hang from the stair structure, one on the lower level, another on the roof level. There is a skylight above the stair, and the metal stair treads are perforated to allow light down into the darkest part of the apartment. At the top of the stair there is a small room that leads outside to the decked area, which contains a mechanism that allows for a bed. The interior form is sculpted using twists, folds, and undulations to create a soft flow of light and action along with the suggested movement of the stair.

1 PERSPECTIVE bulkhead addition + stair
2 roof PLAN
3 VIEW rooftop

1

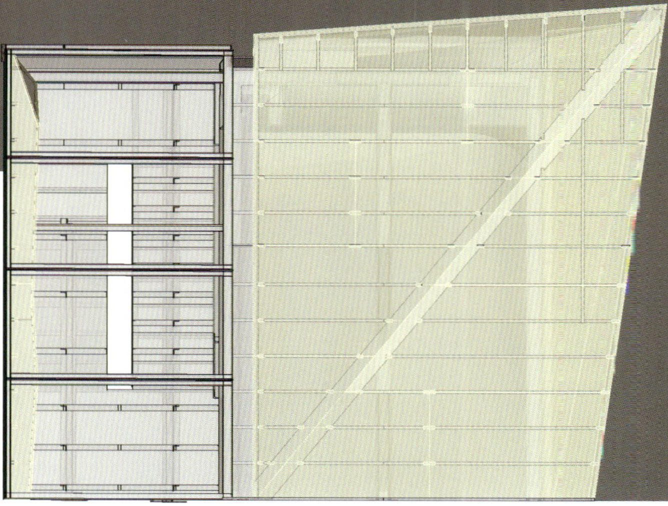

2

3

1

2

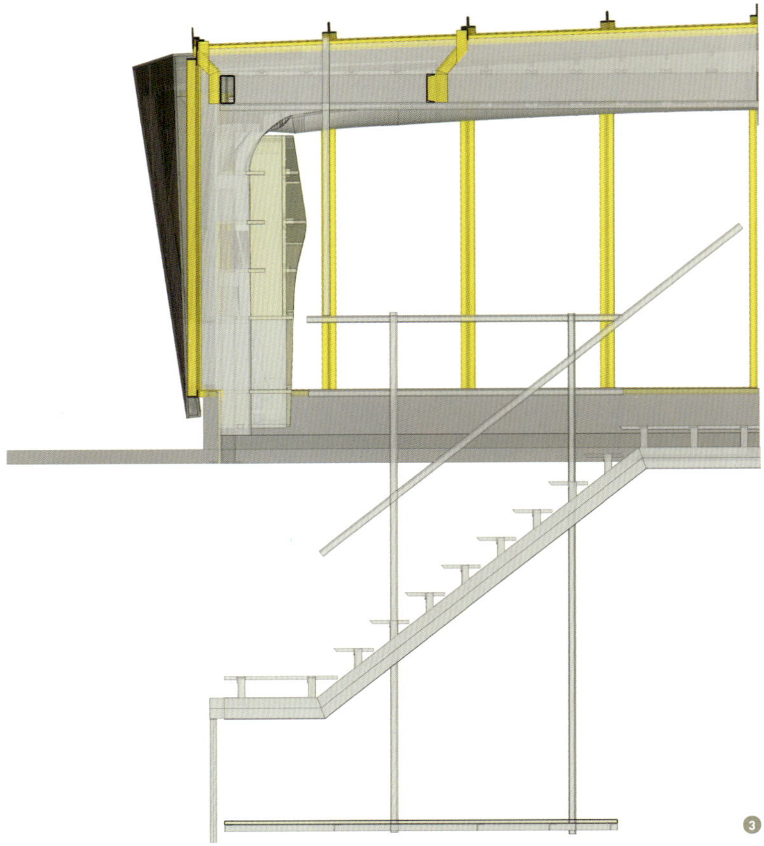

3

1 VIEW looking uptown
2 VIEW outside in
3 SECTION desk, stair, bulkhead
4 VIEW into the bulkhead
5 PLAN apartment

4

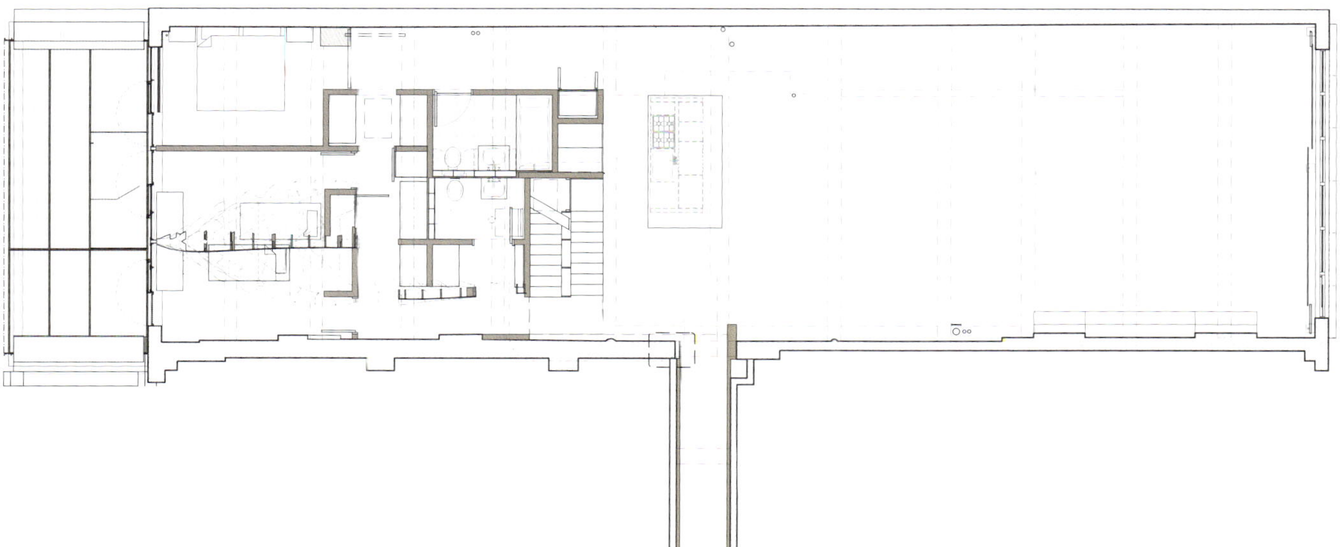

5

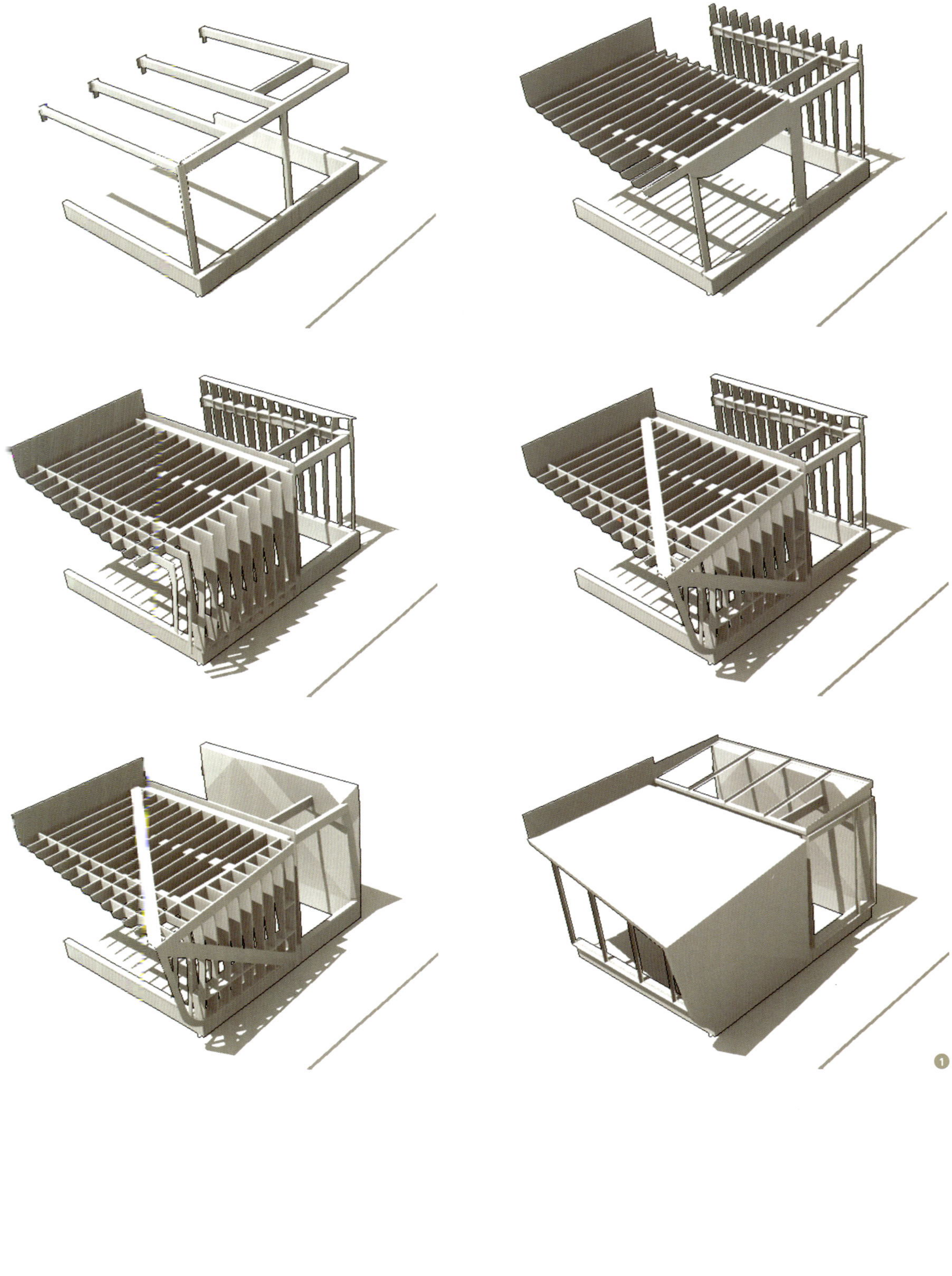

1 AXONOMETRIC bulkhead construction sequence
2 CONSTRUCTION roof structure
3 CONSTRUCTION showing ribbed structure + steel frame
4 VIEW stair bulkhead from below

1

2

3

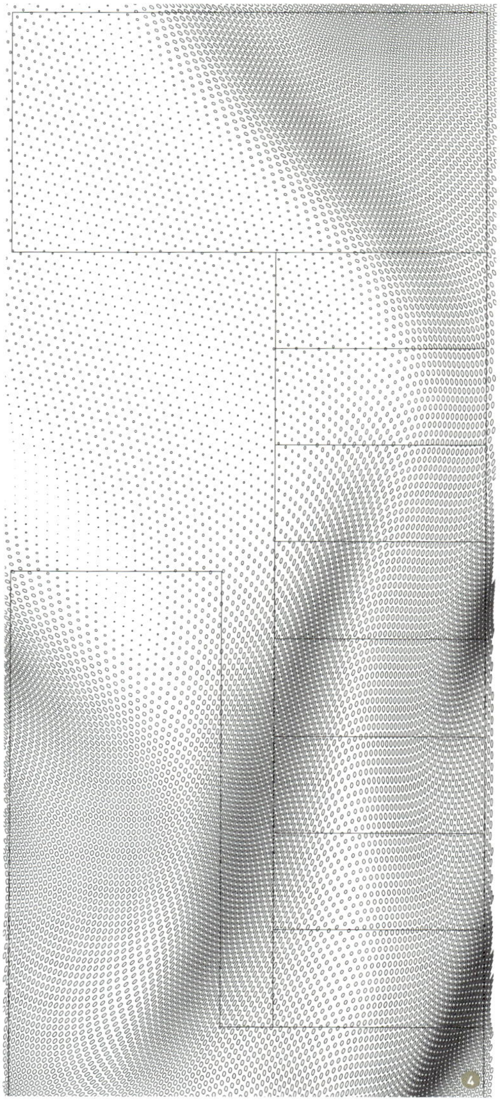

4

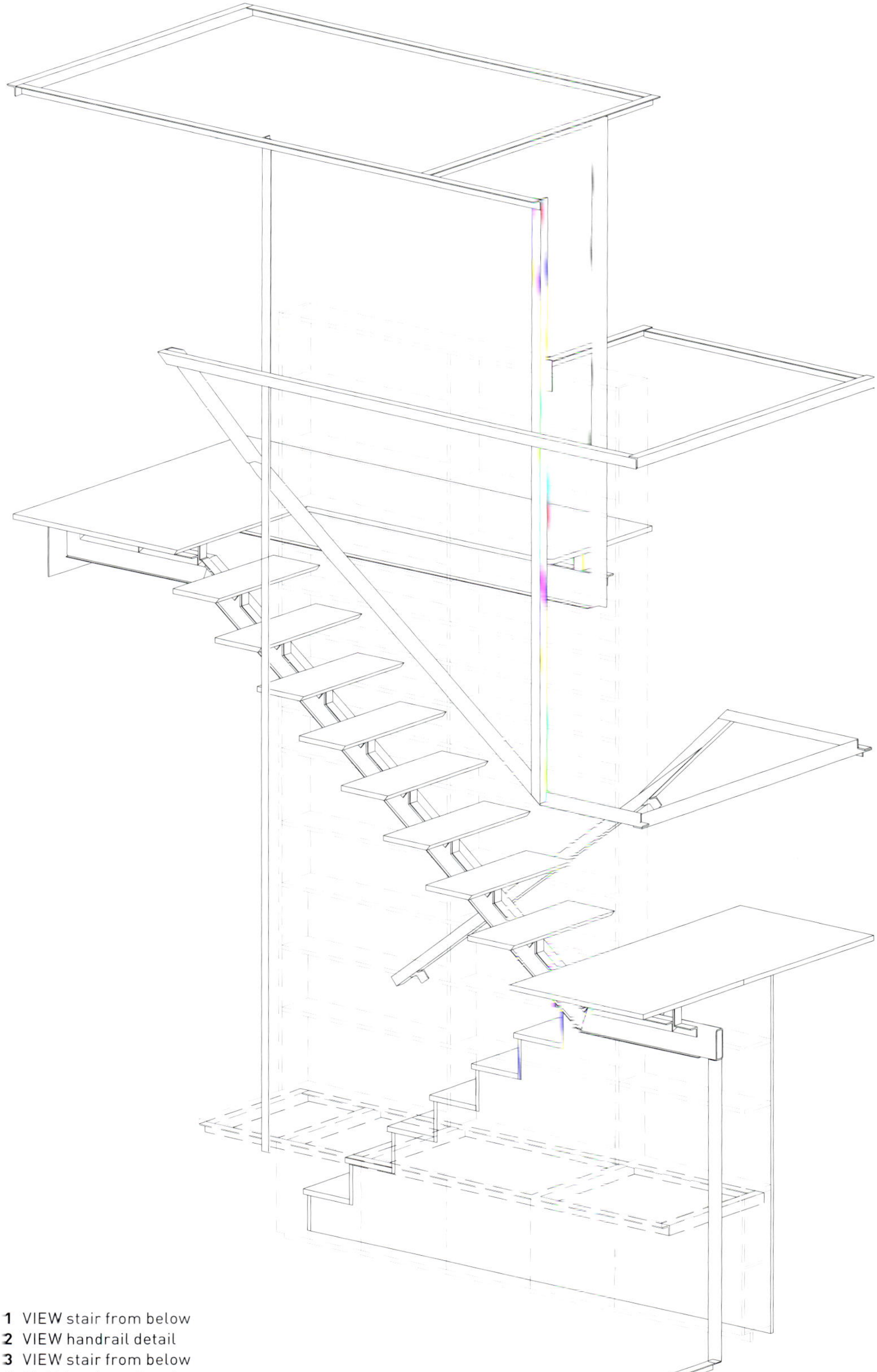

5

1 VIEW stair from below
2 VIEW handrail detail
3 VIEW stair from below
4 PLAN stair perforation pattern
5 AXONOMETRIC of stair

1 VIEW murphy bed up position
2 VIEW bulkhead looking out
3 VIEW shelving
4 VIEW murphy bed detail

1 VIEW below skylight and above stair
2 VIEW skylight support
3 VIEW murphy bed down position
4 VIEW bulkhead inside out
5 VIEW handrail detail

3

4

5

1.5 terminal pop-UP

Barangaroo is a harborside site in Sydney, Australia, named after the wife of the first Aborigine who tried to set up communication between the white settlers and the indigenous people. She disapproved of her spouse's collaborations and remained with her people, but stayed married to him. In the same way the large site is a juncture, half in one camp, half in another. It's being redeveloped from shipping and stevedoring to accommodate commercial and recreational uses. In the interim, the site is in a transitional phase, mostly used as a pop up space for parties and events and SYSTEM was invited to submit design solutions for this interim period.

We developed our idea as an ecology of interconnected use and form at the scale of a large urban site. Ecology, a term first coined by nineteenth-century biologist Ernst Haeckel, describes a system having to do with domestic use and economy. We used the notion of an ecology of activities to populate the site with moments for social interaction. The transition from one use to another and the varying degrees of interaction are in keeping with the history of the site.

We started by mapping the flow of the drop-off and parking at the site, together with the recreational activities of the adjacent urban park and river walk. By charting these, we observed a series of patterns emerging over the site that showed a density of overlapping actions and infrastructure, and imagined these as sites for a casual meeting. Our forms responded to the movement of users creating moments for micro-uses like sitting, taking a drink, resting, with the possibility for social interaction. A social ecology is spread across the site that is in effect at all times of day and night.

1 AERIAL perspective event pavilion
2 PLAN organising pattern with pavilion
3 SITE mapping

1

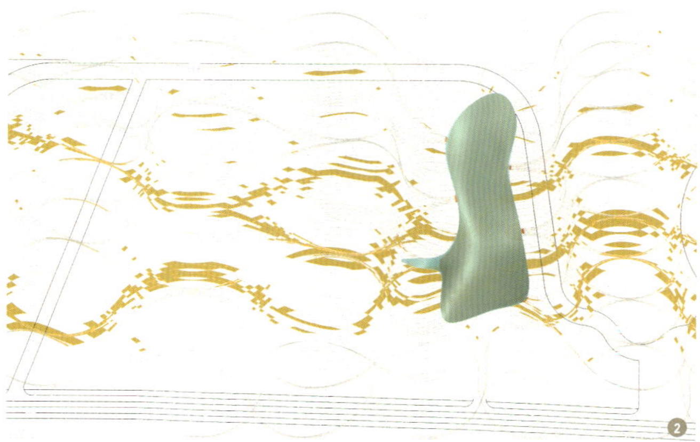

2

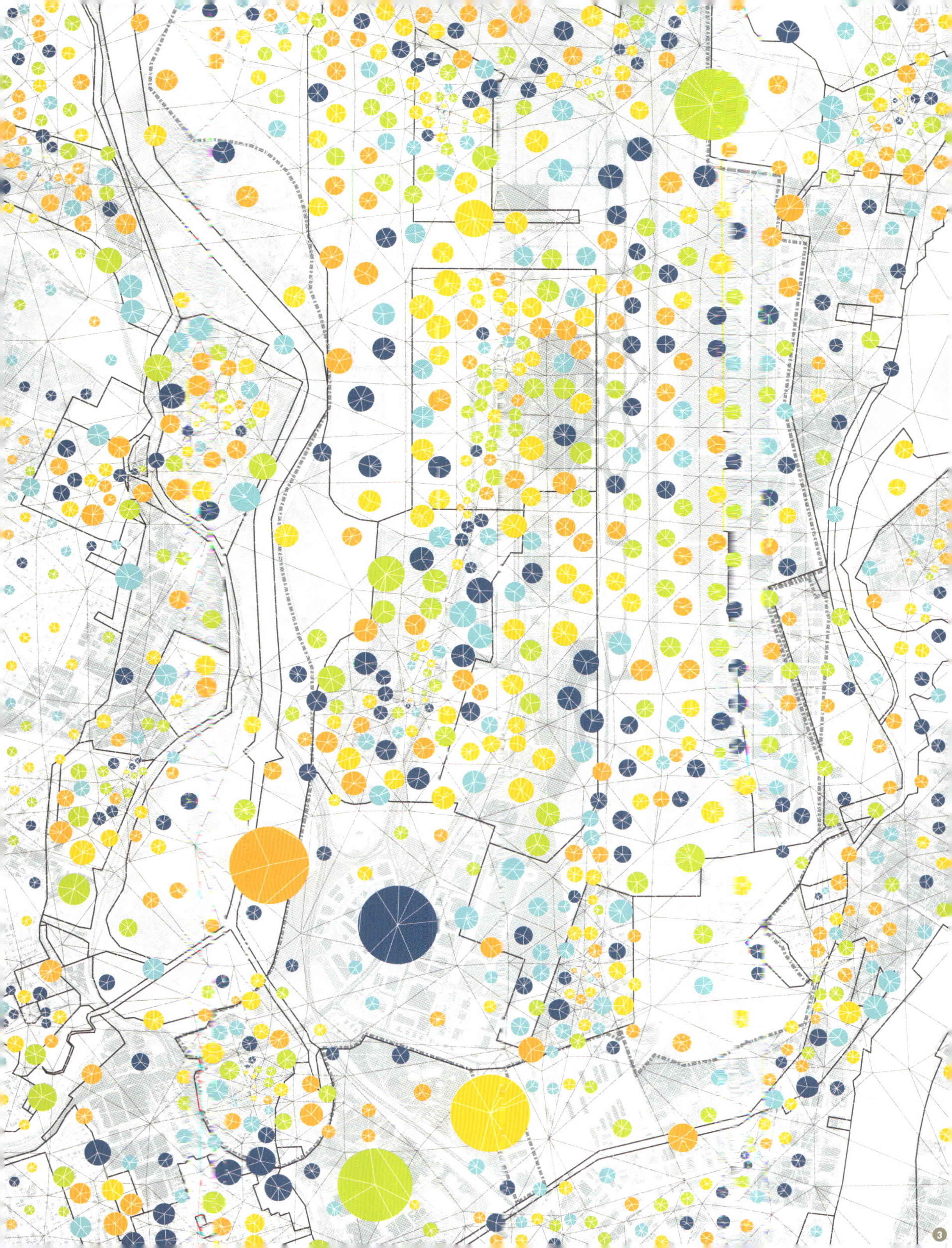

3

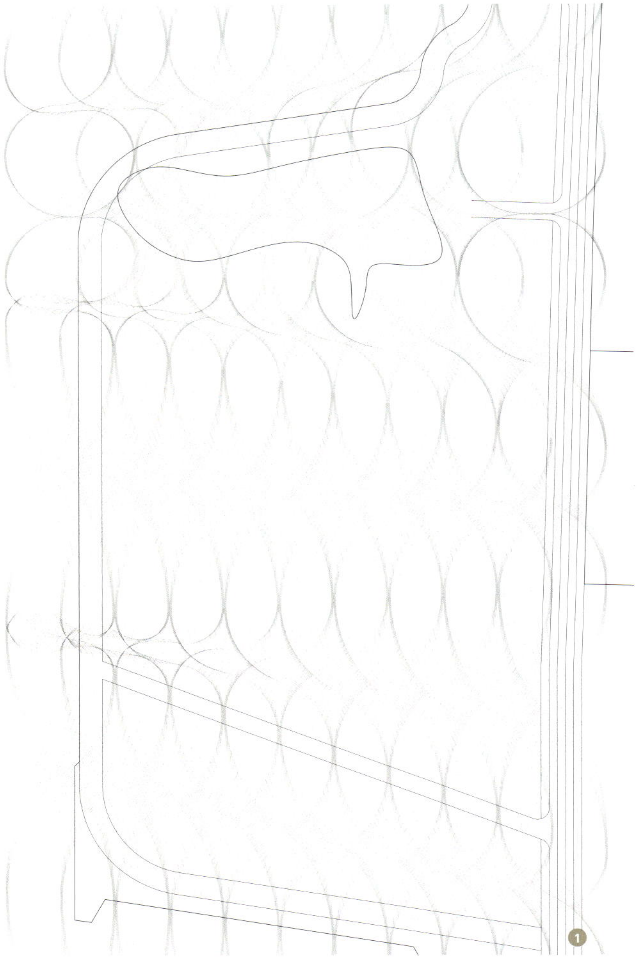

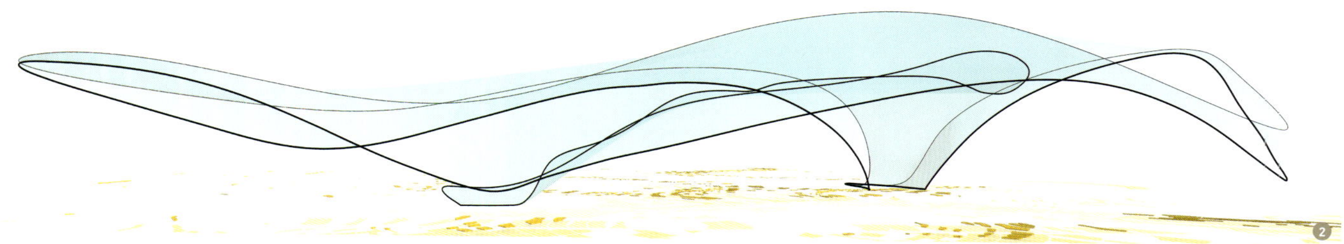

1 DIAGRAM organising grid
2 SKETCH event pavilion
3 RENDERING from water
4 RENDERING from the entrance

3

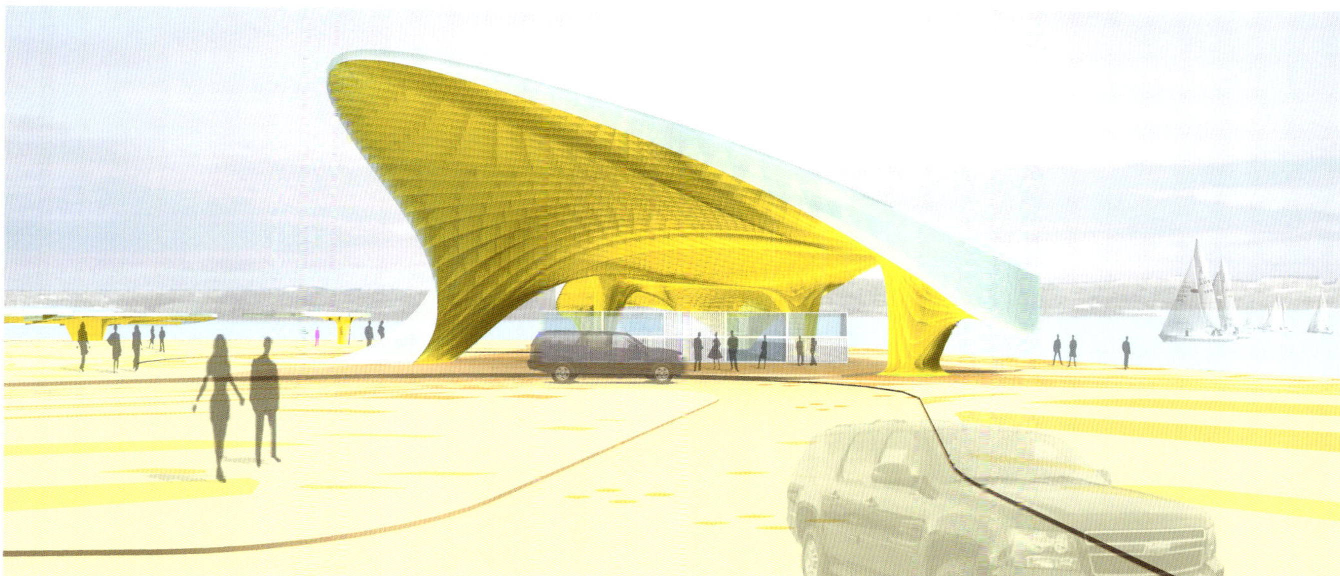

4

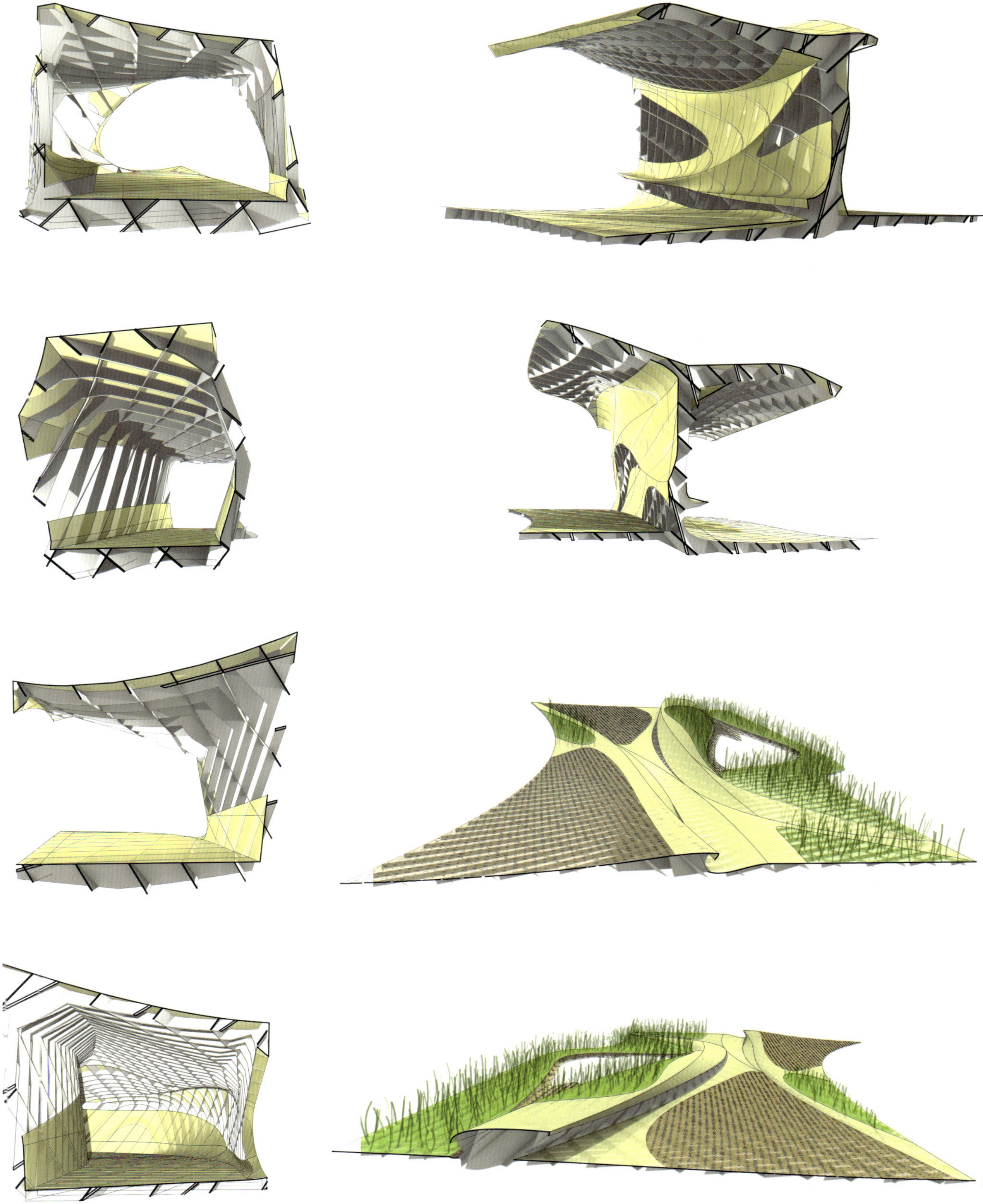

1

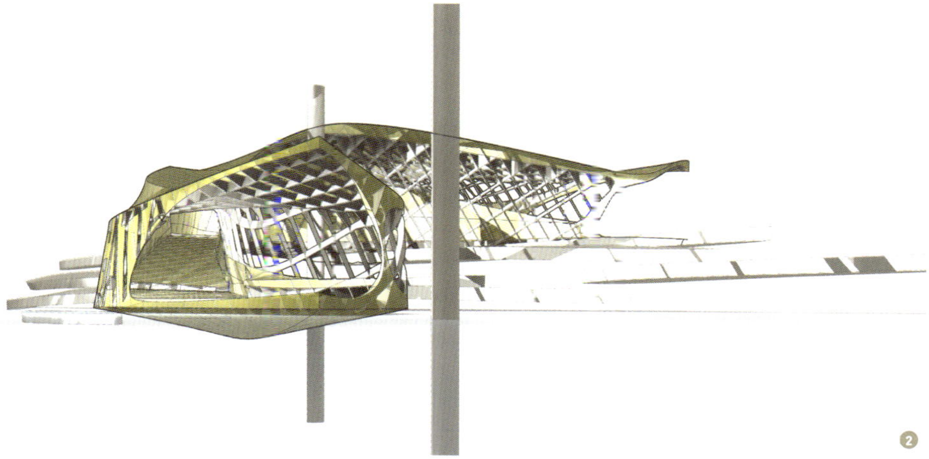

2

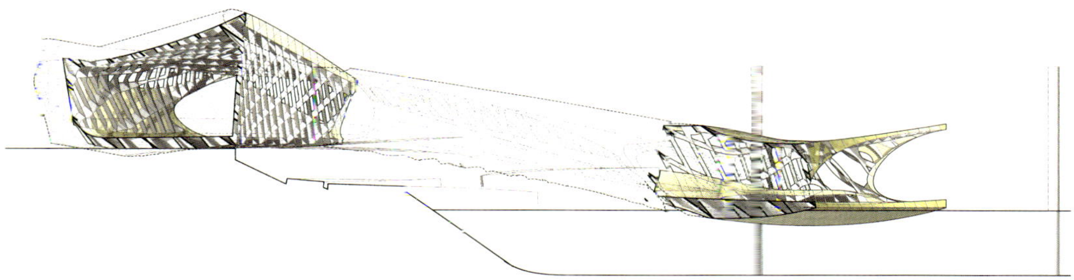

3

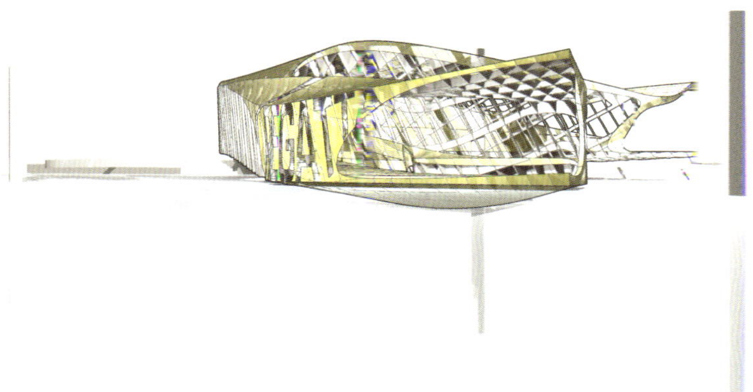

4

1 VARIATIONS of auxiliary structures
2-3 section PERSPECTIVE ferry stop
4 PERSPECTIVE ferry stop

2

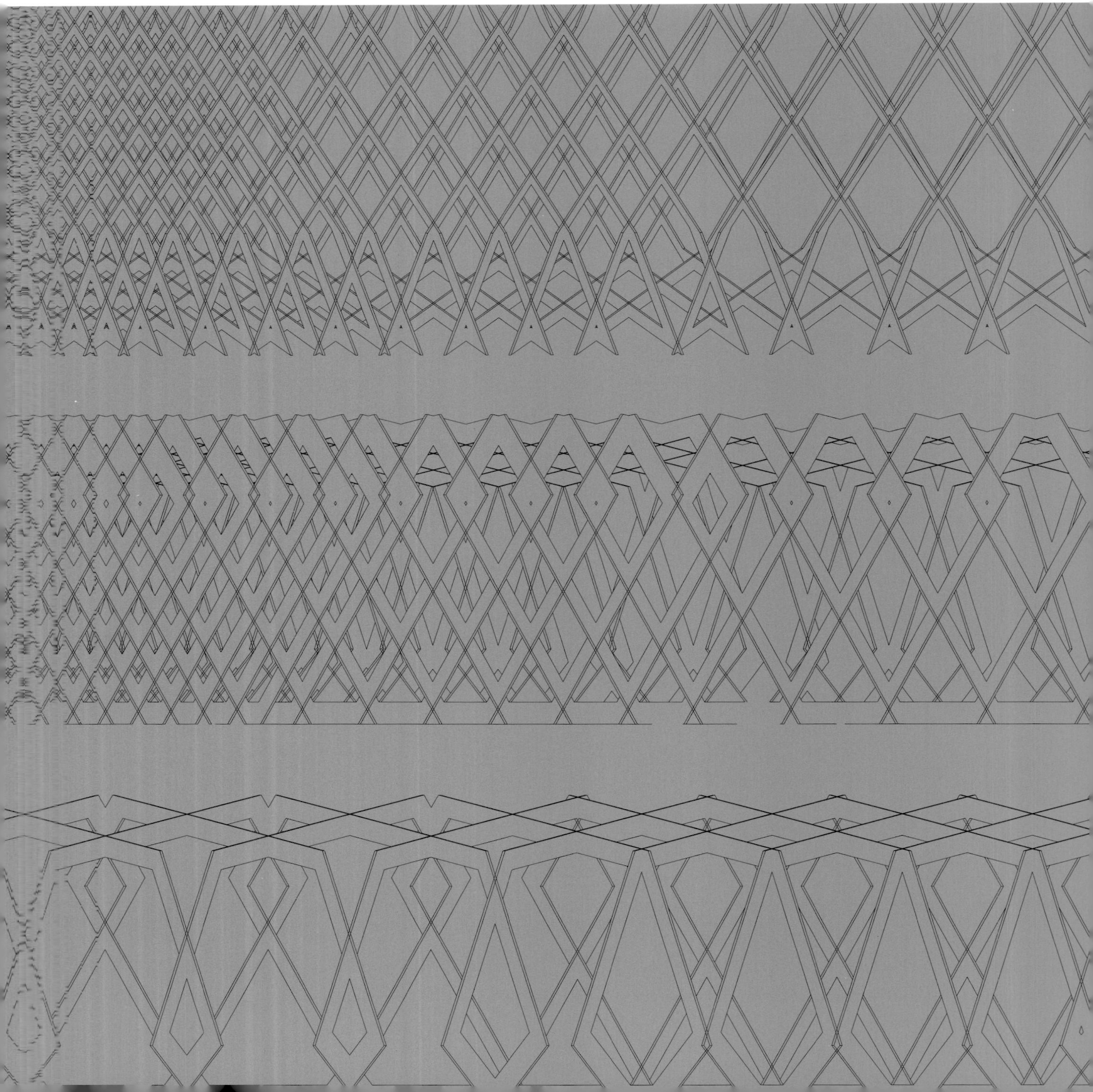

structure + connection

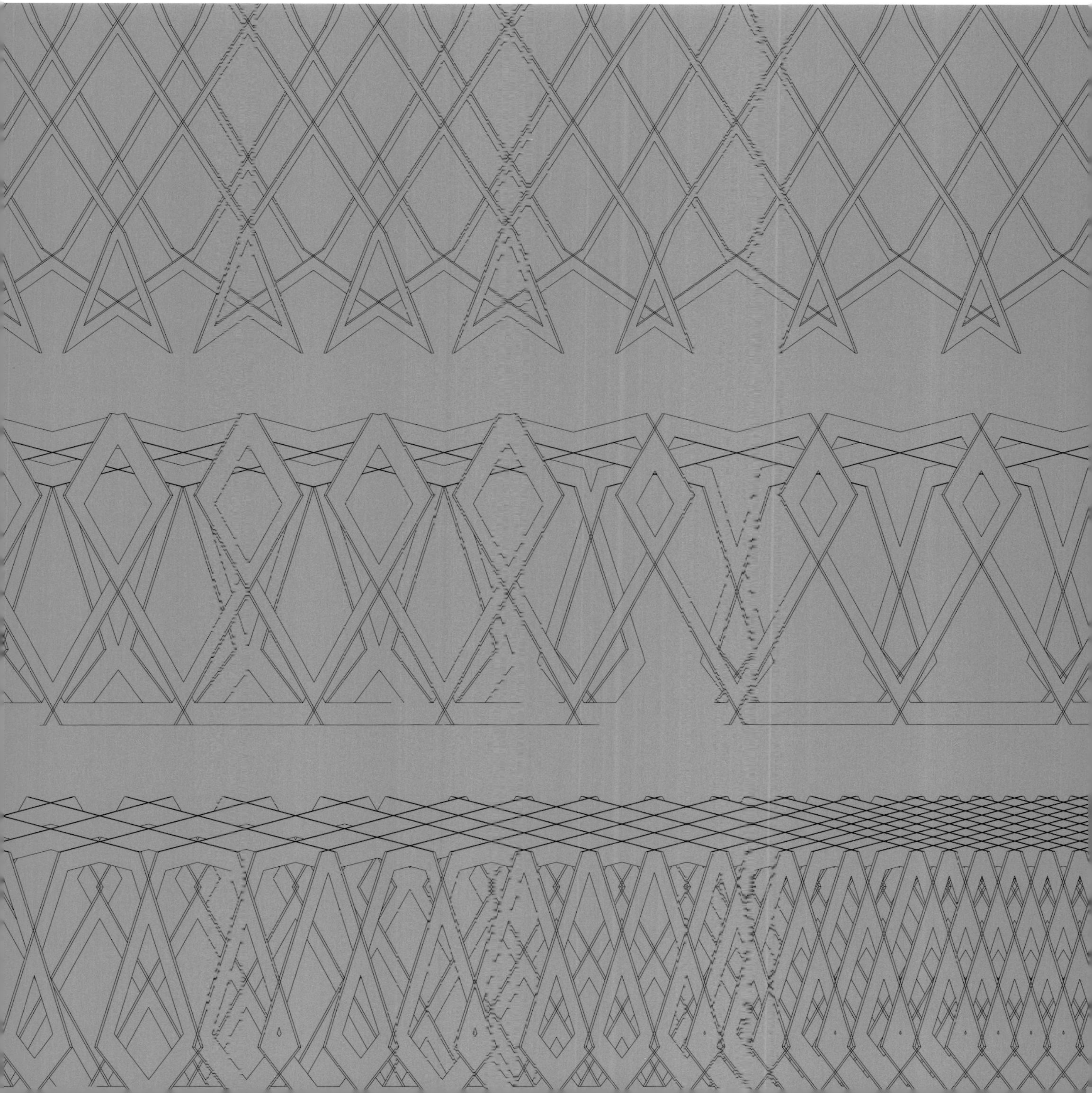

structure + connection

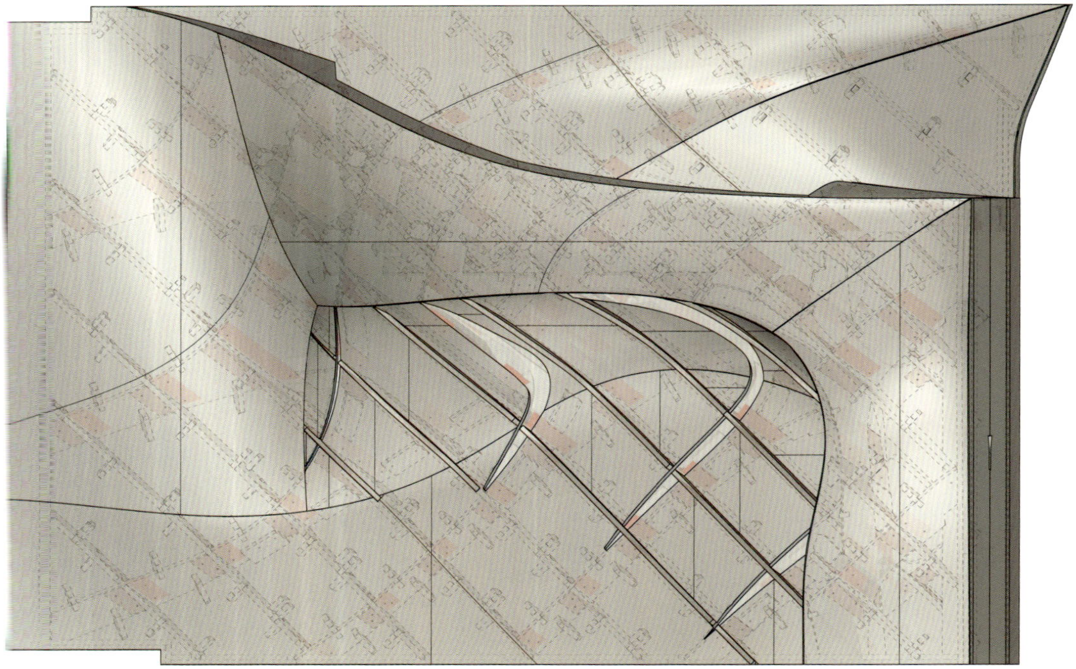

Structure is commonly thought of as the skeleton for form. But what has directed the way SYSTEM builds is an interdependence between structure and form, a symbiosis that binds them so tightly it becomes impossible to separate them. Form is no longer just shape and structure no longer just support; the roles are indistinguishable. As SYSTEM developed its 'kit of parts' method of construction, the interplay between structure, connection and form became ever more intimate. Pushing that idea further, form and structure, skin and skeleton begin to penetrate each other's space and miscegenate.

The Wellfleet project (see p. 056) was designed with a relatively conventional structure: a steel frame with attached cladding and infill walls. Using conventional construction methods, it would have been difficult to reconcile the exterior sloped planes with the stepped planes needed for the organization of the beds, but because steel can be manipulated with precision and accuracy, the frame and cladding could be fabricated offsite. It could then be assembled without the onerous task of measuring and cutting shapes on site. However, it was inescapable that the pavillion designed for temporary visitors was many times stronger and heavier than the light wooden structure of the main house that had sat on top of the hill for more than 50 years. Further innovation was needed.

BURST* (see page 030) was a beach shack, so we approached the structural design in the same way that we might build a model in the studio, by thinking about a network of ribs made of light plywood or chipboard or acrylic for the model) that could be cut with the geometry of the form embedded. The accuracy was still the result of the pieces being factory-made, but there were many more smaller parts. The necessary rigidity came from the juncture of those parts and the plywood skin that connected the ribs together.

The success of this project—not only was it built, it was built again in another location—prompted us to develop this system in further projects to accommodate increasingly complex and subtle formal maneuvers. The 'kit of parts' that was delivered to the very first site is now more precise: it includes ribs, clips, tabs, blocks, seams, and surfaces. The design and production of this kit includes a modeling and scripting operation that would allow us in a later iteration, the KOKODAschool (see p. 086), to produce the digital files necessary to make all the parts of the kit within a couple of hours of making the form for the pavilions.

In these projects, form is literally the exterior surface of the structure. That surface is stretched over a network of ribs and generates the rigidity. The form becomes an expression of the structural forces, and the structure is in turn an expression of the programme. The form narrows and widens according to its structural and programmatic aims. The interplay between the structure and the surface can become more intricate, with ribs poking into or out of the form or form meandering in and out of the ribs. The form is not compromised; indeed it is articulated by the lines of the exposed structure.

There is an enhanced interdependency to this system of design. The physical strength and rigidity of the construction comes from the connection of the surface to the ribs, and from the thickness or depth of the form. The detailing of the elements echo this connectivity so that each of the parts which make up the kit can be influenced by the shape of the surface, and, conversely, the form is influenced by the details of the kit. There is texture to the system that is particular and may be expressed or repressed throughout the project.

The four projects in this chapter are organised counter chronologically, because the first project, KOKODAschool (unbuilt), is the culmination of previous developments in a plywood-woven structure.

2.1 KOKODAschool

1 AERIAL perspective KOKODA school
2 Kokoda Local Village

The high school in Kokoda will serve 320 students, a third of them living on site, in rural Papua New Guinea (PNG). The site is only accessible by foot or 4WD and the journey from the nearest coastal town, Popendetta, involves numerous river crossings. When built, it will be the only high school within a day's bus ride.

The project uses the local village design strategy of grouping together sets of small shelters and connecting the sets via a network of pathways, with social spaces between the groups. The traditional buildings are open-sided to promote cross ventilation and protected from daily rain and sun by overhanging roofs and elevated floors. Our design echoes this low-energy-use approach, with separate pavilions for classrooms, dormitories, and teacher housing clustered adjacent to paths. Residential buildings are lifted higher to provide undercover recreational space, and are shallow to reduce the need for artificial light. Classrooms are less than three feet off the ground to protect them from groundwater while still making them accessible. Water is collected on the roofs for drinking and washing.

Each pavilion is made as a kit of parts that can be assembled locally using the skills within the community. The assembly is repetitive, but each building is unique. The kits use locally manufactured plywood for their structure, exterior sheathing and interior surfaces. Stainless steel connectors, bolts, nuts, and waterproof paint complete the building system, which is engineered to withstand the known forces from floods, earthquakes, and cyclones. The engineered strength comes from assembling the bolts and screws in pre-drilled and numbered holes, an operation easily overseen by the construction manager. No heavy machinery will be used during construction; indeed, none would be available.

The design process employs a purpose-written scripting process that breaks the structures into numbered parts that are cut from plywood sheets using a CNC router that runs directly from the files created by the architects. This allows each building to have its own formal identity with minimal labor. Two inexpensive SHOPbots, proprietary CNC routers able to cut all the parts for the pavilions, are to be shipped to site, accompanied by operators who can train local carpenters in their use—locals gain new, usable skills as they build. PNG produces high quality exterior grade plywood; all the building parts are arranged on the plywood sheets to eliminate waste when cutting. The minimal offcuts are used in landscaping and building blocking.

These design and construction techniques have been developed through many of our prior BURST* projects, but were further refined at a research studio at University of Pennsylvania, which examined the structure and connections. BURST*003 was designed on a field of columns. BURST*008 used continuous moment frames to allow for additional load. At the UPenn research studio, we developed an alternative structural method where the plywood ribbed structure acted as a box truss-like bridge, able to span the length of the building. As a result only two columns at each end of the pavilion are necessary. We were also able to reengineer the steel clip, which is used multiple times throughout each pavilion, reducing the manufacturing cost from $1 to $15 each, not a trivial improvement for projects in a developing country.

1

2

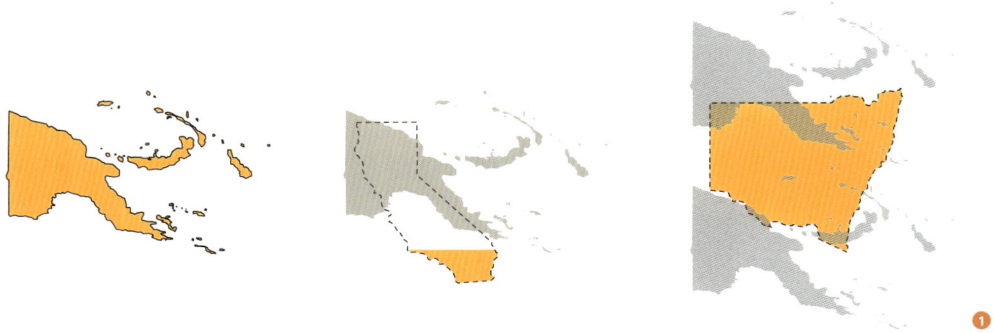

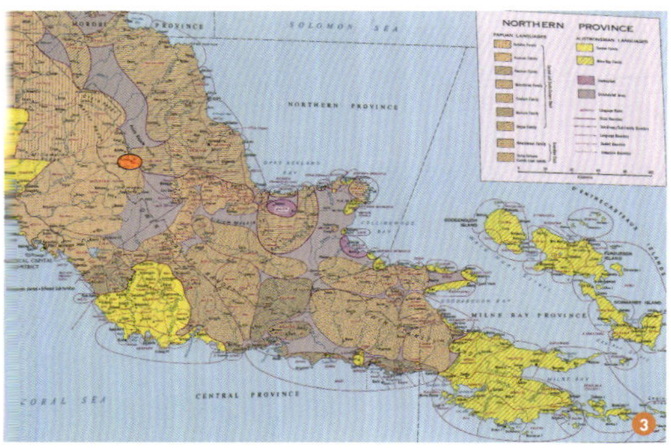

1 SITE map Papua New Guniea in relation to California + New South Wales
2 SITE map topography
3 SITE map regions
4-5 CULTURAL environment
6 SITE plan of village layouts — drawn by Wallace Ruff
7 VIEW Kokoda Villages

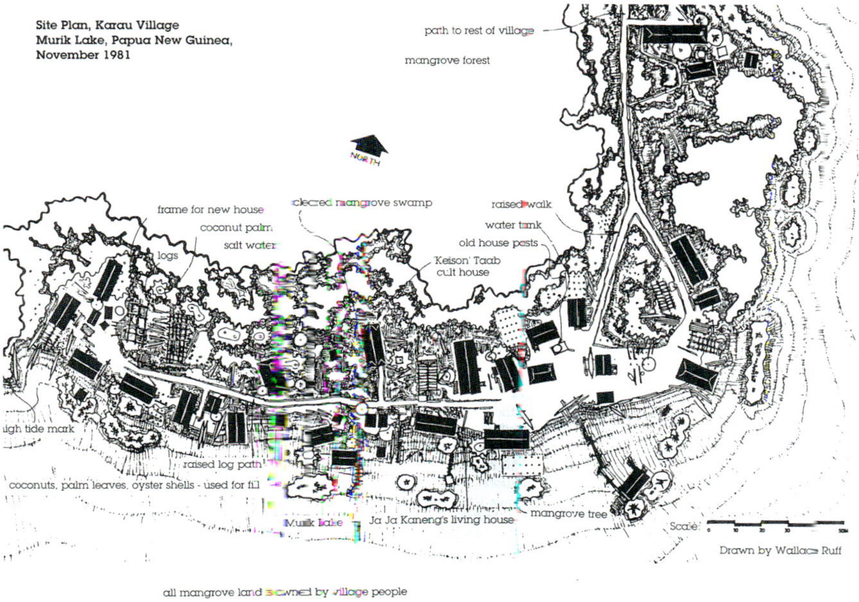

Site Plan, Karau Village
Murik Lake, Papua New Guinea,
November 1981
path to rest of village
mangrove forest
NORTH
frame for new house
coconut palm
salt water
logs
cleared mangrove swamp
raised walk
water tank
old house posts
'Keison' Taab
cult house
igh tide mark
raised log path
coconuts, palm leaves, oyster shells - used for fil
Murik lake
Ja Ja Kaneng's living house
mangrove tree
Scale:
Drawn by Wallace Ruff
all mangrove land is owned by village people

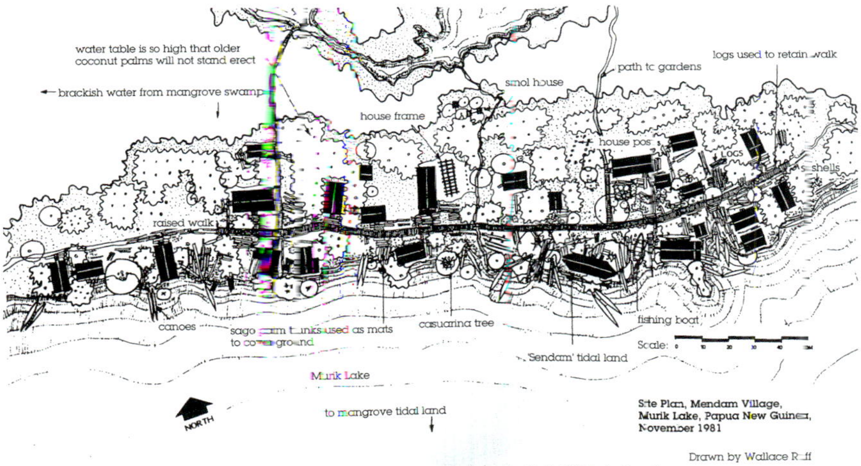

water table is so high that older
coconut palms will not stand erect
brackish water from mangrove swamp
path to gardens
logs used to retain walk
smol house
house frame
house pos
shells
raised walk
canoes
sago palm trunks used as mats
to cover ground
casuarina tree
fishing boat
'Sendam' tidal land
Scale:
Murik Lake
NORTH
to mangrove tidal land
Site Plan, Mendam Village,
Murik Lake, Papua New Guinea,
November 1981
Drawn by Wallace Ruff

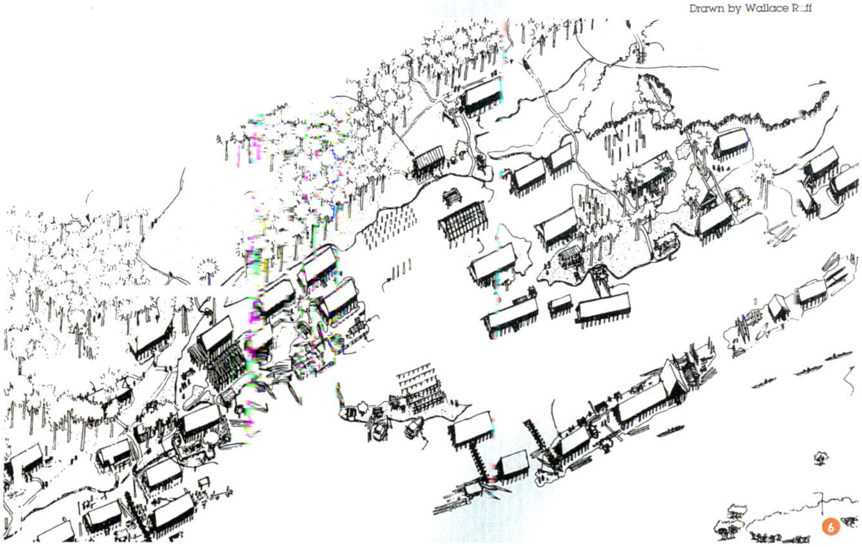

6

7

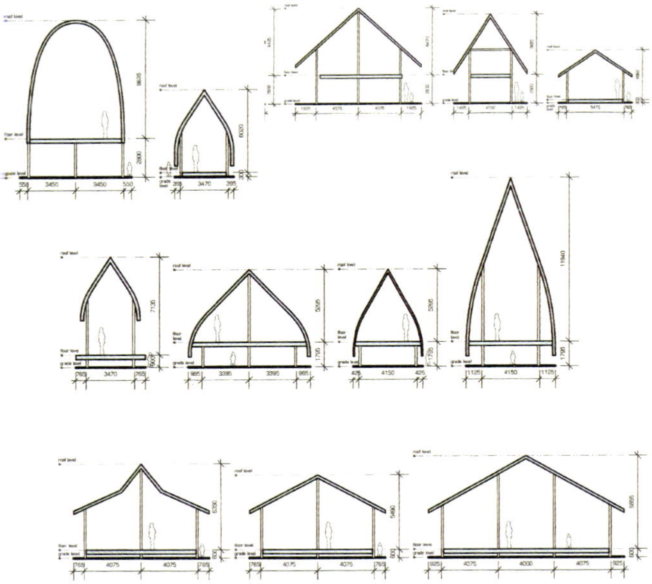

Indigenous building sections

1

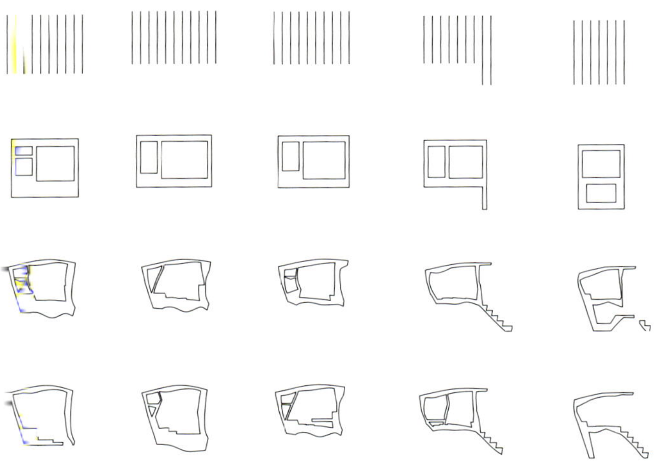

2

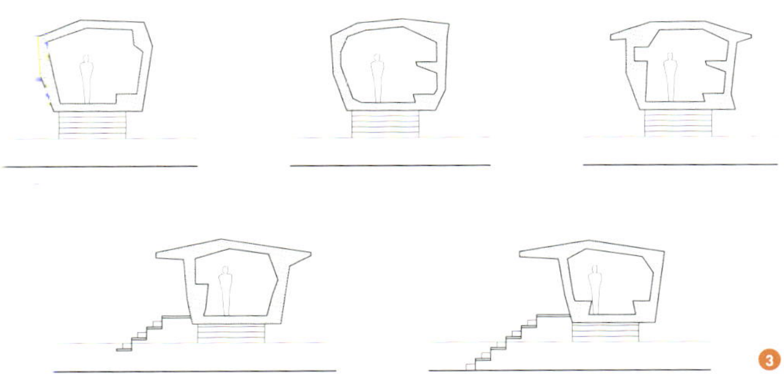

3

STUDENT DORMITORIES

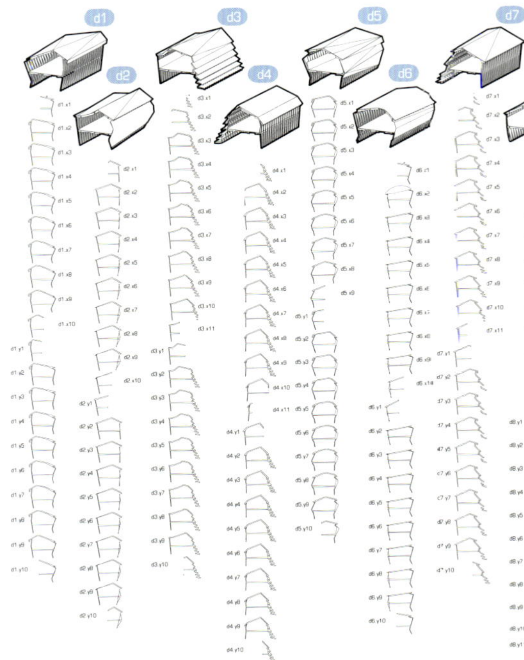

VOCATIONAL

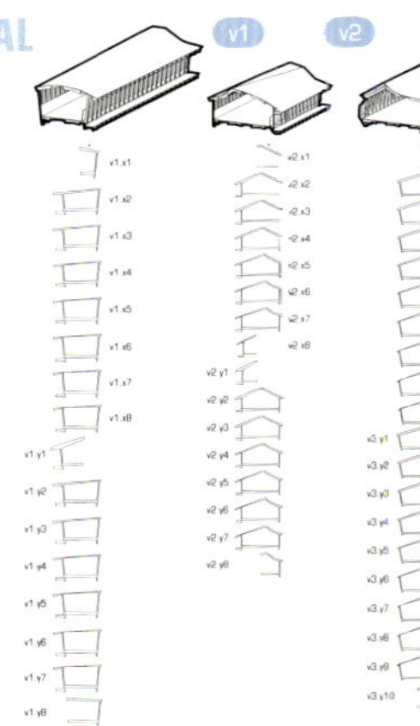

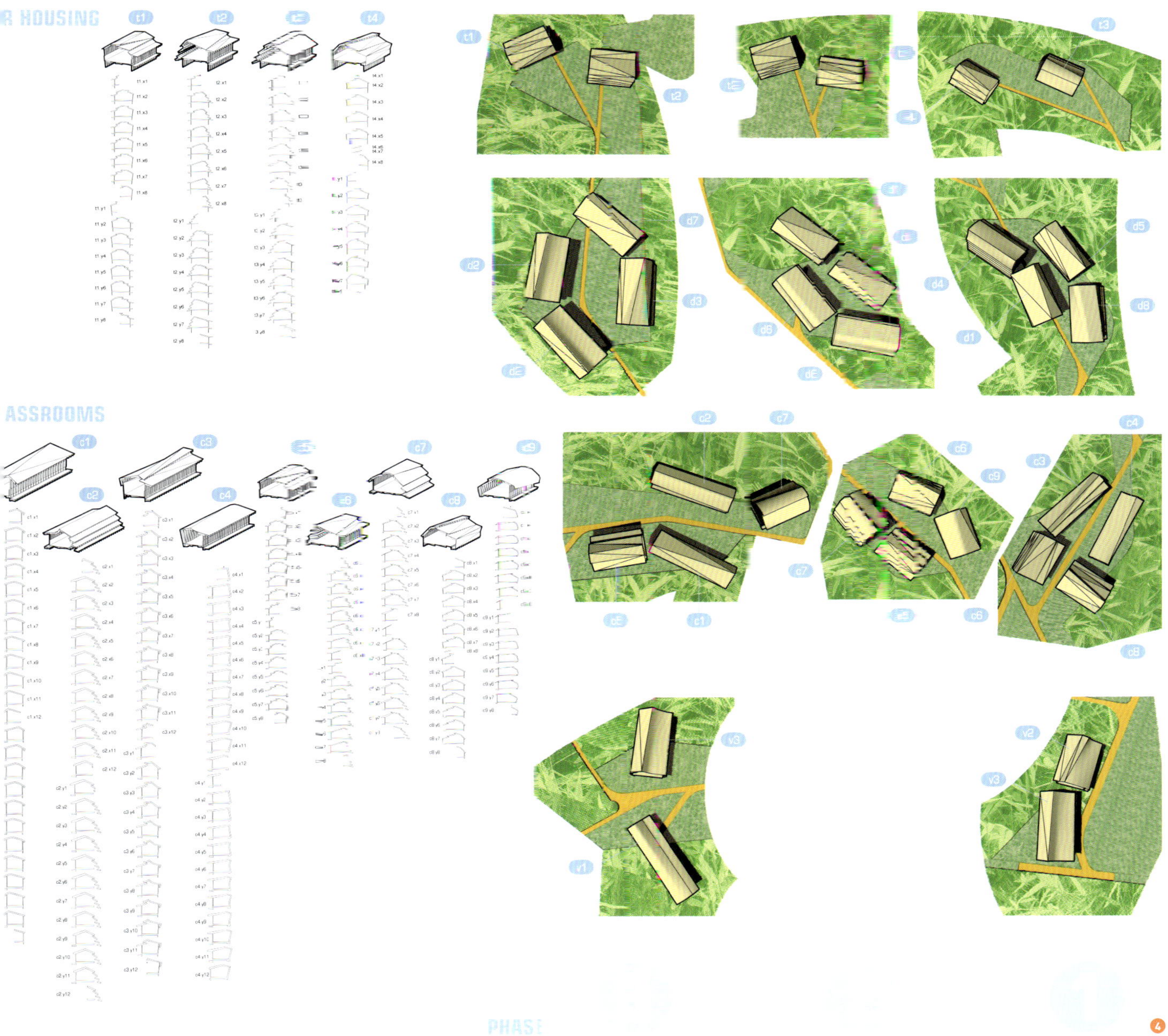

1 CULTURAL environment — indigenous building sections
2 DIAGRAM generating of Kokoda school typologies
3 DIAGRAM school typologies
4 BUILDING typology structural ribs + arrangement
5 EXISITING structural conditions

1 RENDERING classroom section
2 PERSPECTIVE undercroft view
3 AXONOMETRIC site planning
4 INDEGENOUS materials

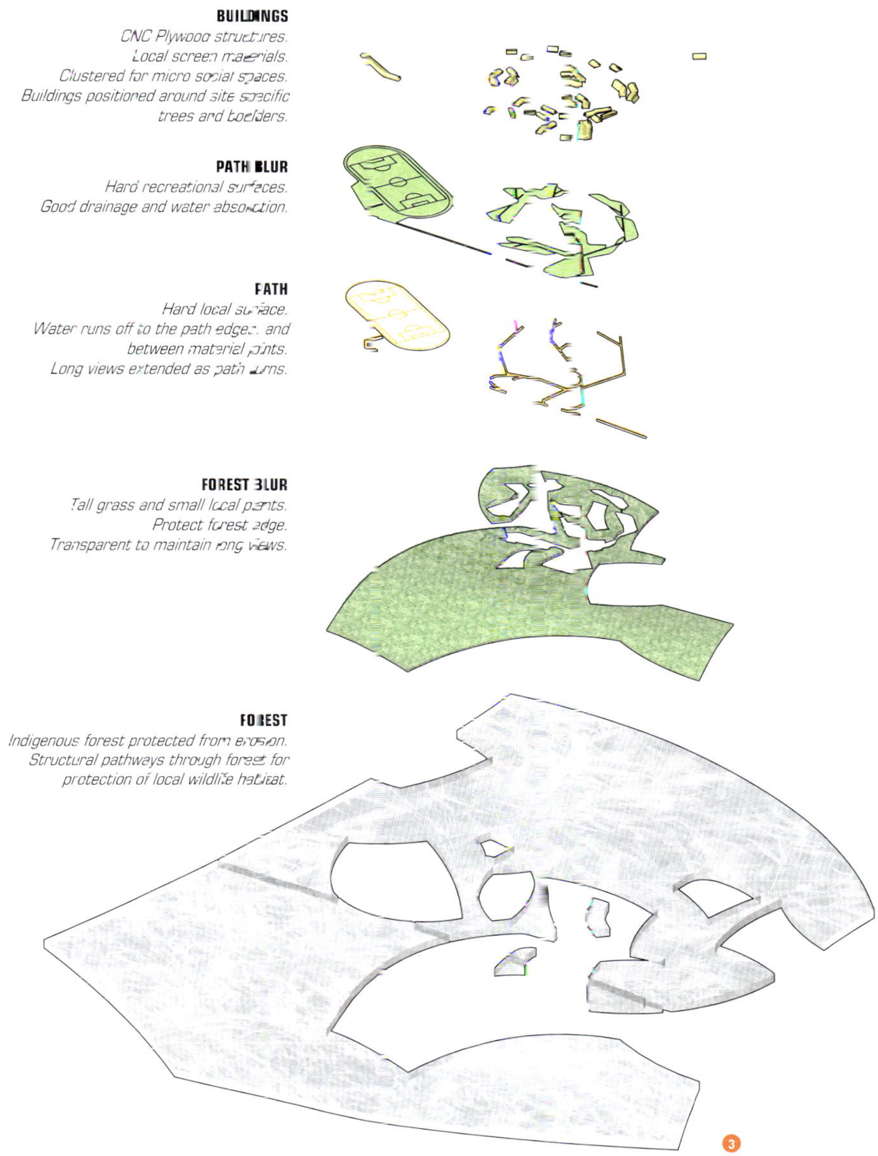

BUILDINGS
CNC Plywood structures.
Local screen materials.
Clustered for micro social spaces.
Buildings positioned around site specific trees and boulders.
PATH BLUR
Hard recreational surfaces.
Good drainage and water absorption.
PATH
Hard local surface.
Water runs off to the path edges and between material joints.
Long views extended as path turns.
FOREST BLUR
Tall grass and small local plants.
Protect forest edge.
Transparent to maintain long views.
FOREST
Indigenous forest protected from erosion.
Structural pathways through forest for protection of local wildlife habitat.
3

4

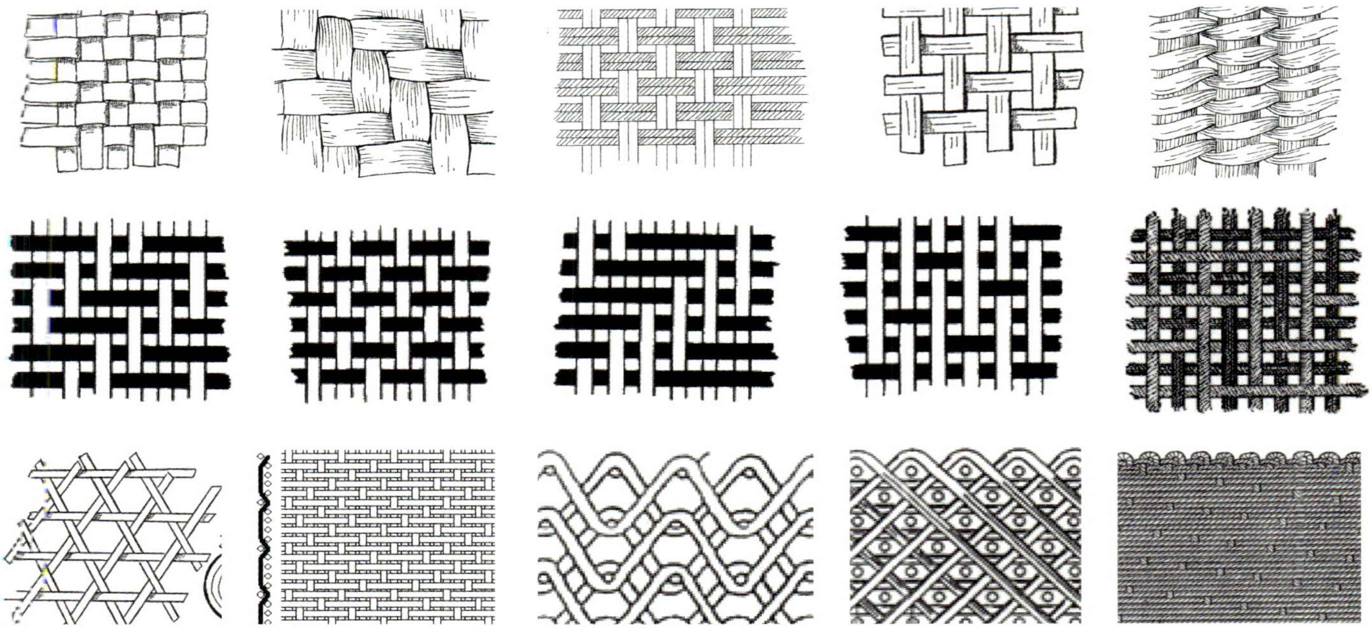

1

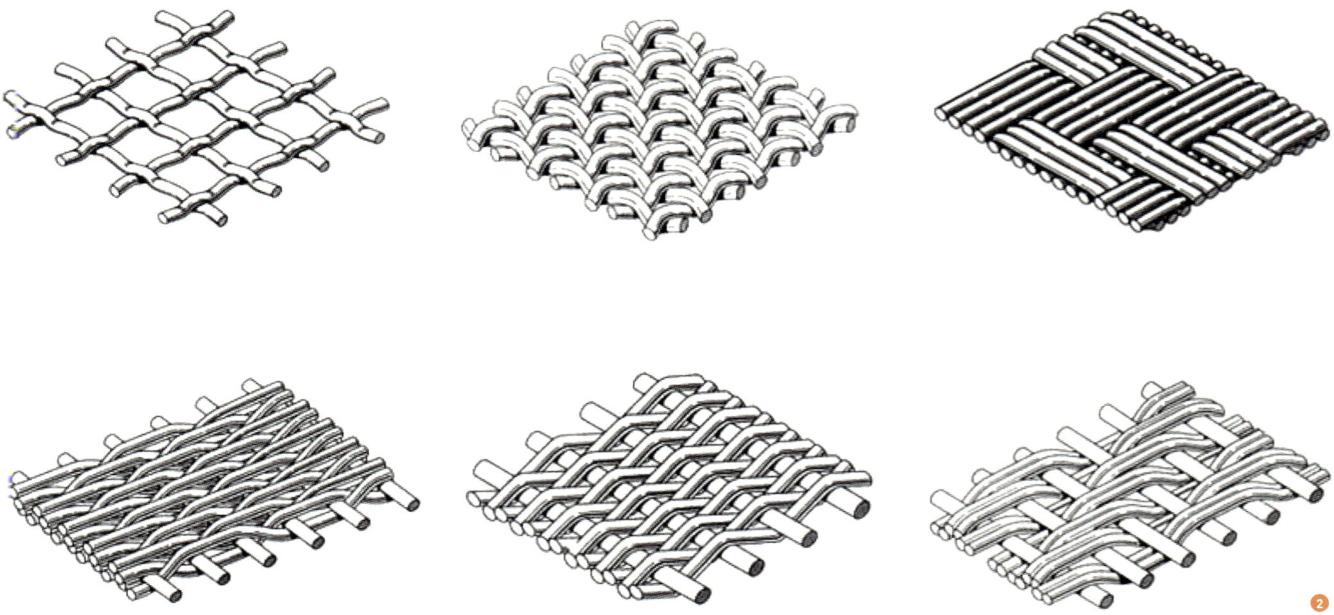

2

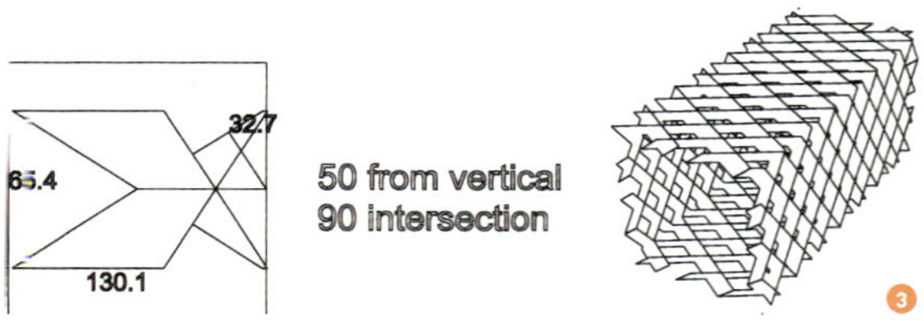

3

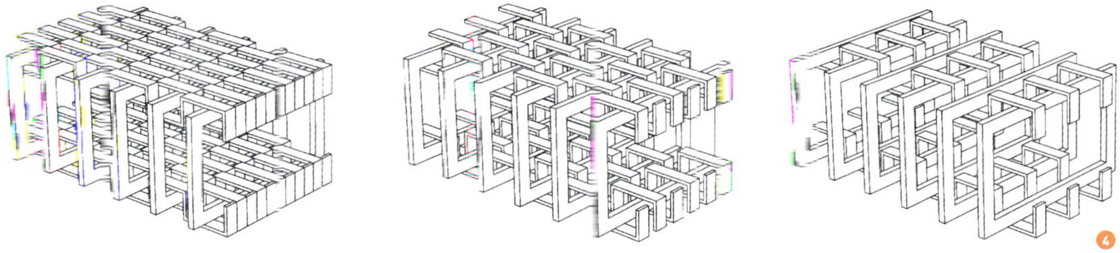

4

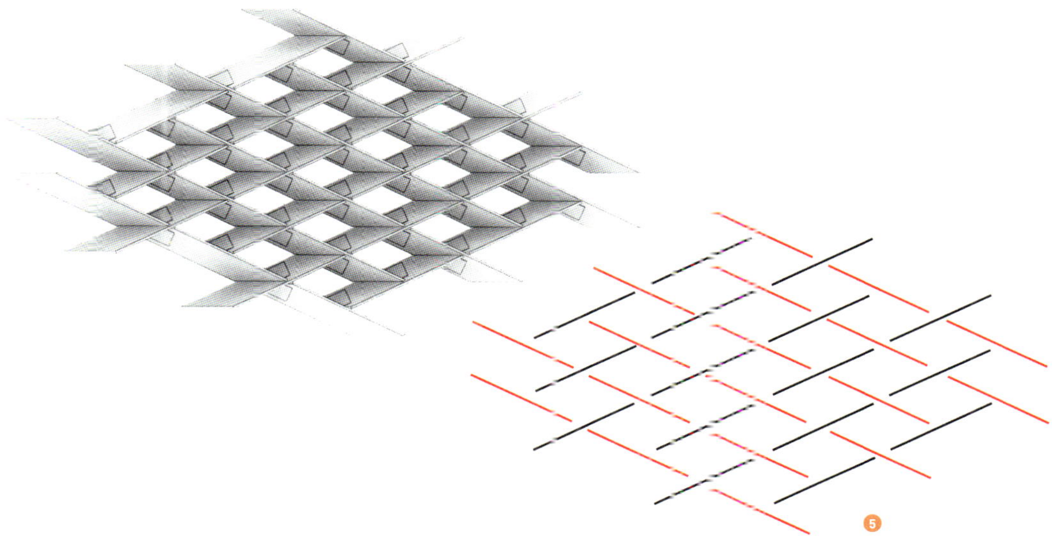

5

6

7

1 This PATTERNS weaving techniques — compiled by UPenn Research Lab
2 DIAGRAM structural grid orientation — drawn by UPenn Research Lab
3 AXONOMETRIC structural box truss — drawn by UPenn Research Lab
4 AXONOMETRIC structural weaving
5 DIAGRAM pinwheel construction technique — drawn by UPenn Research Lab
6 VIEW Hokoda Villages
7 CONSTRUCTION structural rib prototype

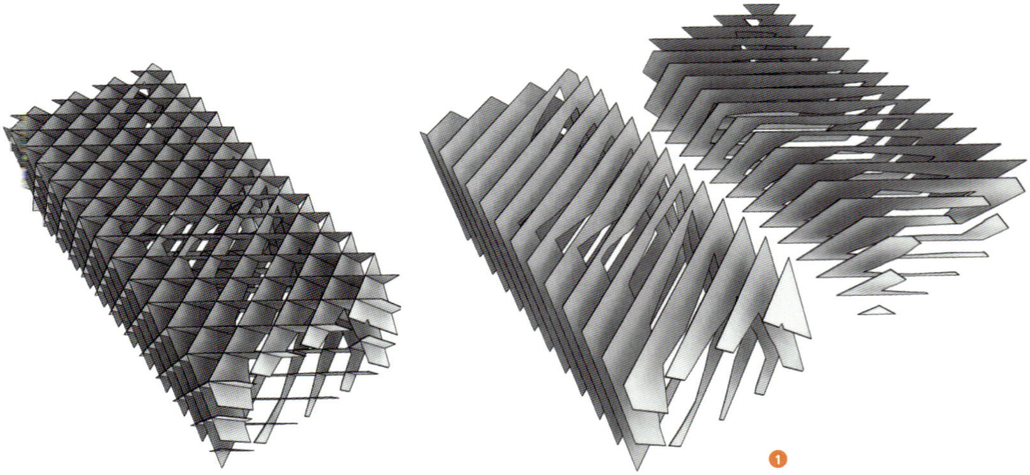

1

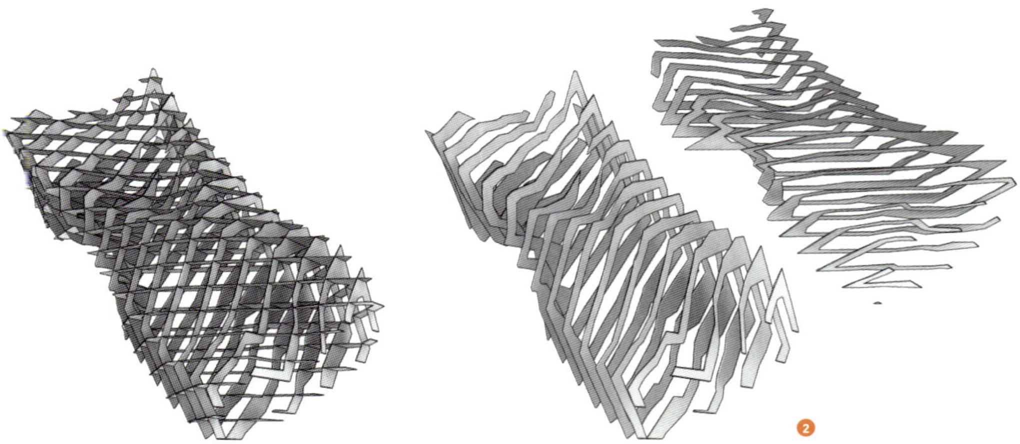

2

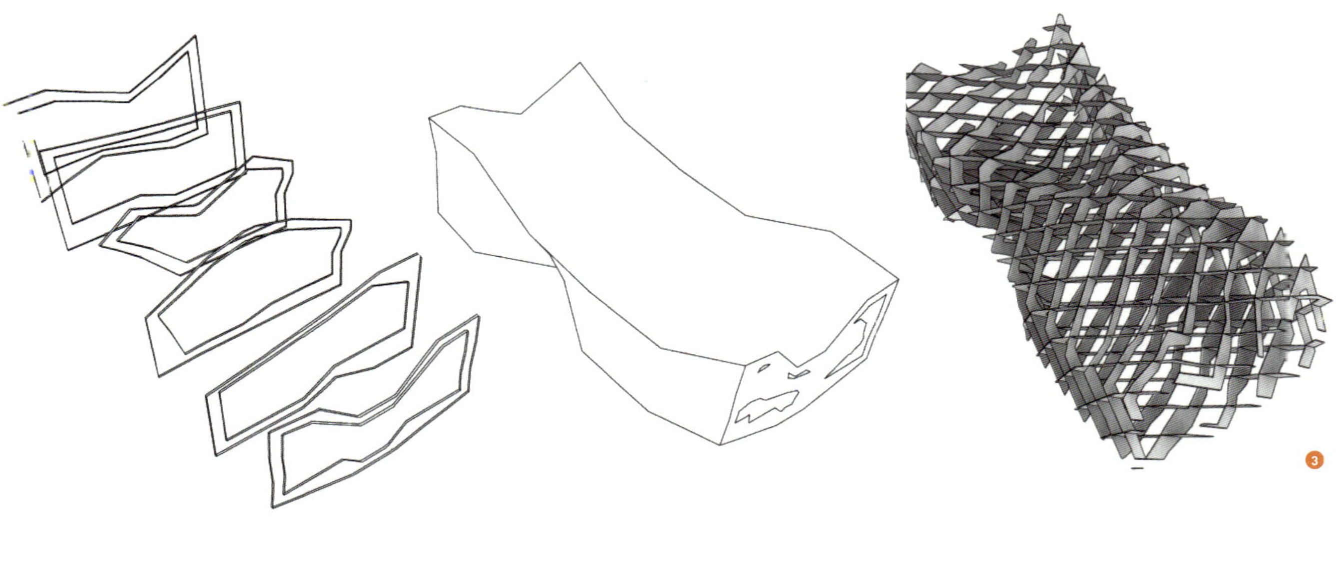

3

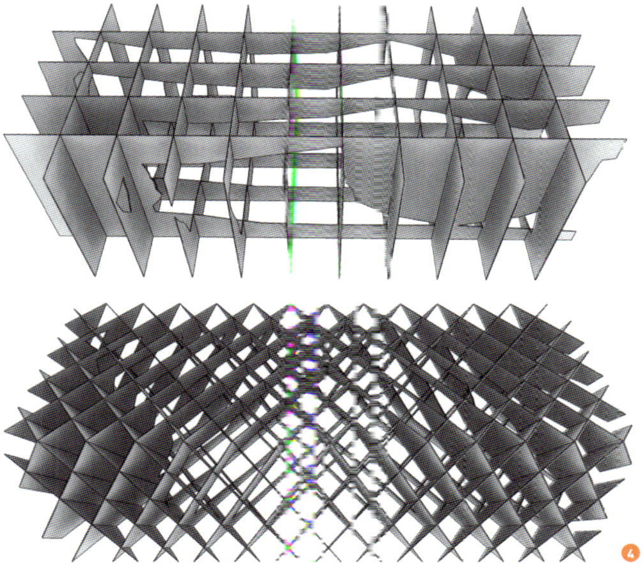

4

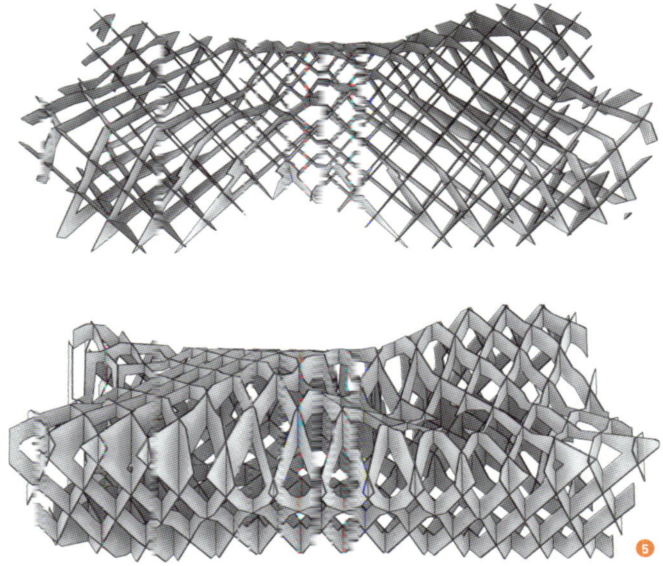

5

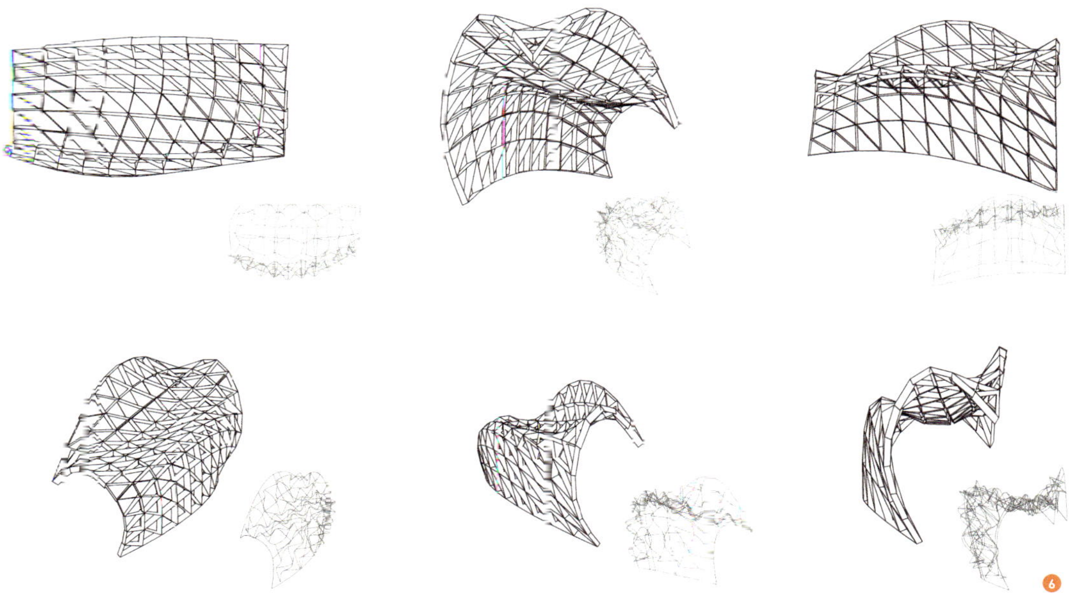

6

1-3 UPENN Research Lab Structural Rib Experimentation — Box Truss
4-5 STRUCTURAL rib orientation experiments
6 STRUCTURAL surface experiments

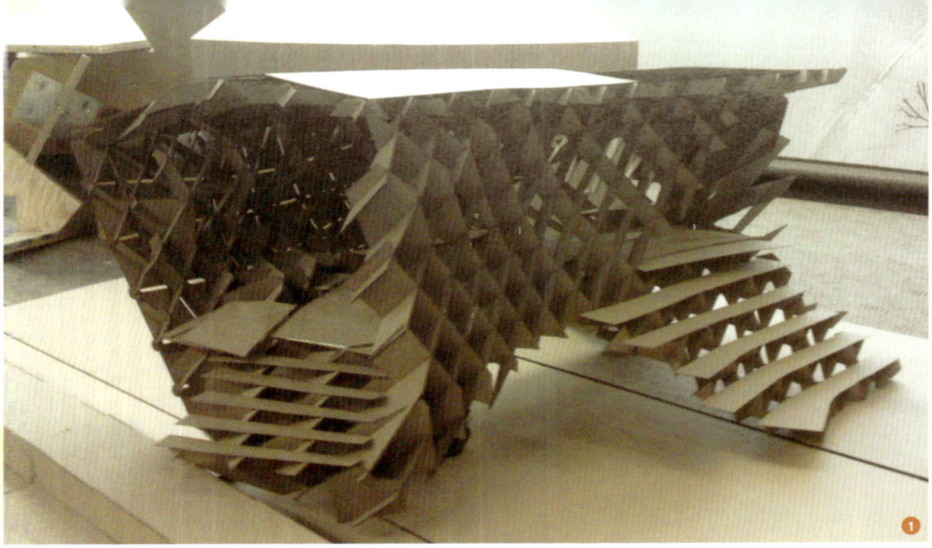

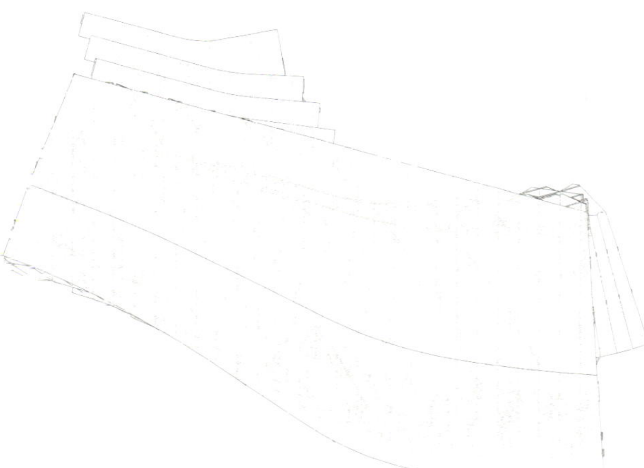

5

1-2 MODEL ¼" = 1' scale
3 MODEL half full size scale
4-5 MODEL interior
6 MODEL pavilions pieces showing ribs + clips + tabs + skin
7 roof PLAN
8 RENDERING exterior of KOKODAschool Pavilion

2

6

7

8

1

3

2

4

1-4 CONSTRUCTION chunks being assembled
5-6 CONSTRUCTION process
7 MODEL half full scale completed
8 MODEL interior under construction

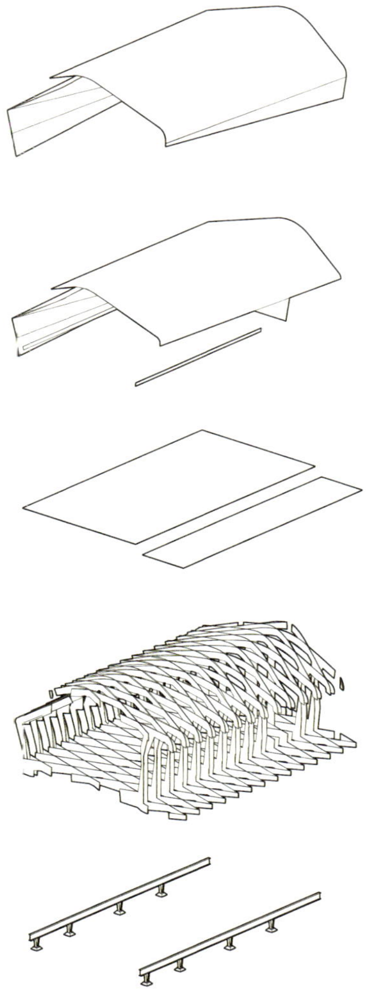

EXTERIOR SKIN
2 Layers of 3/4" thick plywood: 118 sheets (total for both layers)

INTERIOR SKIN
1 Layer of 3/4" thick plywood: 71 sheets

FLOOR
2 Layers of 3/4" thick plywood: 78 sheets (total for both layers)

RIBS
1" plywood 104 sheets

FOUNDATION+MOMENT FRAMES
Steel beams and legs on concrete footings

TOTAL PLYWOOD SHEET COUNT
Sheet size: 1.22m by 2.44m
267 sheets 3/4" thick plywood
104 sheets 1" plywood

KOKODAschool*classroom building material calculation* 1

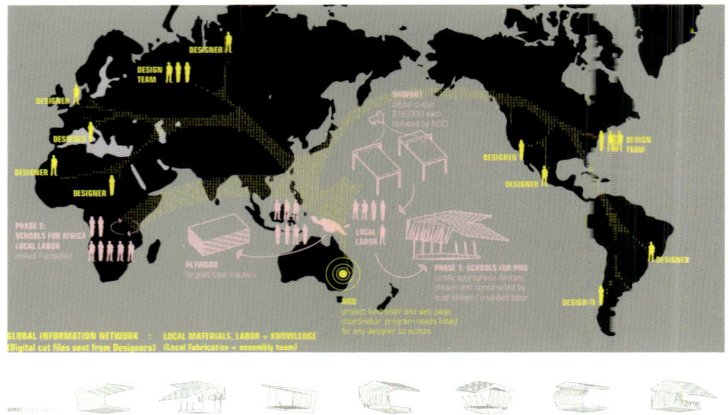

2

3

4

5

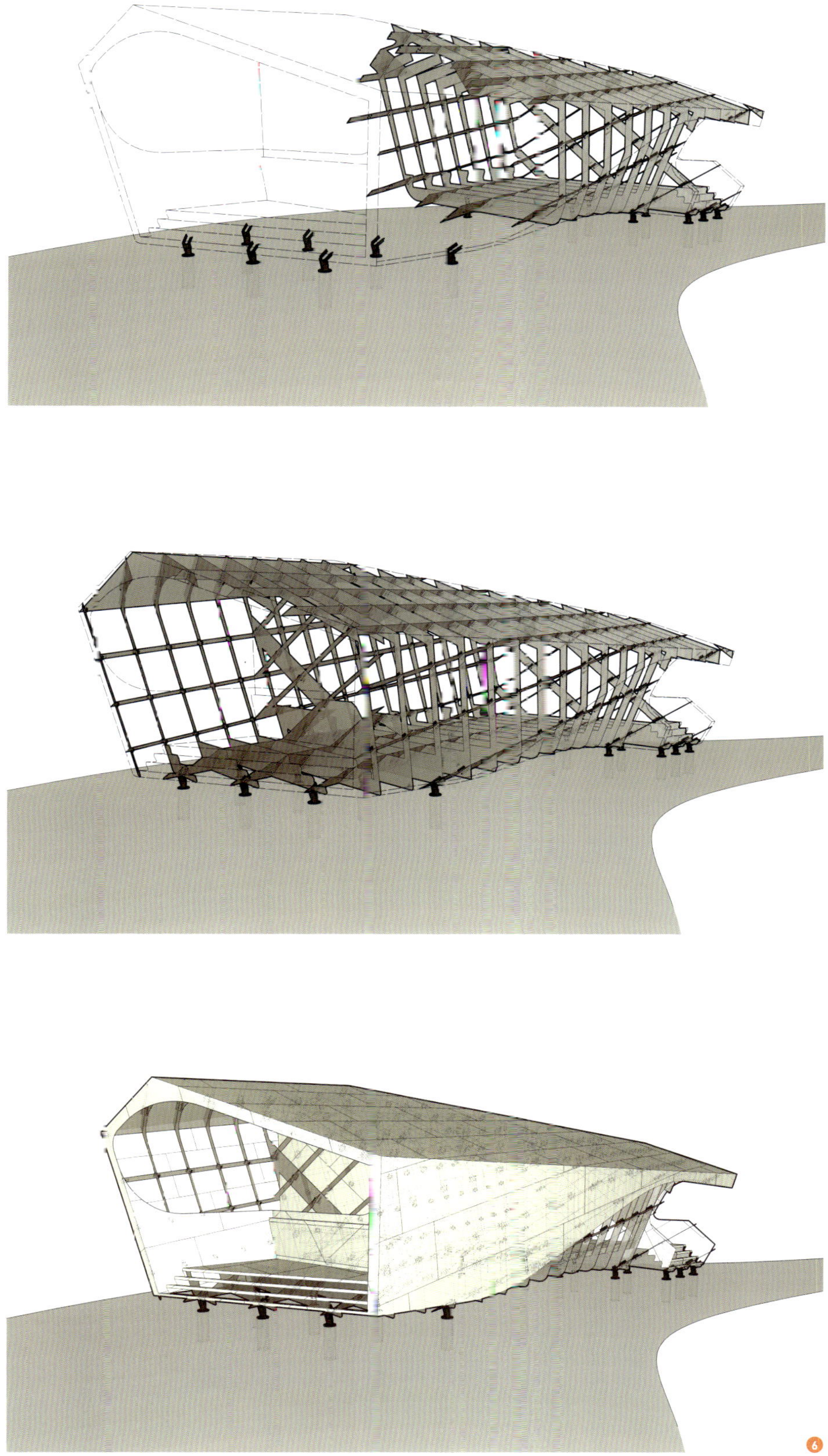

6

1 AXONOMETRIC pavilion parts
2 DIAGRAM global supply network
3-5 VIEW local plywood materials + fabrication tools
6 PERSPECTIVE pavilion sequence

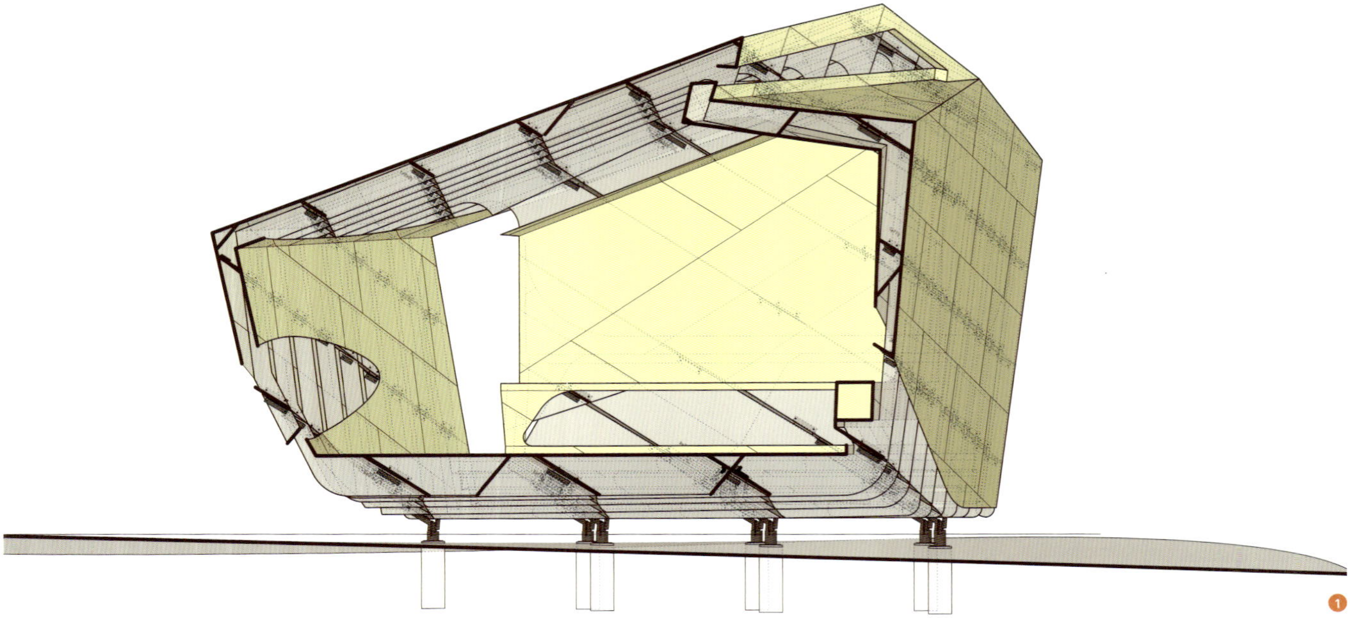

1

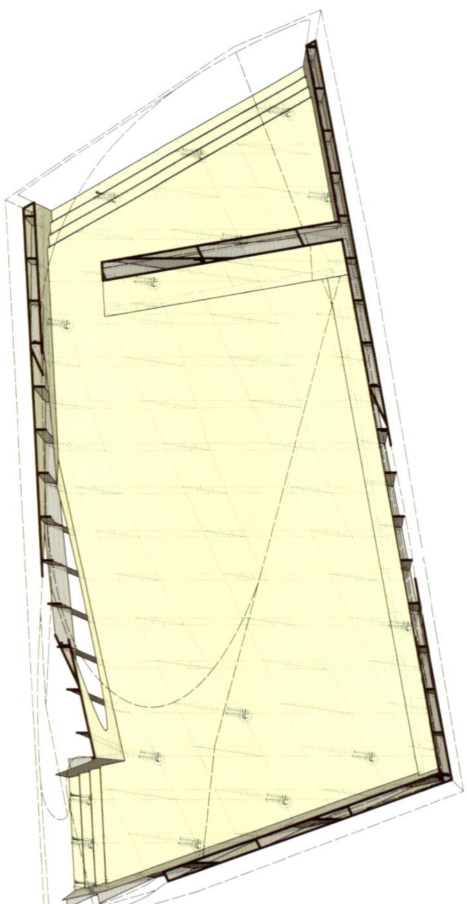

2

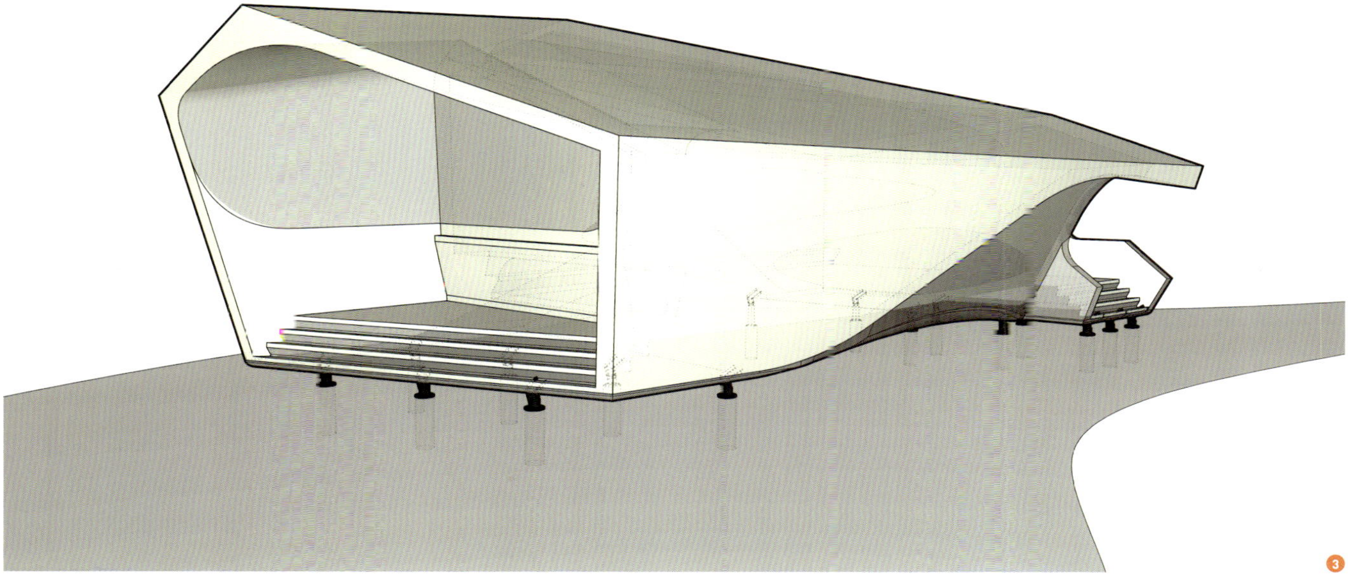

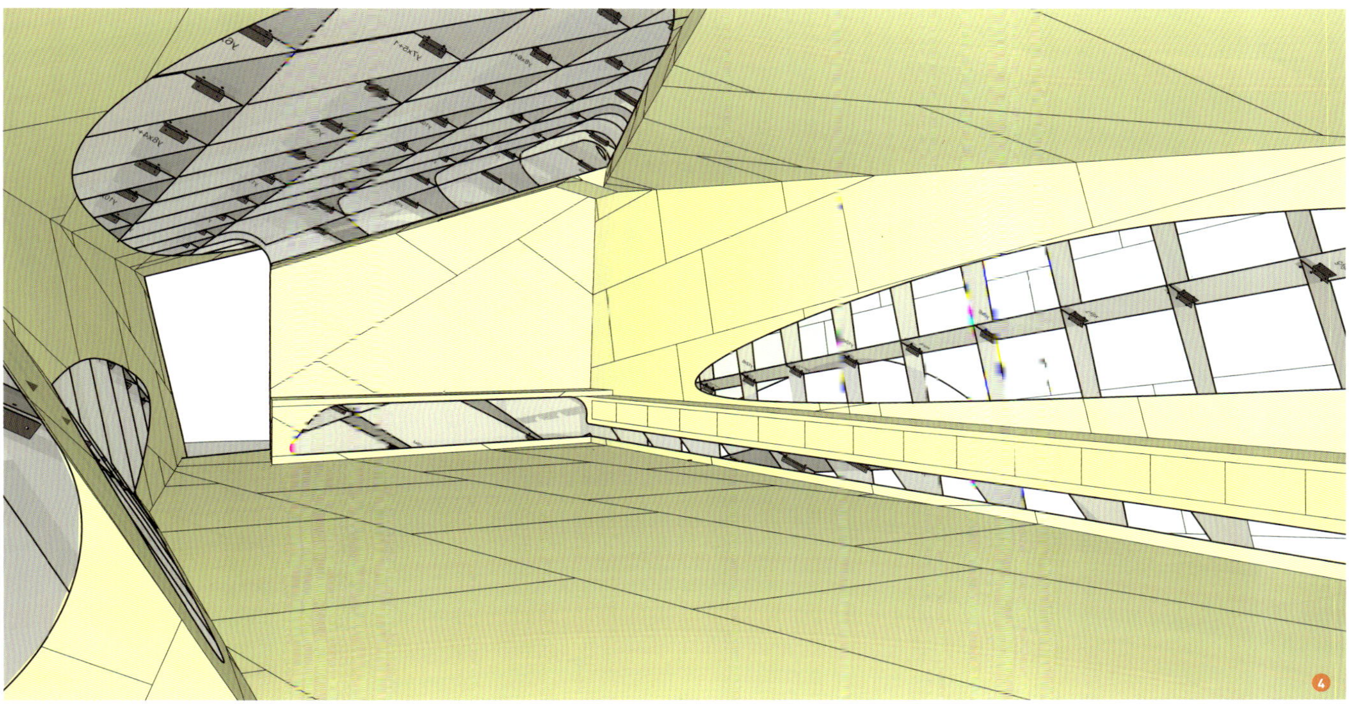

1 SECTION classroom prototype
2 PLAN prototype
3 PERSPECTIVE exterior
4 PERSPECTIVE interior

2.2 boats 2E + 2N

Two adjacent apartments had similar challenges: to create two children's bedrooms in a narrow space that had access to an exterior deck, light, and air. Both spaces had 11-foot ceilings, enough—in New York City, at least—to create a mezzanine. The form of each project is very similar. The rooms are divided by a highly curved wall that also contains the mezzanine and closet space. This wall is vertical and thin where it meets the windows, to maximise the potential light and view into each room. As it moves away from the glass it bulges as if the hull of a boat were emerging out of the other wall. Atop this hull sits the mezzanine, which can be used for sleeping or storage. The programme of these rooms is resolved into a single smooth construction.

These two projects helped further SYSTEM's research into construction using a kit-of-parts. The wall in 2E is clad on one side with smooth plywood, while the other side leaves the structural ribs exposed, giving each room very different surface and spatial qualities. Both sides of the wall in 2N are clad but the surface recesses into the structural ribs, which then appear as diagonals in the surface, visually reinforcing a direction embedded within the form.

The orientation of the structural ribs used in 2E is rotated in two directions making the connection between the ribs unique, (BURST* used repetitive joints). We achieved this by having the CNC milling machine cut the ribs to make the joint. In this project we explored the splice joint, using a repetitive formed metal clip. This created a structural connection along the path of the rib, making it longer and relieving the connection of two ribs from having to provide substantial structural support.

The kit for 2N implemented many of the discoveries made during the UPenn research studio, including the rib orientation and clip design. We used this project to develop scripting protocols for all of the kit parts, so the production of each element could be easily repeatable for any form. This made the production of digital cutting files fast and accurate, eliminating the need for drawing and modeling construction pieces. The kit expanded to include tabs that locked the twisting surfaces to the ribs, blocks that supported the surface parts that exposed the structural ribs, and seams that strengthened and articulated the fold lines in the surface geometry.

The early projects of SYSTEM used a folded geometry consisting of large triangular planes to make the form. This was largely a response to the flat sheet technology pervasive in the building industry, and the rudimentary software we were using at the time. As the software and our facility with it progressed, so did the experimentation with materials. We added curves to the folds, and twists to the curves. The desire is to have a greater range of surfaces at our disposal, in the quest to communicate through form. As the ability to use more complex geometry increases, so also does the challenge for coherence, and it is at this moment that drawing becomes critical to the work. The definitions in drawing—line, shade, and points—provide the basis for coherence within a complex form. Profile lines and defining points are used to create the form while lines on and through the surface provide a visual clarity and legibility.

1 PLAN boats + existing conditions 2E
2-3 SKETCH boat 2N
4-5 PLAN — showing structural rib + skin 2N
6 exploded AXONMETRIC boats 2E + 2N showing profiles

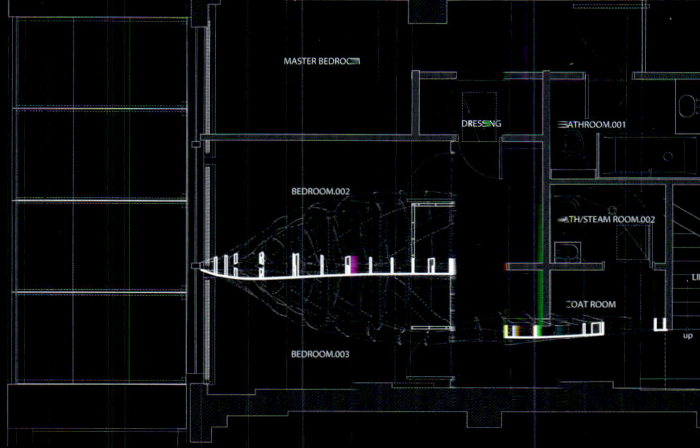
DRESSING
BEDROOM.002
COAT ROOM
BEDROOM.003
up

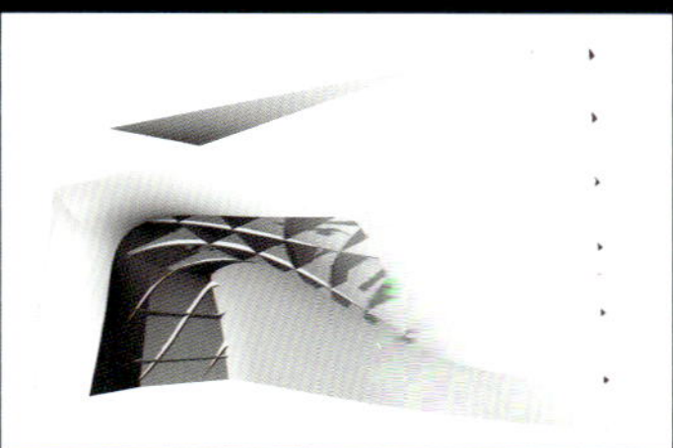
2

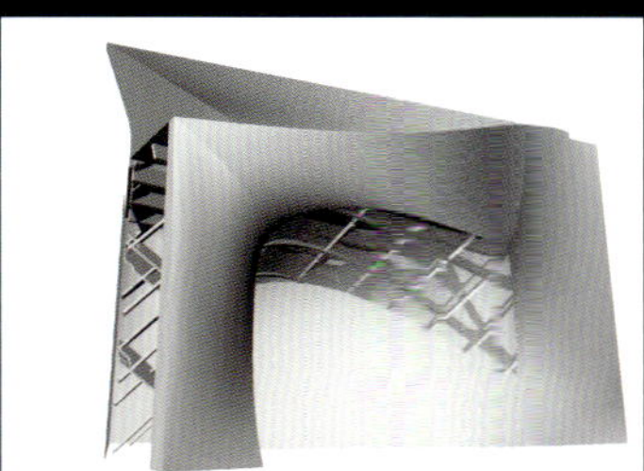
3

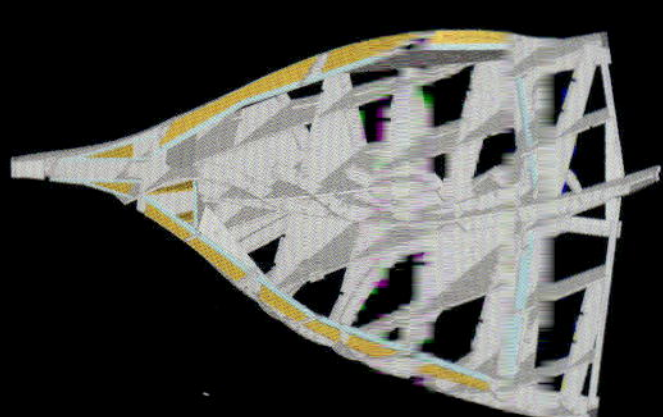
4

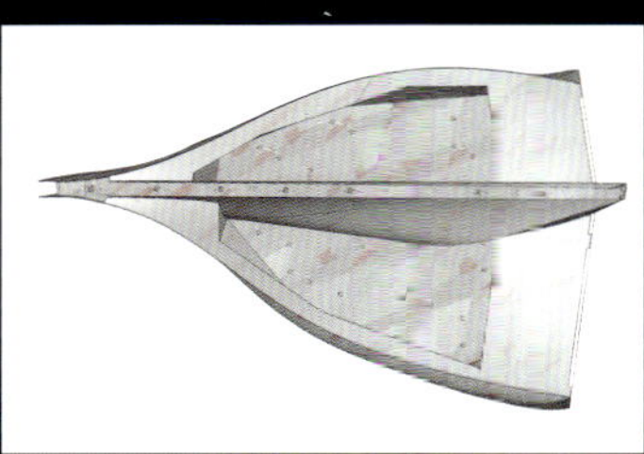
5

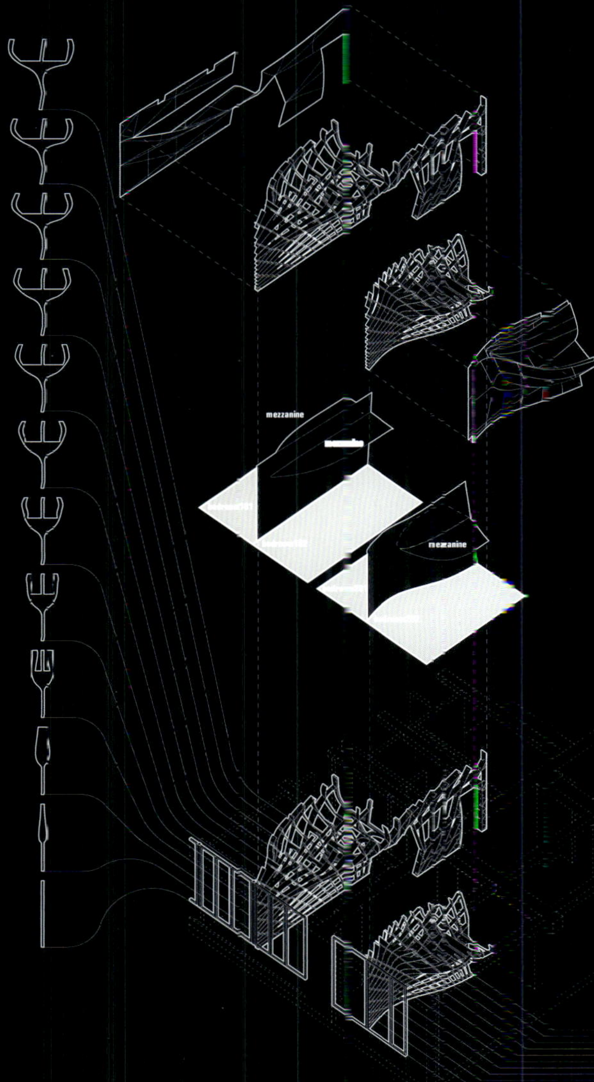
SKIN
RIBS
SKIN
mezzanine
mezzanine
PROGRAM
SITE

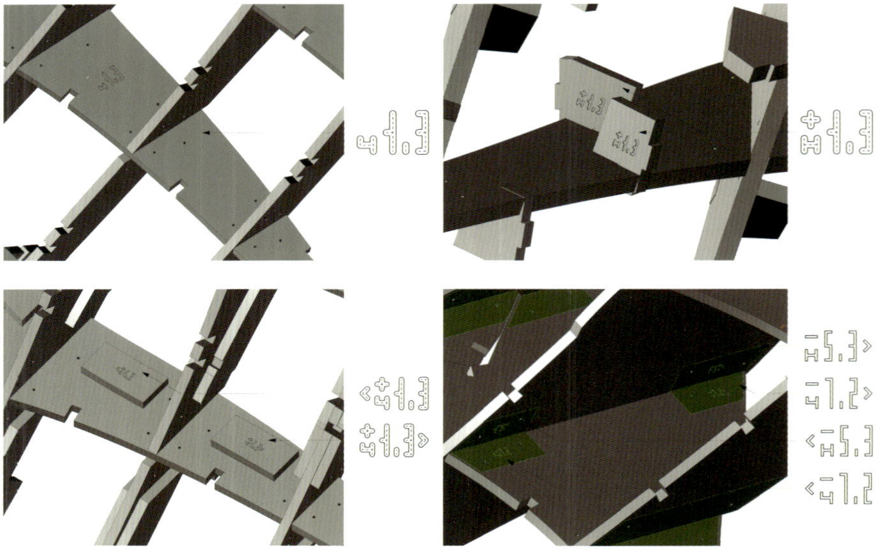

1 ASSEMBLY structural ribs, tabs, blocking + clips
2 CONSTRUCTION ribs
3 CONSTRUCTION tabs
4 ASSEMBLY construction parts
5 ASSEMBLY clips boat 2N
6-7 STURCTURAL ribs 2N

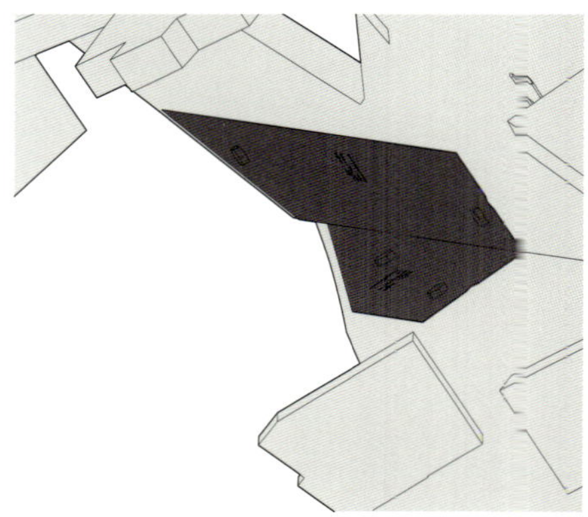

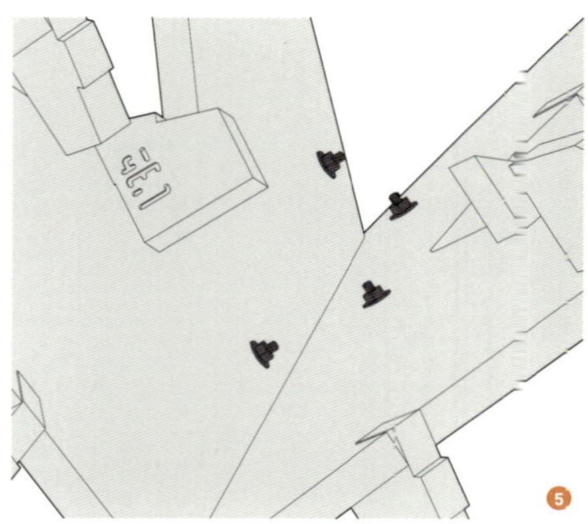

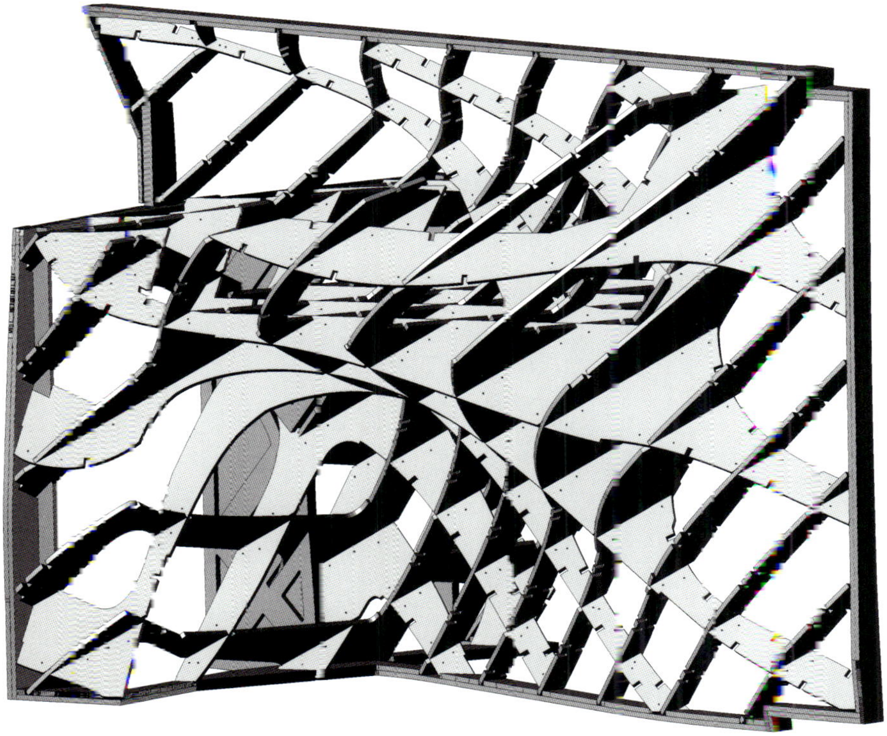

6

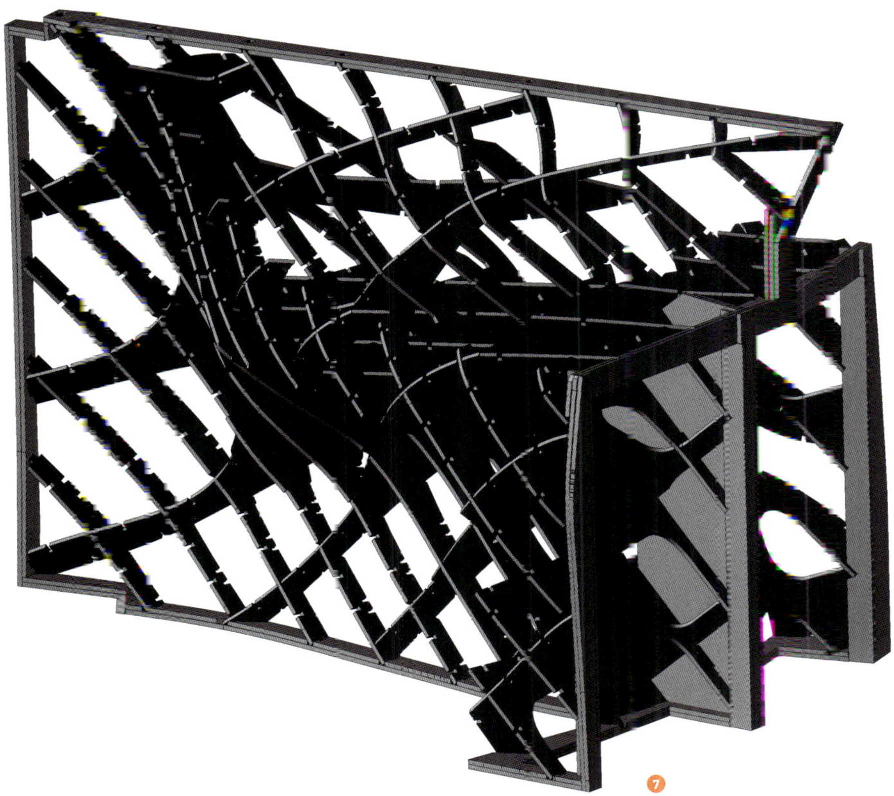

7

1 ASSEMBLY closet
2 LASER cut clip files
3 LASER cut skin stitching
4-7 CONSTRUCTION connections
8 CODING steel connecting clips

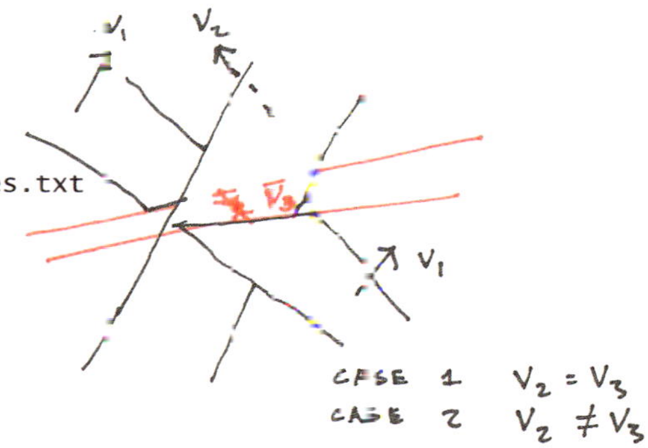


```
clip maker notes:

inputs:

joint lines
xSrfs
ySrfs


for each joint line ->

srf1 = srf that intersects joint line
srf2 = srf of opposite set that is closest to mid point of joint line


border1 = offset curves of srf1 border minus curve that is same as joint line
          extend ends 12 inches
border2 = offset curve of srf2 border

move border1 in direction of srf1 1/2 inch
move border2 in opposite direction of srf2 1/2 inch

move joint line in direction of srf1 1/2 inch

clipEnd1 = copy joint line in direction of srf2 3 inches, extend ends 12 inches
clipEnd2 = copy joint line in direction of srf1 3 inches, extend ends 12 inches

clipEdge1a = copy border1
clipEdge1b = copy border1

clipEdge2a = copy border2
clipEdge2b = copy border2

clipEdge1aFoldPt = intersection (clipEdge1a, joint line)
clipEdge2aFoldPt = intersection (clipEdge2a, joint line)

        edgeAFoldPt = closest point to joint line midpoint
        if not same as edgeAfoldPt ->
                offset clipEdge to meet edgeAfoldPt

        for each clipEdgeA ->
                clipEdgeAEndPt = intersection (clipEdgeA, clipEnd)
                split clipEdgeA with edgeAFoldPt and clipEdgeAEndPt
                        clipEdgeA = curve in set with endPts matching edgeAFoldPt
and clipEdgeAEndPt

        midPt = joint line midPt
        split joint line with edgeAfoldPt
                joint line = curve in set closest to midPt

        midPt = clipEnd1 midPt
        split clipEnd1 with clipEdge1aEndPt
                clipEnd1 = curve in set closest to midPt

        midPt = clipEnd2 midPt
        split clipEnd2 with clipEdge2aEndPt
                clipEnd2 = curve in set closest to midPt

repeat for b set

clipSrf1 = srfFromEdges (clipEdge1a, jointLn, clipEdge1b, clipEnd1)
clipSrf2 = srfFromEdges (clipEdge2a, jointLn, clipEdge2b, clipEnd2)
```

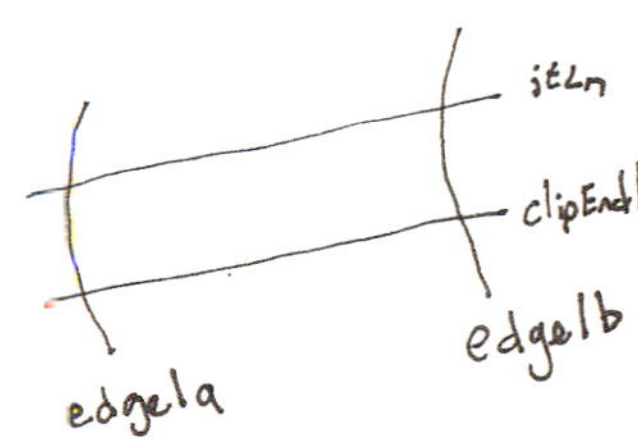

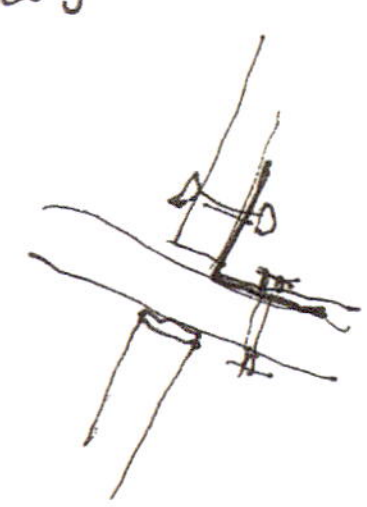

1

1-2 CONSTRUCTION 2N skin
3 boat 2N
4-7 ASSEMBLY sequence for ribs a + b + c

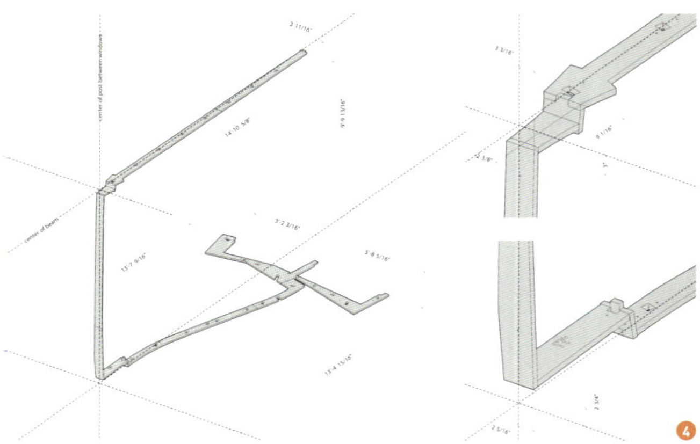

4

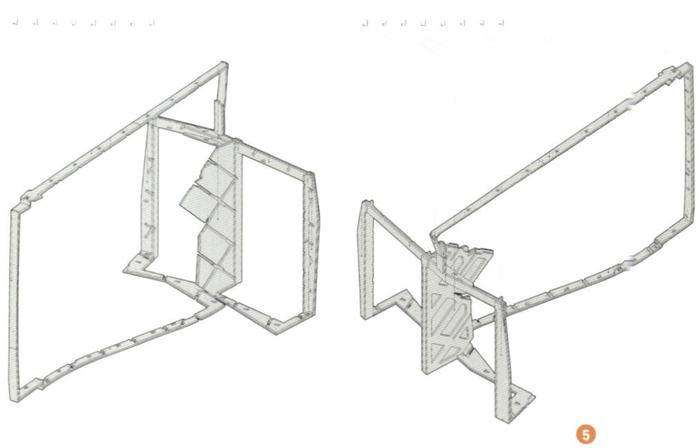

5

2

3

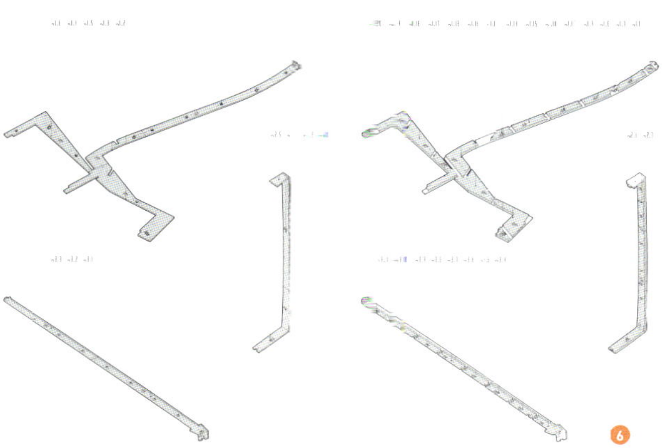

6

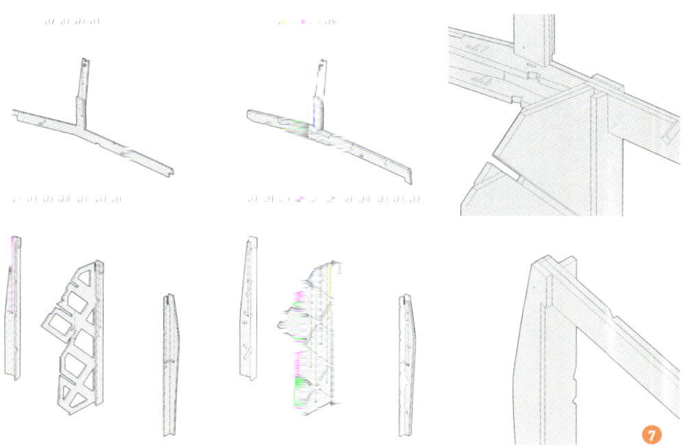

7

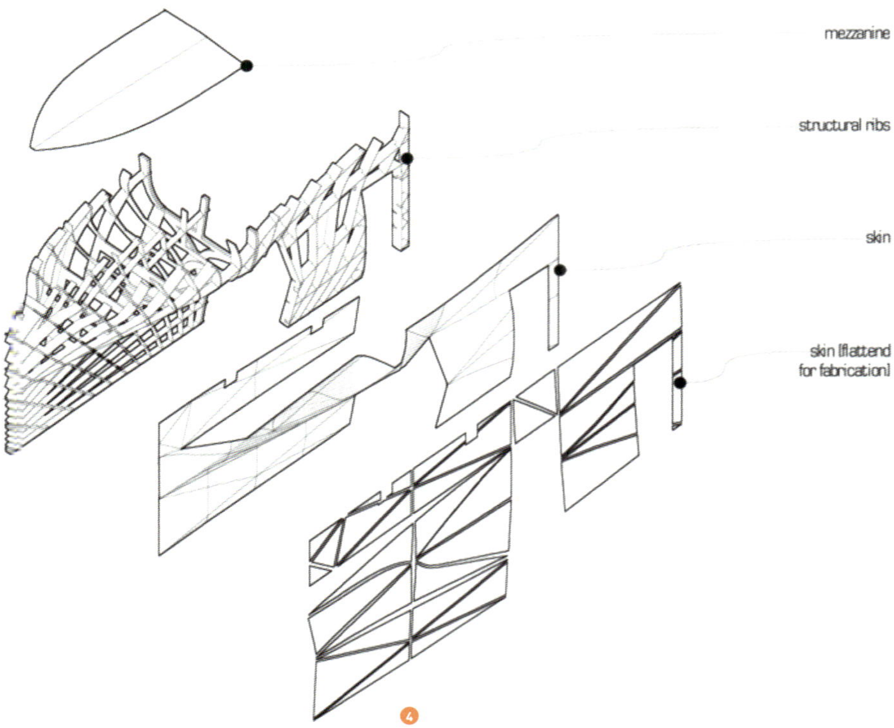

1-3 CONSTRUCTION ribs + splice clips 2E
4 exploded AXONOMETRIC surface elements
5 VIEW plywood ribs in place 2E
6 CONSTRUCTION boat 2E ribs and skin

6

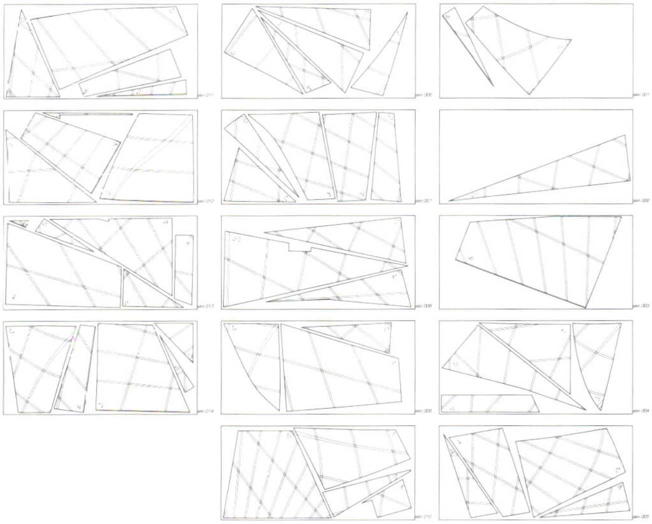

1

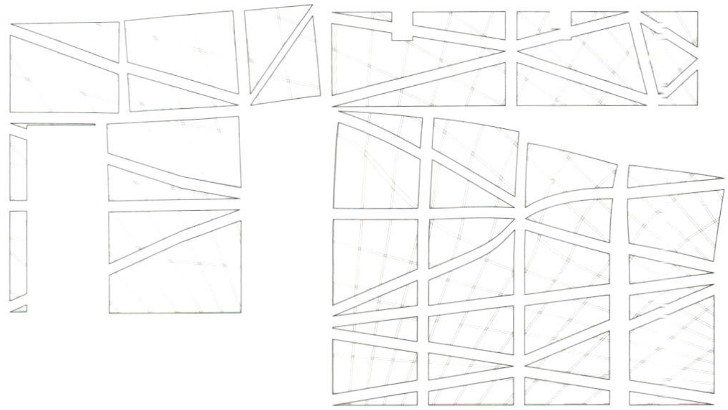

2

3

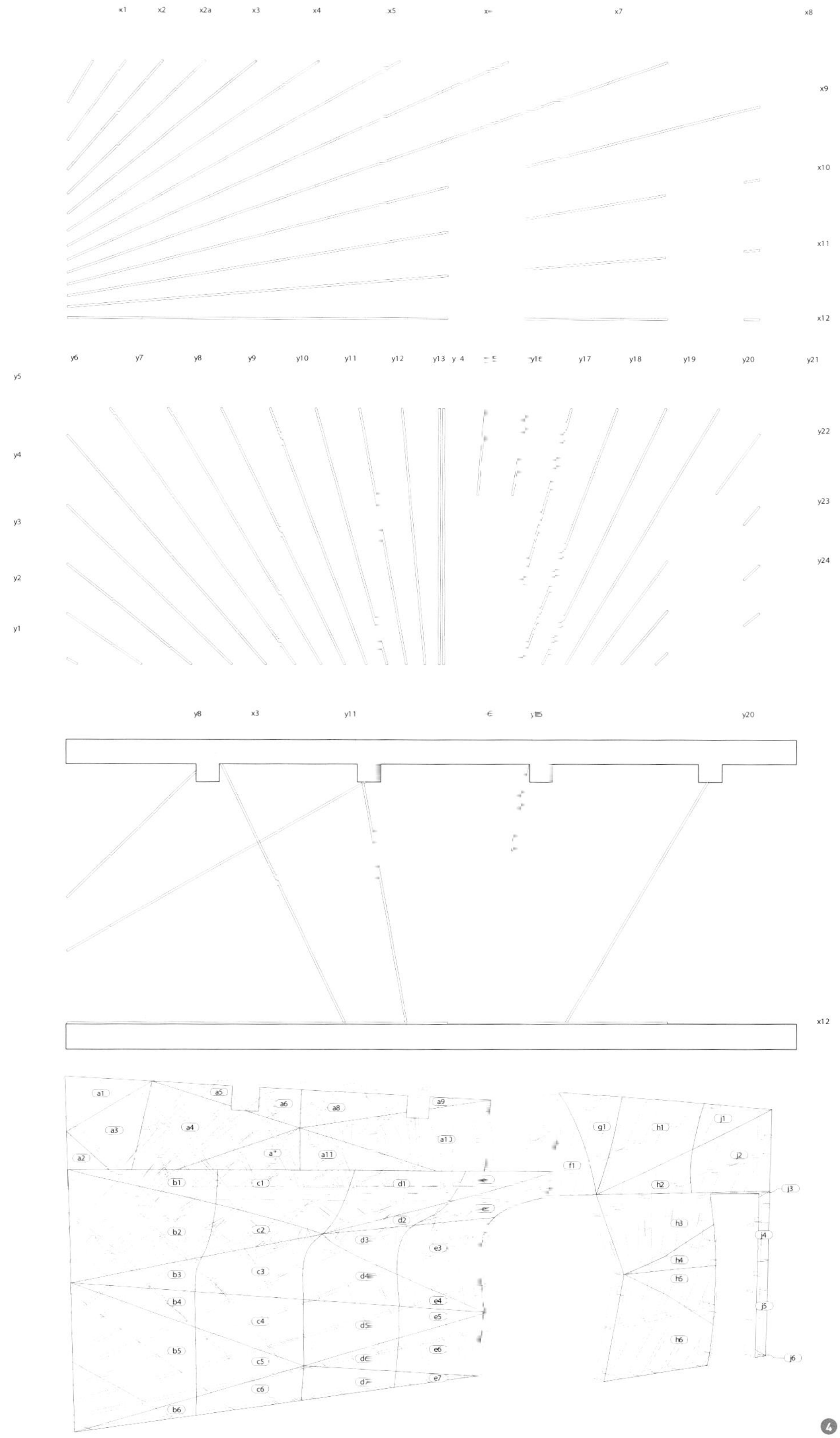

1 ASSEMBLY nested sheets
2 ELEVATION skin parts
3 VIEW boat occupied 2N
4 ELEVATION boat 2E geometric setup

2.3 Burst*008

With Douglas Gauthier

BURST*008 was a commissioned work by the Museum of Modern Art (MoMA) for the exhibition Home Delivery: Fabricating the Modern Dwelling, which showcased innovative and groundbreaking methods of home construction. Our contribution, designed and built with Douglas Gauthier, was an amended version of BURST*003 for which we further developed the construction method and the adaptability of its design.

BURST*003 had been designed and built using precision-cut plywood parts connected by metal clips. While this method had never been accomplished at this scale before, and was only made possible by contemporary machinery and software, it followed an historic arc in domestic architecture.

In the US, balloon-framed construction started to have an impact on residential construction around the turn of the twentieth-century. Advances in lumber cutting meant that there was a predictability to the size of wood that could be ordered and delivered. A house could thus be planned before the material arrived on site. The steel nail had already made joining lumber faster, particularly if the nail were attached to a plywood sheet that could provide lateral stiffening to the system of framing. In a way, the BURST* system was a response to contemporary versions of these historic developments.

As the MoMA exhibition was to be open to the public and classified by the New York City building authorities as a place of public assembly, the project had to be designed for double the structural loads of the first BURST*003, which was a single family house. This had little impact on the form of the project as the structure was already extremely rigid, but by weaving the structure more tightly, or, in other words, adding a few more grid lines, the desired strength was achieved. The project was to be constructed in just six weeks in midtown Manhattan with the aid of a crane.

We had discovered while building the Australian BURST* that the stainless steel connectors could act as hinges, allowing the pre-assembled structural ribs to fold flat and unfold like a concertina. We trucked the skeletal structure in three tight chunks on a truck bed, lifted them onto the site and—while they were suspended on the crane—unfolded the chunks to full size. From there, they were lifted into place. Custom-designed connectors such as the ones we used, manufactured for a specific building or building type, were an idea that had developed in Europe particularly in the fabricated constructions of Jean Prouvé. BURST* combined traditions from both sides of the Atlantic.

The first BURST* had been designed to be exquisitely responsive to the weather of the site, so we wanted the exhibit to respond to the site and weather of New York City. This meant substantial insulation, which was achieved by using SIPS (structural insulated panels) as the exterior surface of the form instead of raw plywood. Using a CNC router on a 20 by 80-foot bed carved out notches for the structural ribs on the inside layer of OSB (oriented strand board) and foam, leaving only the outer layer of plywood. These large skin elements were then fitted over the ribs, each of which slotted into one of the notches. This locked the ribs in place and held the structure rigid. We used steel moment frames to support the project off the ground and these doubled as support during the construction.

1-2 VIEW BURST* in the city Home Delivery: Fabricating The Modern Dwelling

1

2

1 CONSTRUCTION steel support
2 CONSTRUCTION plywood ribs packaged for transport
3-4 CONSTRUCTION plywood rib delivery
5-7 ASSEMBLY on site

3

4

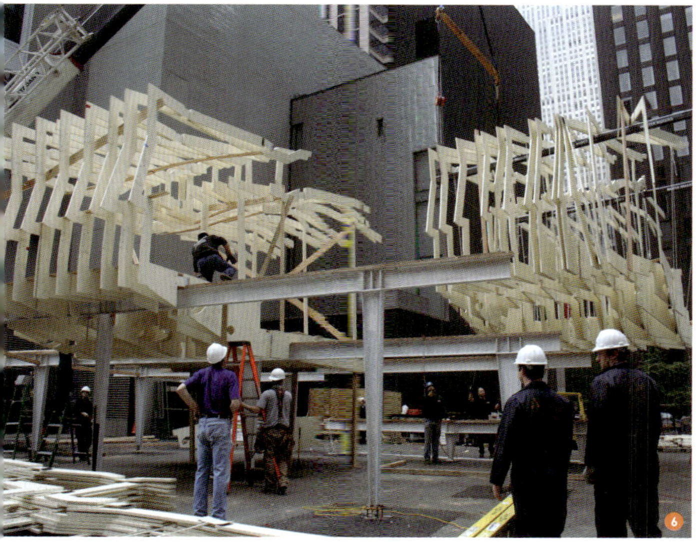

6

7

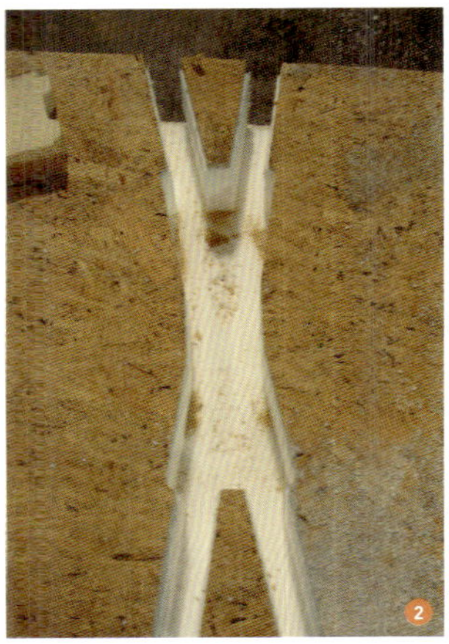

1 ASSEMBLY floor clip
2 VIEW rounted SIPS panel
3 ASSEMNLY rib + clip
4 VIEW bleacher structure
5-6 ASSEMBLY on site
7 PROCESS CNC routers SIPS panel

5

6

7

1

2

3

1 VIEW BURST* profile
2 CONSTRUCTION of facade
3 CONSTRUCTION BURST* window
4 VIEW BURST* details
5 VIEW BURST* window
6 VIEW exhibition site

2.4 fulcrumSTAIR

Jeremy Edmiston & Douglas Gauthier partners

fulcrumSTAIR is a counterweighted cantilevered stair that connects a first floor duplex apartment with the garden below. The painted steel frame creates a strong and visually light support for a deck and holds a horizontal pivot rod that balances the stair. To avoid blocking the light to the apartment below the deck, the surface of the deck was fabricated from a perforated stainless steel sheet. This was made structural by folding another sheet of the same material into a profile of extended row of zigzags and attached underside. This fabrication also spanned the steel members of the supporting frame.

To activate the stair, one unlocks and opens the gate, steps down onto the landing then steps off the landing onto the top step, transferring just enough weight to start the staircase moving. At that point the timid may step back onto the landing and watch as the staircase slowly descends to the ground, where it will stay until gym weights attached to the other side of the stair are given a push downwards. This will slowly raise the staircase and complete the cycle.

One of the concepts that propelled this project was the reverse transition between nature and industry. Those who wish to enter the garden must first traverse the mechanical device, as if connecting with nature is permitted only after negotiating with the machine.

1 RENDERING fulcrumSTAIR
2 VIEW perforated decking
3 VIEW details
4 VIEW fulcrumSTAIR up
5 VIEW fulcrumSTAIR down

3

CU
4

5

3

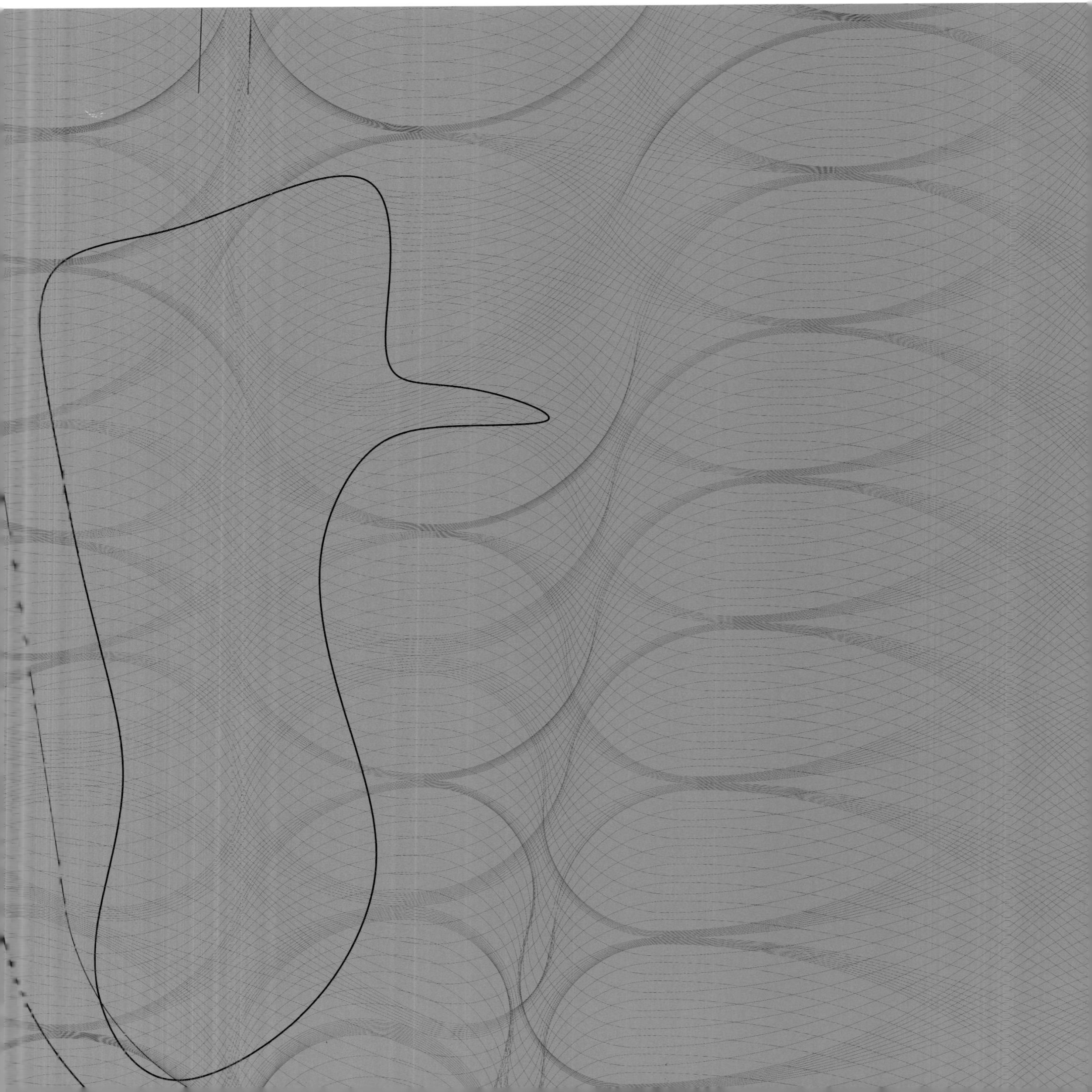

perforation + pattern

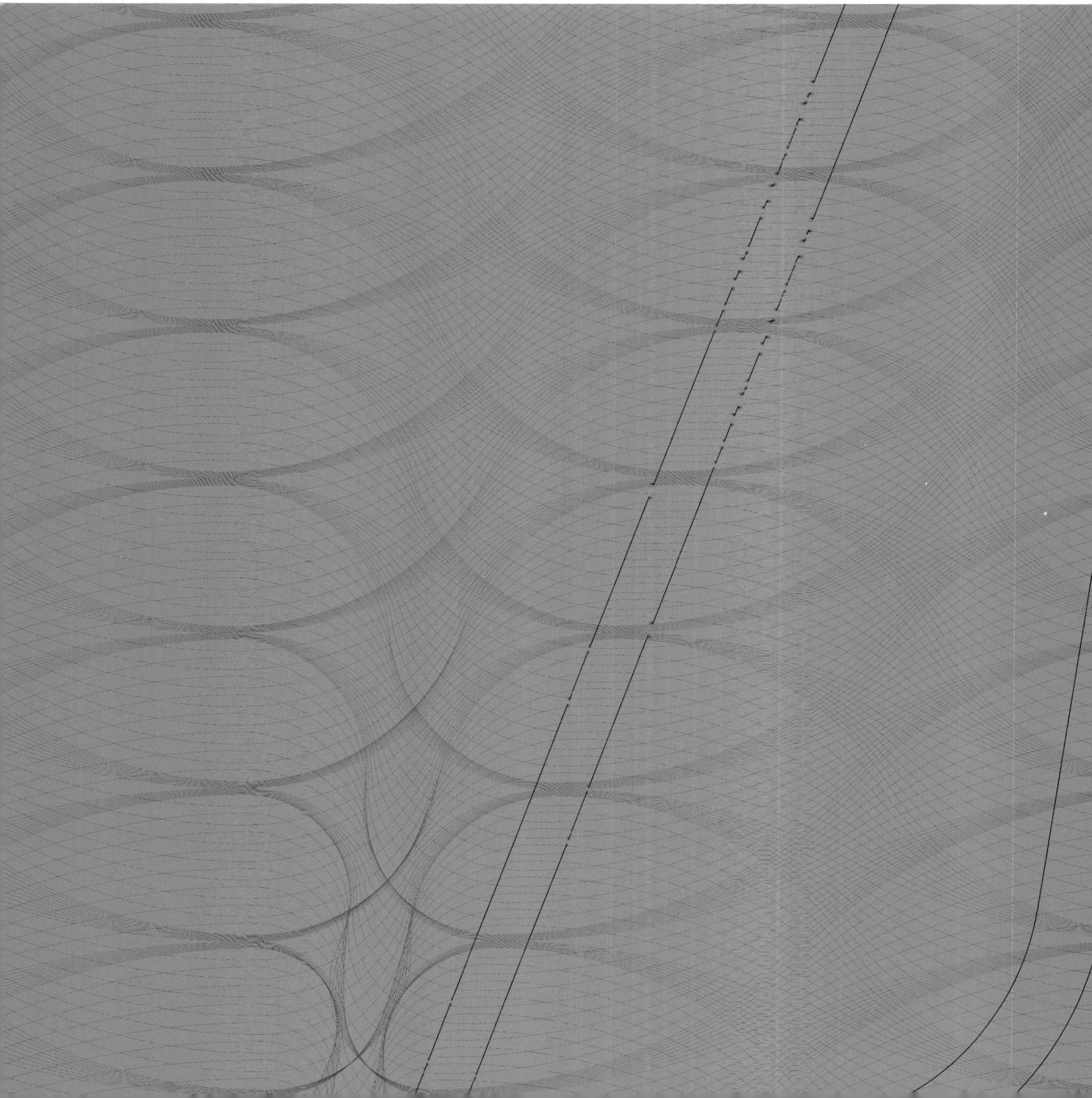

perforation + pattern

The measure of form is usefulness. The measure of structure is its strength. How then do we measure pattern? It is measured in the response it elicits, how much feeling it creates, how much it moves its beholders. Without feeling, it becomes difficult, if not impossible, to really occupy a place.

Just as form and structure are symbiotic, so enmeshed that it's hard to tell which is the cause and which is the result of any design decision, pattern is both the author and the product of its environment. Pattern is not applied, but integral to the other inter-relationships in the project. It's not just about material and it's not just about form; it's a whole other expression of the space.

As SYSTEM developed its iterative method of design, form-making, and construction, it followed a similar path for the creation of surfaces of patterns and perforations. The technology that allows us to implement rules of form, geometry, structure and construction in generating a surface also allows us to generate patterns using a combination of scripted code and complex geometries. The formation of these surfaces is a catalyst for creating patterns that eventually take on the contours of these surfaces and become three-dimensional.

In metropolitan apartments, light is often the currency for habitability. The idea that a pattern is able to respond to the micro-conditions of the natural and artificial lighting led to SYSTEM's experimentation with allowing the surface to reveal more subtle changes within a space. In Lattice 3N (page 158), steel is perforated in an arrangement that's both a result of the conditions in the apartment and also changes those conditions. The perforations become larger and the lattice more lacy at the edge of the screen that is closer to the window. On the other edge, close to the front door of the apartment, the holes are sparser and smaller. This has the effect of movement, of carrying anyone entering the apartment into the room as their eye is drawn from dark and solid to light and open.

Movement—imagined or implied—has been one of SYSTEM's guides to pattern creation. It seemed to us that if a pattern was a way to 'read' hidden forces within a place, then these forces were kinetic; they did not desire static resolution in the structure of form, but were rather seeking an expression of change. Patterns were therefore about moments of density, or compression, moments that were gradually opening up or suddenly tightening.

The software that we were using for these patterns is based on a grid geometry. We were forming and reforming and deforming grids, but trying to create a surface that spoke about constant and unexpected change. We were tied to a structure that was fully deterministic.

We discovered one way of loosening the grip of the grid in the aA SHELTER in Manhattan. In the shelter, the pattern on the floor is not only that of the material, but also a design of lines and markings that are milled into the material. These lines allow a large empty space to seem dynamic and occupied, so that users, who might initially be wary of entering a space where they might not intrinsically feel welcome, are drawn in. The pattern gives the impression that something is already going on and they will not be alone. The lines extend up the contoured wall, which does actually move and the pattern reinforces the geometry of the wall almost as if it were marking out the contours of a map.

Sometimes patterns can cause the opposite of movement. At the shelter, the markings on the floor often cause people to pause to wonder at their meaning. A wide variety of users have told us of the narratives they have invented about the pattern, evidence perhaps that pattern gives the surface depth.

3.1 aA SHELTER

1 SKETCH curve geometry
2 reflected ceiling PLAN — wall panels in open position
3 LOGO aA SHELTER
4 VIEW operable panels in closed position

aA SHELTER is a 1600 square foot interior space on the street level of a church building on the Upper West Side of New York City. The church was established in 1830 to minister to the needs of the city's poor and homeless. This mission continues today.

The room is multi-purpose; it's used for gathering and dining (up to 80 people eat a sit down meal there at least once a week), as well as sleeping, social, medical, and psychiatric services for the itinerant community. But it had become dilapidated. The homeless in New York City are constantly on the move and the architecture of the renovation sought to acknowledge and 'write' their transience into the surfaces and structure of the space.

The space is laid out using an unfamiliar measuring system that places the homeless, visitors, and shelter workers on an equal footing. As the space has very limited access to daylight and no direct sun, the design fills the space with fluorescent light, paints the existing surfaces of the room white, then suspends a laser cut perforated ceiling below the light source. This has the effect of changing the light quality as people move around the room. The new ceiling, floor, and walls are in a honey butter colour.

The back wall is contoured and movable so that it can accommodate items that need to be stored behind it, while not blocking a window on the western wall. The geometry further relaxes the vertical so that visitors might lean up against it, sit on it, and move around it. A pattern of lines articulates the changing geometry on the wall, and these reverberate through the ceiling and floor until, at the entryway, they return to parallel.

aA SHELTER is primarily built from construction-grade plywood finished in an industrial grade epoxy and is a contemporary version of an adjacent historic wood paneled room. Every piece of the new construction is a specific and different shape imprinted with information about what it should connect to, so that volunteers can assemble the pieces as they would a puzzle.

The design used scripting and digital modeling to generate the forms, patterns, lines, and details. Each piece of the floor, wall, and ceiling was modeled for fabrication and drawn for assembly by the architects. A community of workers, ranging from high-end technologically sophisticated fabricators to homeless men, came together to execute the design and create the room, many of them donating their time.

When SYSTEM was designing this project, it seemed to us that many lives were converging on this space in the city, and these lives were often lived without stable coordinates. So we developed a coherent geometry (without a grid), that used lines in a single continuous direction, meandering through a created topographic space. The pattern of these lines tell stories of the space and articulate the divisions within the material of the project. At the plane of the ceiling, the lines turn to perforations, diffusing the light across the space. The continuous change in the pattern affords a textural intensity to build up and subside, and we choreographed this to pre-figure an imagined use of the space. Each project detailed in this chapter similarly has its own textural creations rendered in light.

3

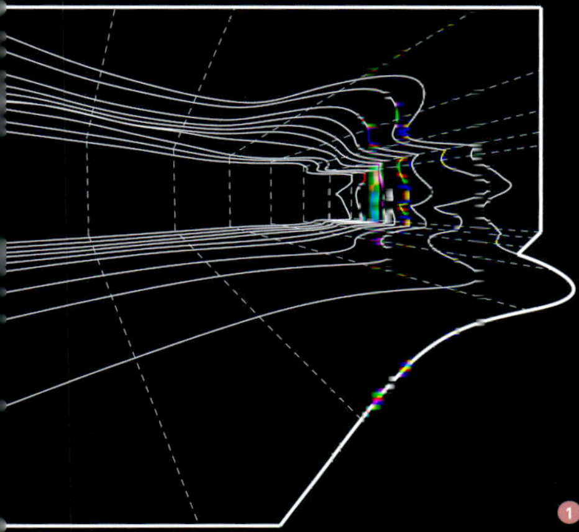

1

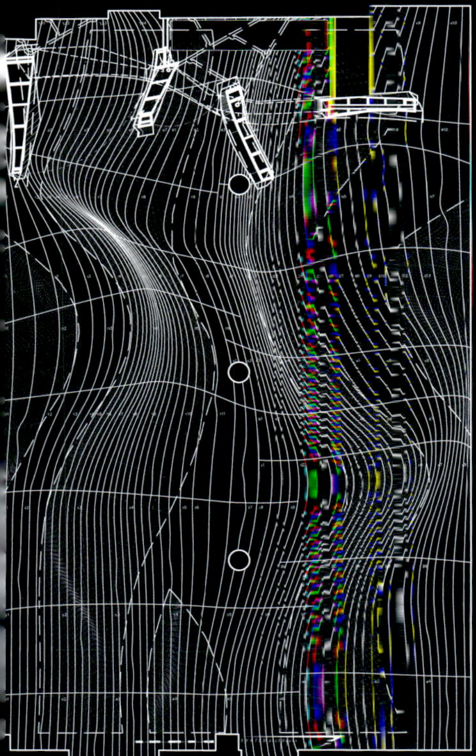

2

4

1

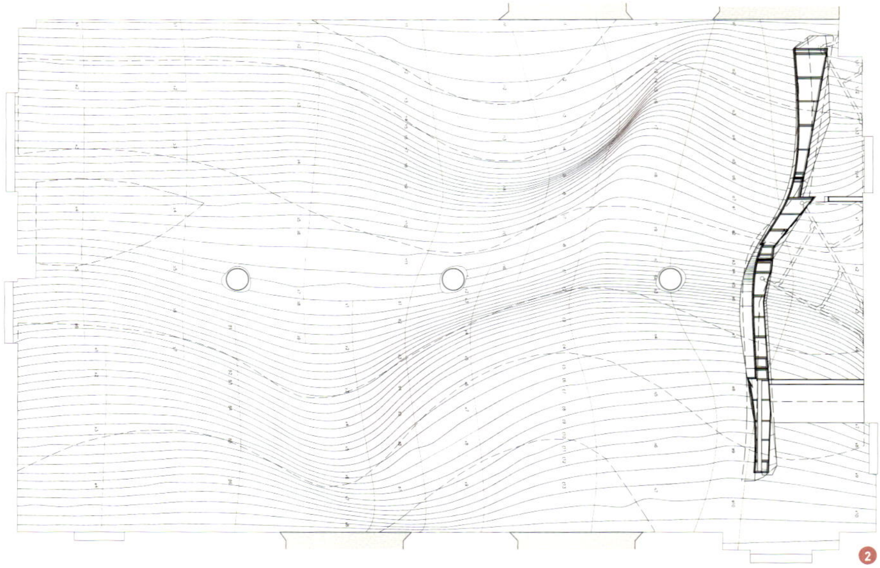

2

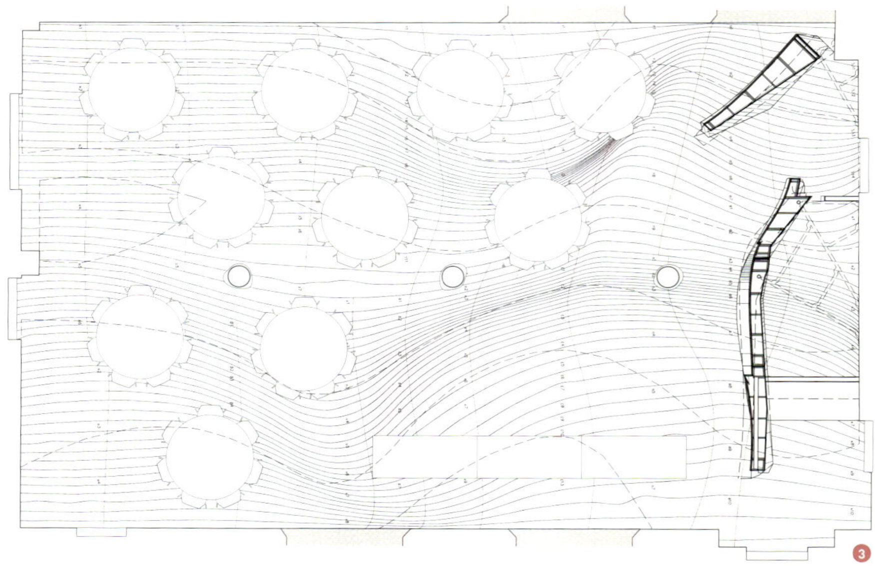

3

1 DIGITAL sketch — variation setout lines
2 PLAN — wall panels in closed position
3 PLAN — wall panels in closed position + table arrangements
4 exploded AXONOMETRIC interventions highlighted

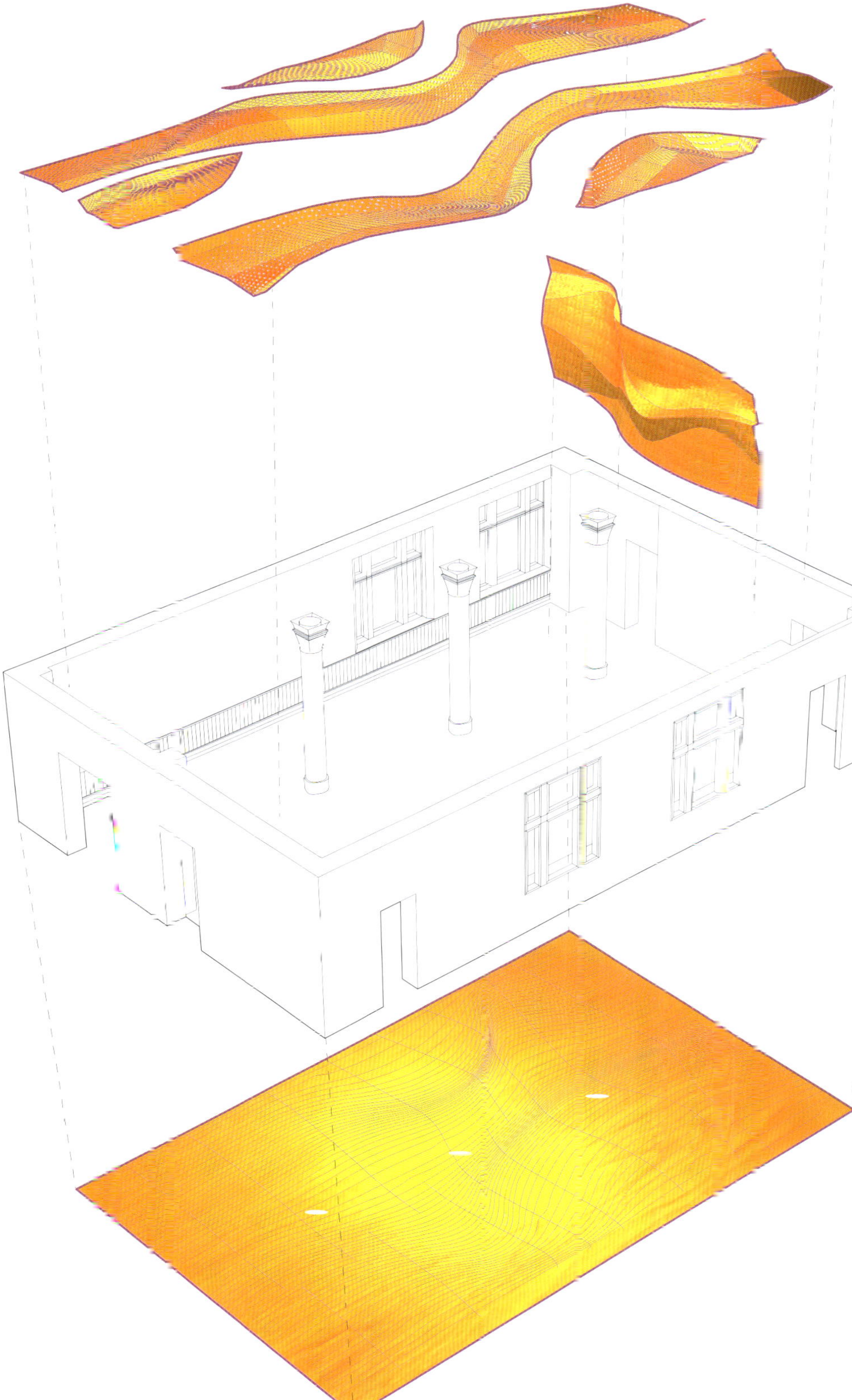

4

1

2

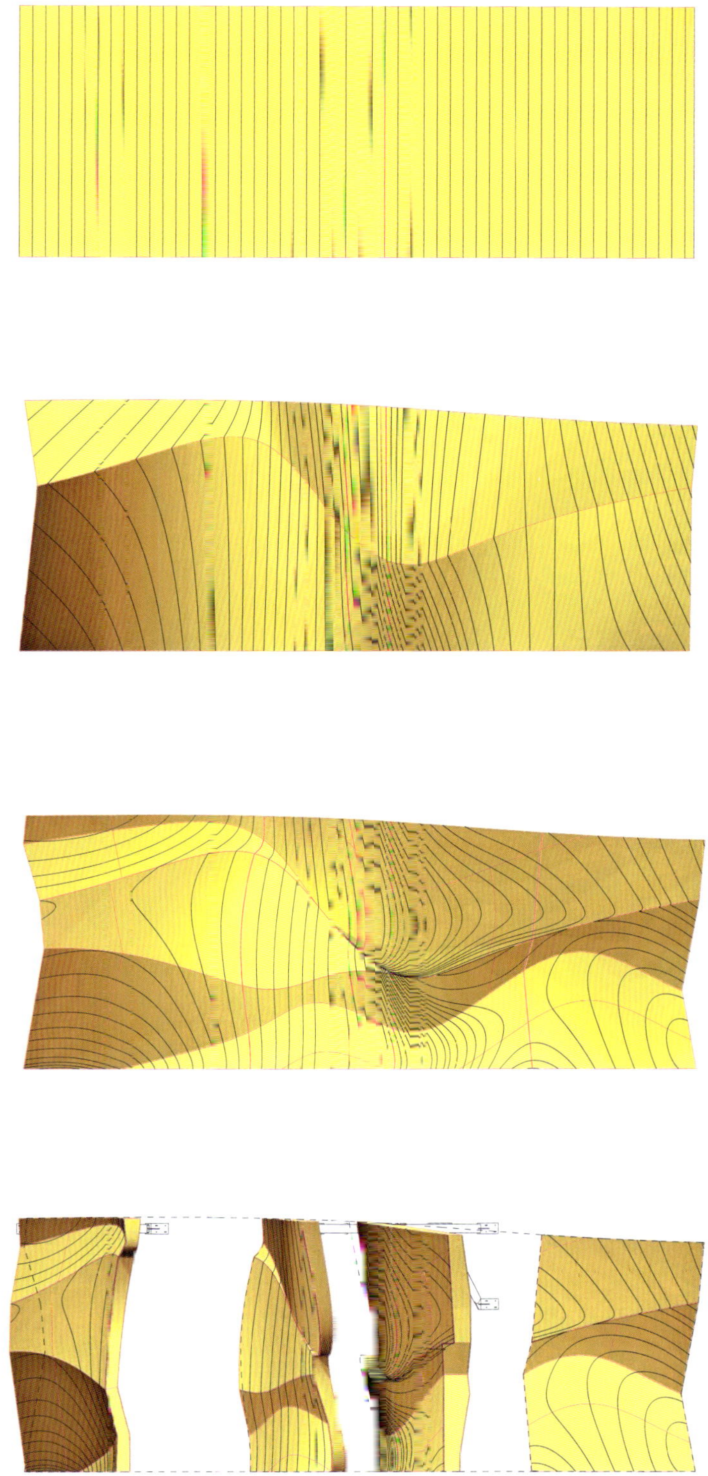

3

1 ELEVATION — curved and folded geometry
2 VIEW wall elevation detail
3 AXONOMETRIC + ELEVATION — development of the topographic organisation

1 PERFORATION light screens
2 PERSPECTIVE fields of lines become segments of perforated light screen

1

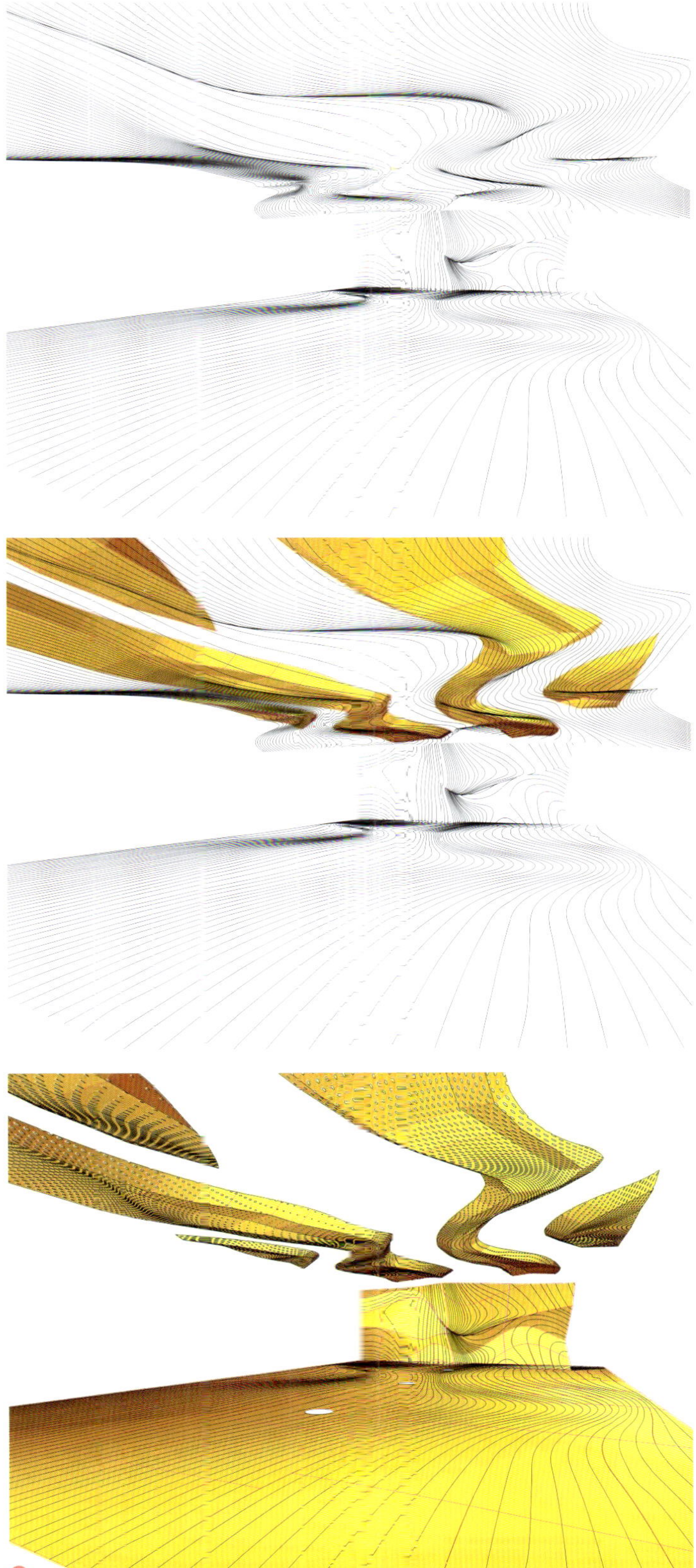

2

1 VIEW operable panels
2-3 PERFORATION ceiling details
4 VIEW operable panels open

4

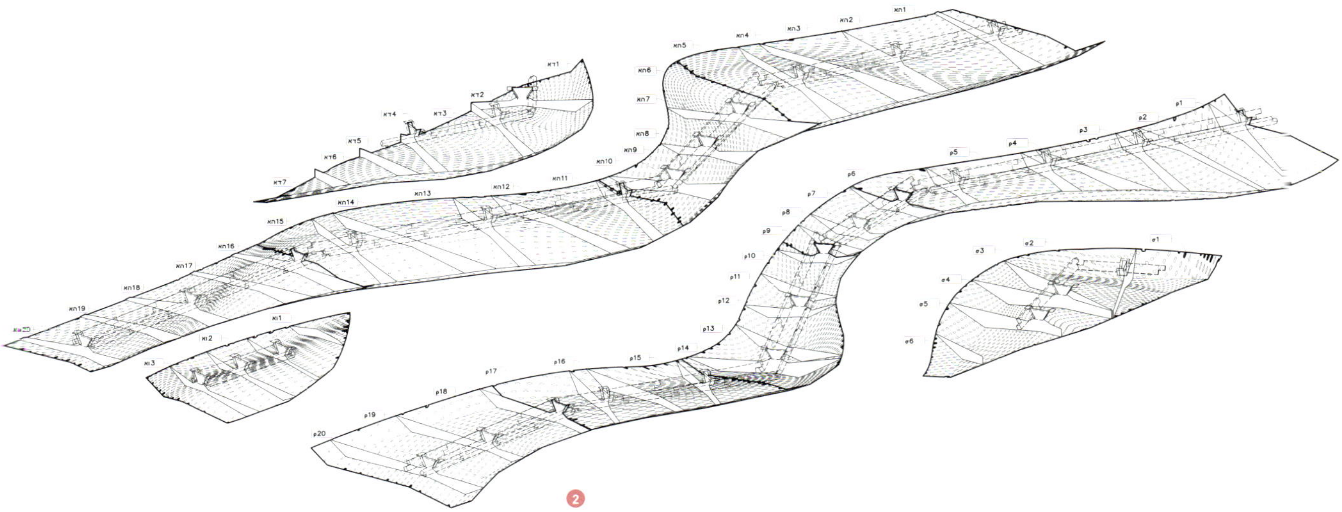

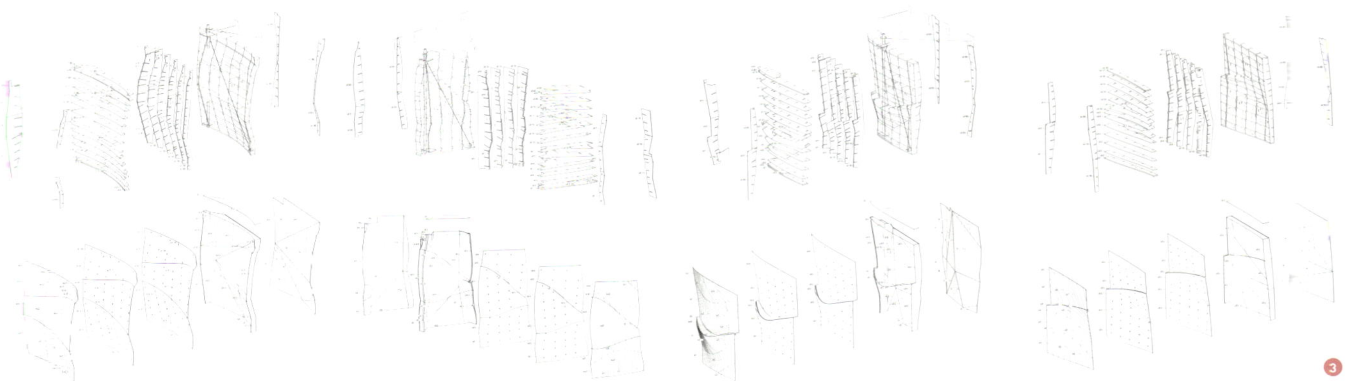

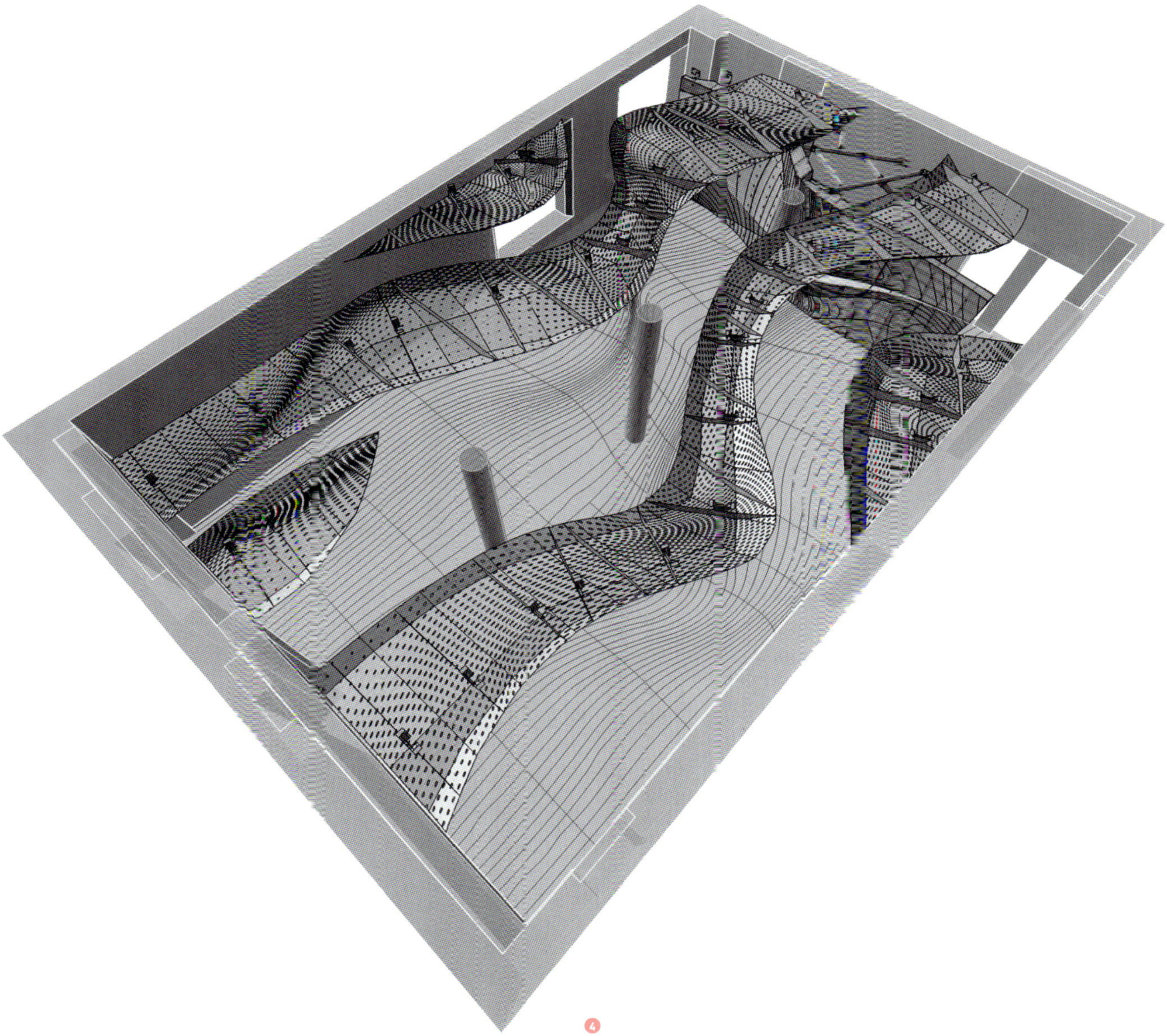

4

1 AXONOMETRIC ceiling panels with fabricated parts + supporting fins
2 exploded AXONOMETRIC assembly of panel #01, #02, #03
3 AERIAL perspective room interventions
4 PERSPECTIVE view from above the space

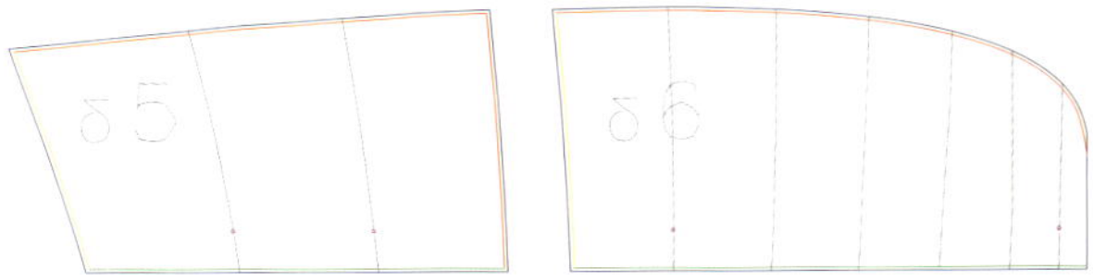

LAYERS (LINE COLOR)

BORDER_EDGE (BLUE) -- 3/4" full depth cut at edge of part
BOTTOM_NOTCH_TOP_SCORE_CL (YELLOW) -- center line of 0.09" deep by 1/4" wide score cut *and* center line of 3/8" deep by 1/4" wide notch on back side of board (routed manually)
BOTTOM_NOTCH_CL (GREEN) -- center line of 3/8" deep by 1/4" wide notch on back side of board (routed manually)
TOP_NOTCH_CL (RED) -- center line of 3/8" deep by 1/4" wide notch
TOP_SCORE_CL (GRAY) -- center line of 0.09" deep by 1/4" wide score
FULL_DRILL_HOLES_0.125"_DIA (MAGENTA) -- full depth 1/8" diameter drilled hole

REF_ONLY_4x8_SHEET (CYAN) -- outer edge of plywood and plywood number (no cut)

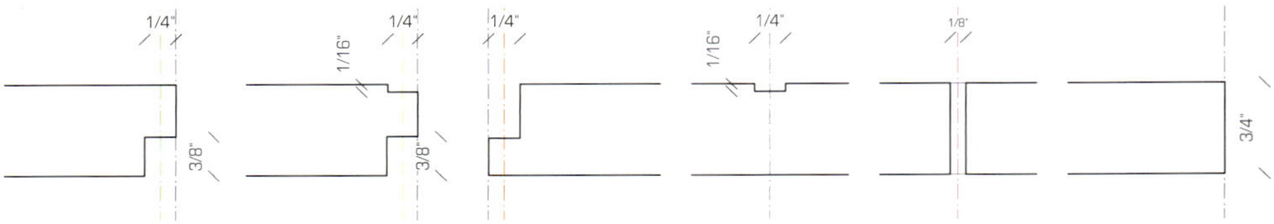

1

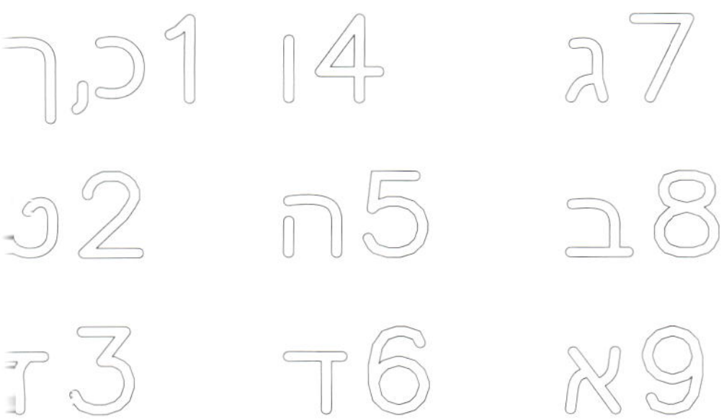
2

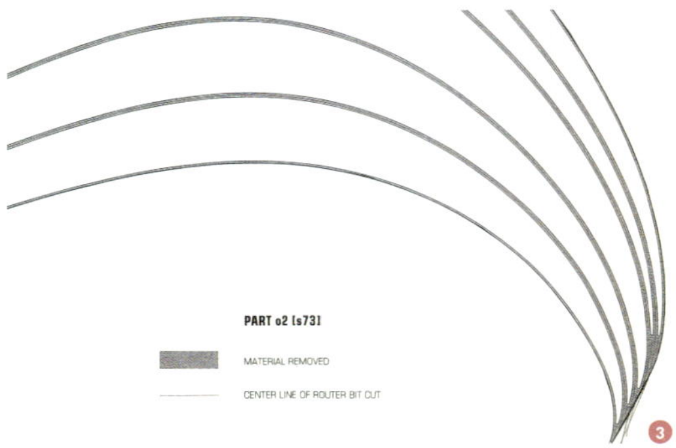

3

4

5

1–3 ASSEMBLY — floor detials
4–5 CONSTRUCTION of floor
6 PLAN — plywood floor panel segments

6

1

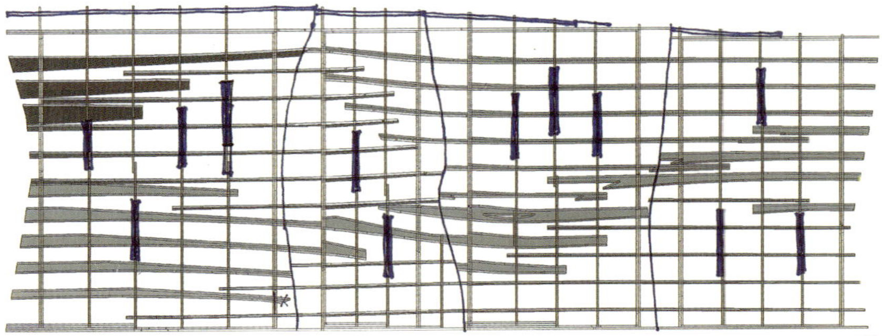
3

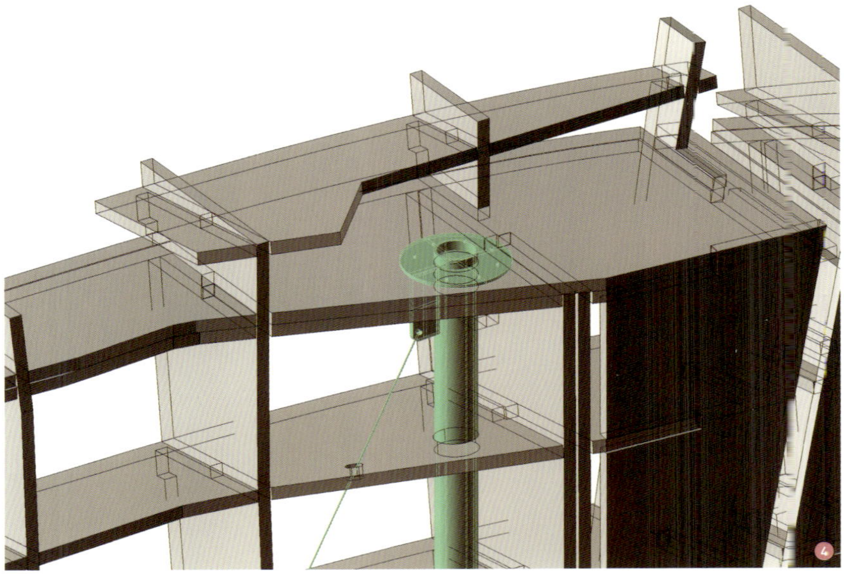
4

2

5

1 VIEW backside of wall structure
2 CONSTRUCTION operable panel
3 ELEVATION — structural ribs + splines
4 PERSPECTIVE — pivot detail top
5–6 CONSTRUCITON wall panel
7 CONSTRUCTION steel support structure
8 exploded AXONOMETRIC plywood floor panel segments — wall panel: structural y-ribs + x-ribs

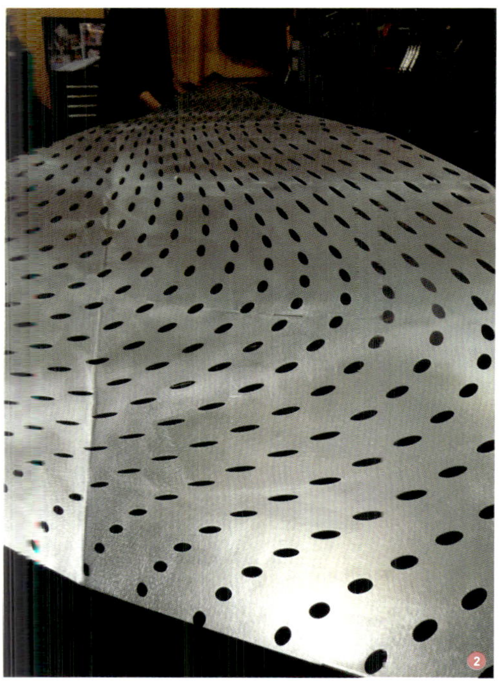

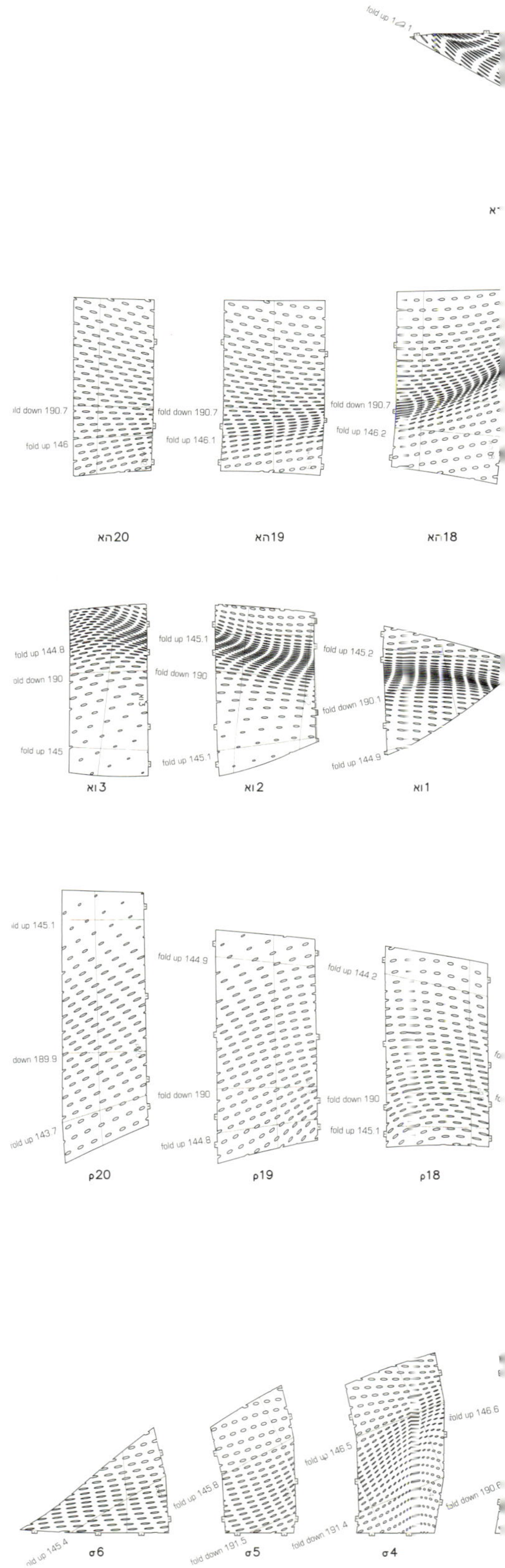

1-2 NEW perforated lighting screen
3 PLAN lighting screens unfolded

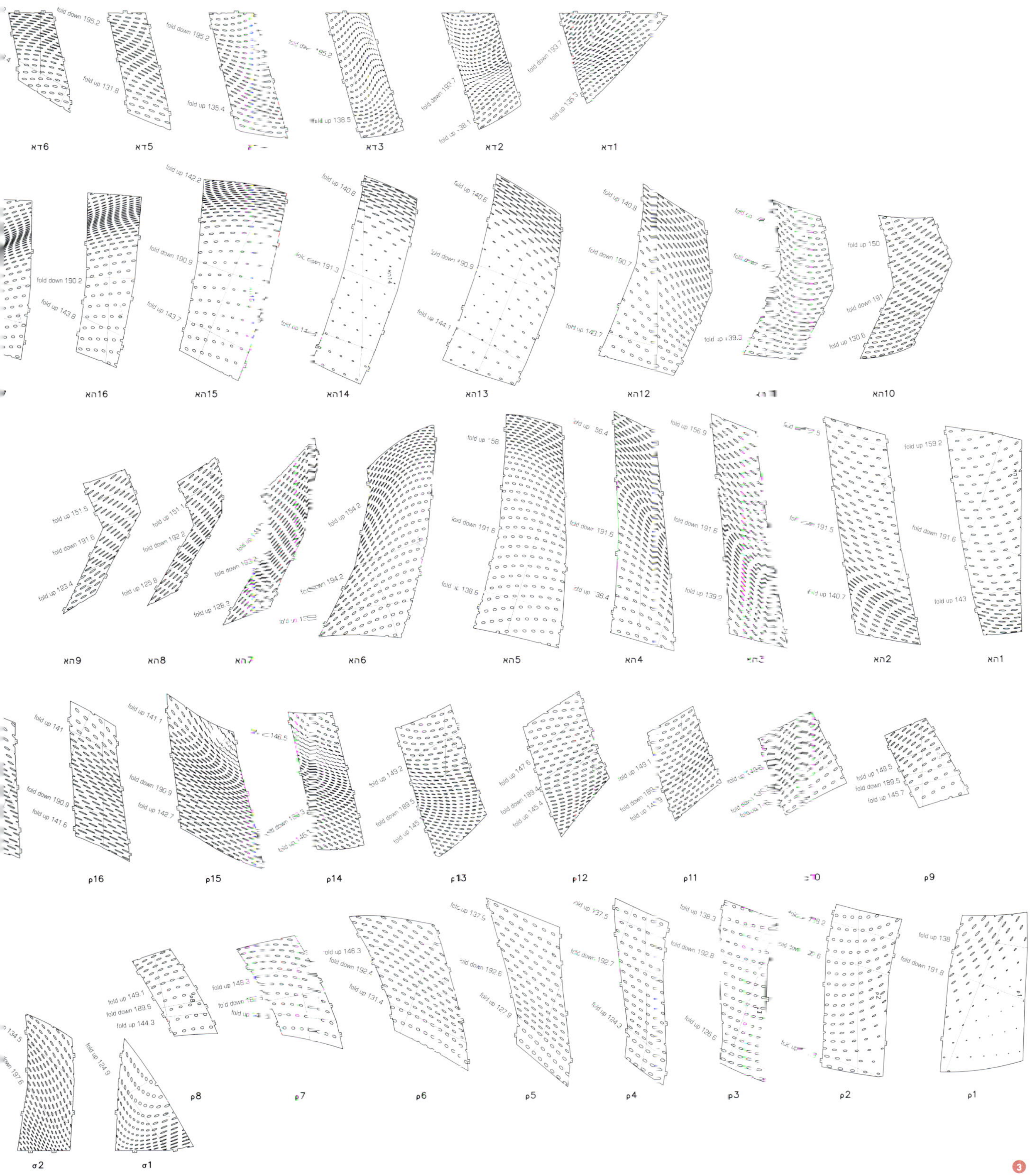
fold down 195.2
fold up 131.8
fold up 135.4
fold down 193.7
fold up 138.5
fold down 193.7
fold up 142.2
fold down 190.9
fold up 143.7
fold down 190.2
fold up 143.8
fold up 140.8
fold up 140.6
fold down 190.9
fold up 144.1
fold up 140.8
fold down 190.7
fold up 150
fold down 191
fold up 130.6
fold up 151.5
fold down 191.6
fold up 123.4
fold down 192.2
fold up 125.8
fold up 126.3
fold up 154.2
fold down 194.2
fold up 158
fold down 191.6
fold down 191.6
fold up 156.9
fold down 191.6
fold up 139.2
fold up 140.7
fold up 159.2
fold down 191.6
fold up 143
fold up 141
fold down 190.9
fold up 141.6
fold up 141.7
fold down 190.9
fold up 142.7
fold up 149.2
fold down 189.5
fold up 147.6
fold down 189.4
fold up 145.4
fold up 149.1
fold up 149.5
fold down 189.5
fold up 145.7
fold up 149.1
fold down 189.6
fold up 144.3
fold up 148.3
fold up 146.3
fold down 192.4
fold up 131.4
fold up 137.5
fold down 192.6
fold up 127.9
fold down 192.7
fold up 124.3
fold up 138.3
fold down 192.8
fold up 126.6
fold up 138
fold down 191.8
fold up 124.9
ρ16
ρ15
ρ14
ρ12
ρ11
ρ9
ρ8
ρ7
ρ6
ρ5
ρ4
ρ3
ρ2
ρ1
σ2
σ1
3

1 VIEW shelter meal
2-3 VIEW wall panels with perforated lighting screen

3.2 cMcF

1 VIEW interior wall patterning
2 VIEW patterning detail

The lobby of a penthouse apartment in a new high-rise residential building in New York City presented an interesting challenge. The space had a utility and it met all the many regulations of the building's co-operative board, but it needed character. We were only permitted to use paint, so we decided to work with qualities of paint that enhance surface. The pattern we devised envelops the floor, walls, and ceiling in an arrangement of matte, low sheen, and high gloss finishes. The effect was transformative but the subtleties of the articulation almost defy documentation. Photographer Albert Vecerka painstakingly adjusted the lighting to pick up the surface changes and compiled an image from more than 20 different exposures to reveal the interactions between the light and paint.

The pattern continued on the terraces as perforated outdoor furniture, designed to articulate the way the space would be used

2

1-2 MODEL perforation
3 MODEL deck furniture
4 PLAN alternate patterns
5 MODEL deck furniture

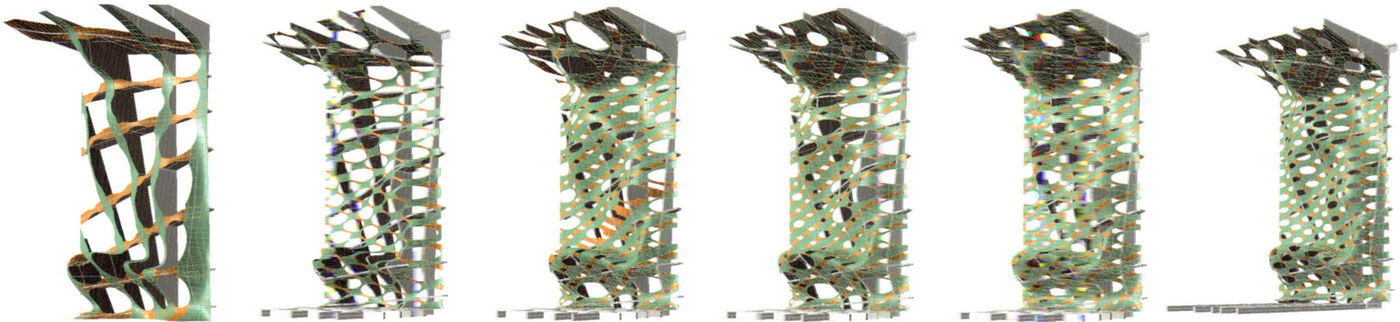

3

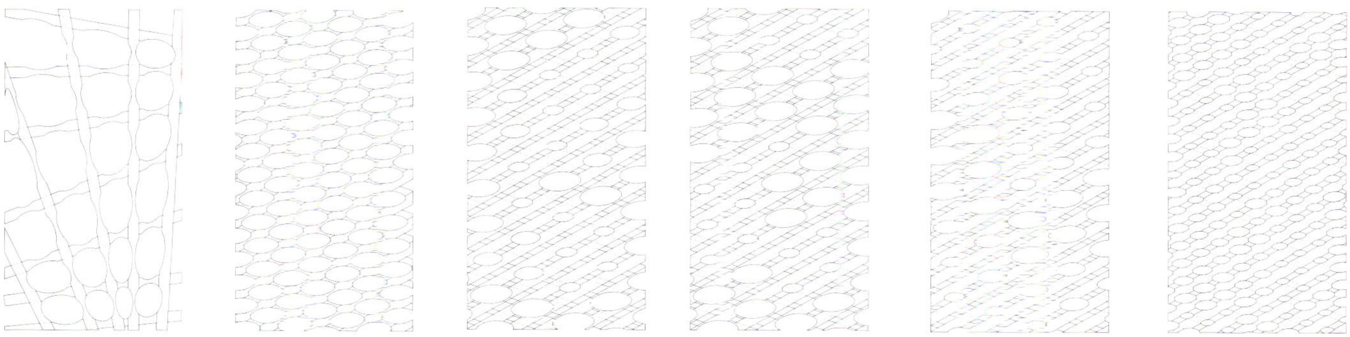

4

5

3.3 lattice 3N

This project is a loft apartment in a converted manufacturing building in New York City and uses a series of moveable perforated screens to make divisions in the space. The perforations allow the pattern of a surface to become three-dimensional.

One wall of the bedroom is milled from three-inch thick laminated plywood with a changing motif that punctures the screen with a variety of shapes. The panels of the wall conceal a walk-in closet and bathroom behind and can be lit from either side in different ways according to the way in which the room is being used.

The perforations are created by joining a pattern of shapes at the back of the panel to a slightly adjusted pattern at the front of the panel. The interplay between the two patterns changes, so that it sometimes appears as if the pattern is disassembling and reassembling when observers stand in different parts of the room. The front surface of the panels is also sculpted to make a wall that is not defined by its straight verticality.

In the main loft space of the apartment, a laser-cut steel framed metal screen separates two rooms. The steel frames slide sideways, permitting the pattern to be re-configured at will. The complexity and mutability of the surface is the product of two defined shapes that break the confines of the grid, and changes based on the relationship between the natural light from the windows and the folded surface of the screen. Metal ribs support the screen and its folded geometry, and the ribs are lasercut with an indentation where each rib meets a perforation in the surface. This gives the perforation a negative form as it crosses the moment of support. The pattern changes—dramatically at times—along the surface, shifting between a moiré effect and a flatness, as adjustments are made to the positioning of the two defined shapes. This screen balances the effects of the light from the space behind with the reflected light from the space in front.

1 VIEW lighting through perforations
2 VIEW perforated plywood screen
3-4 PERFORATION CNC plywood details

2

3

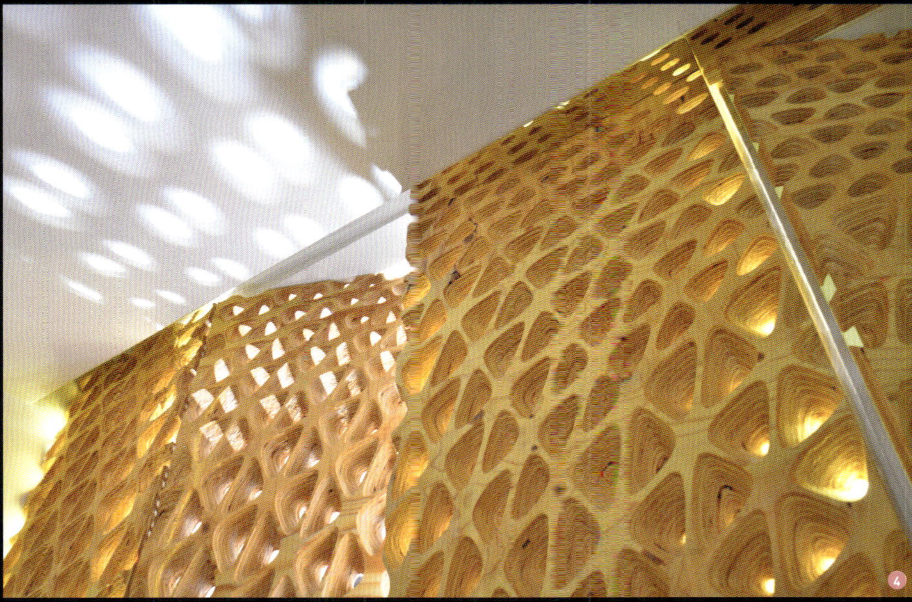

4

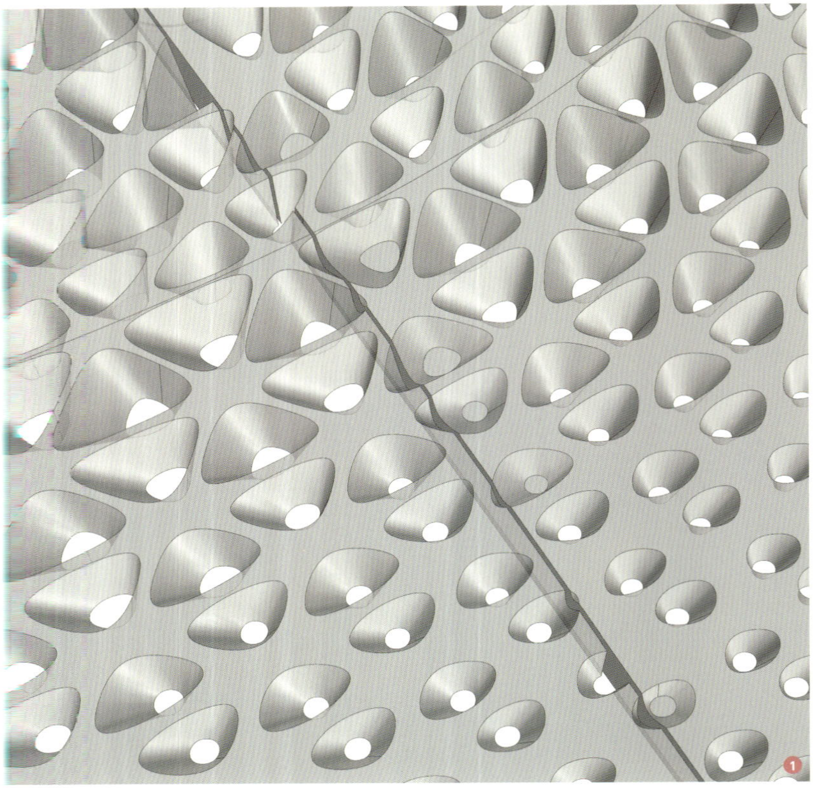

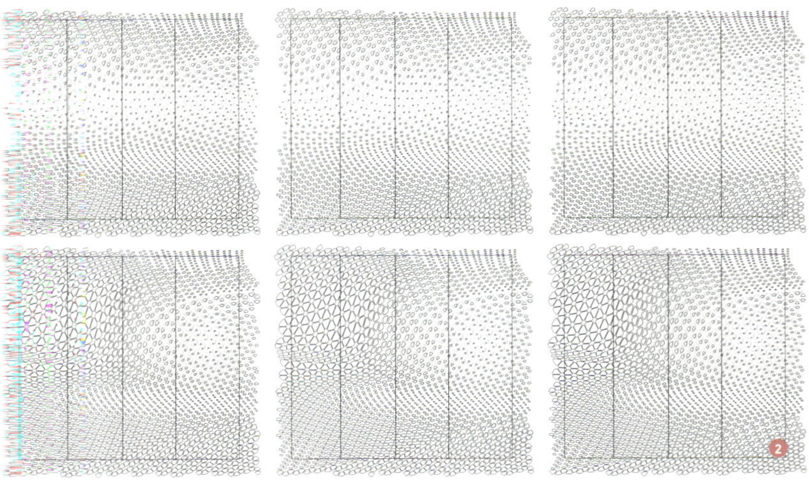

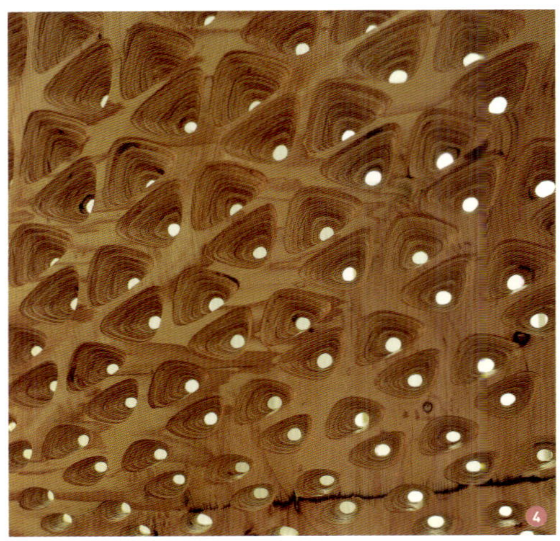

1 PERSPECTIVE plywood screen details
2 PERFORATION plywood screen wall — options #08, #01, #18, #19
3 CONSTRUCTION CNC mill creating cuts for plywood panel
4 PATTERN details
5–6 PATTERN studies

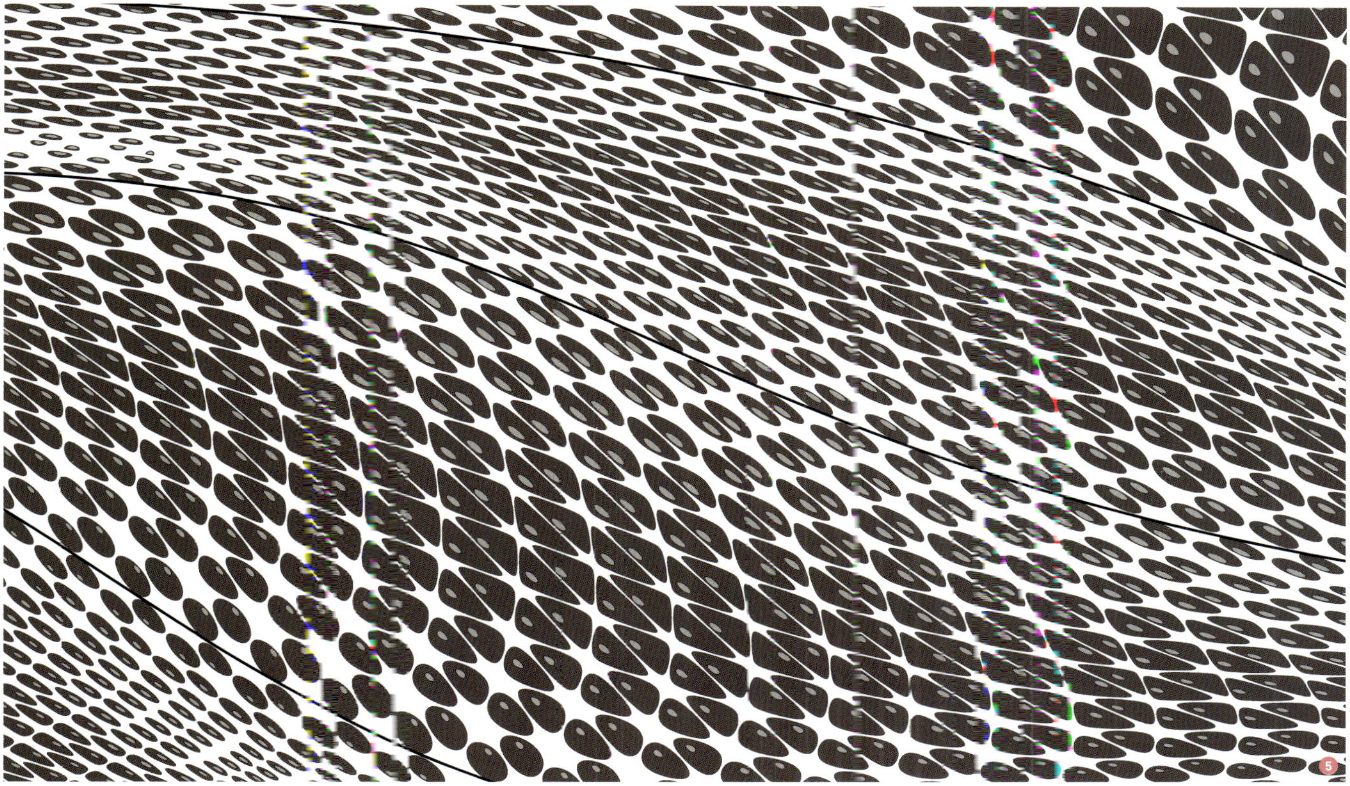

5

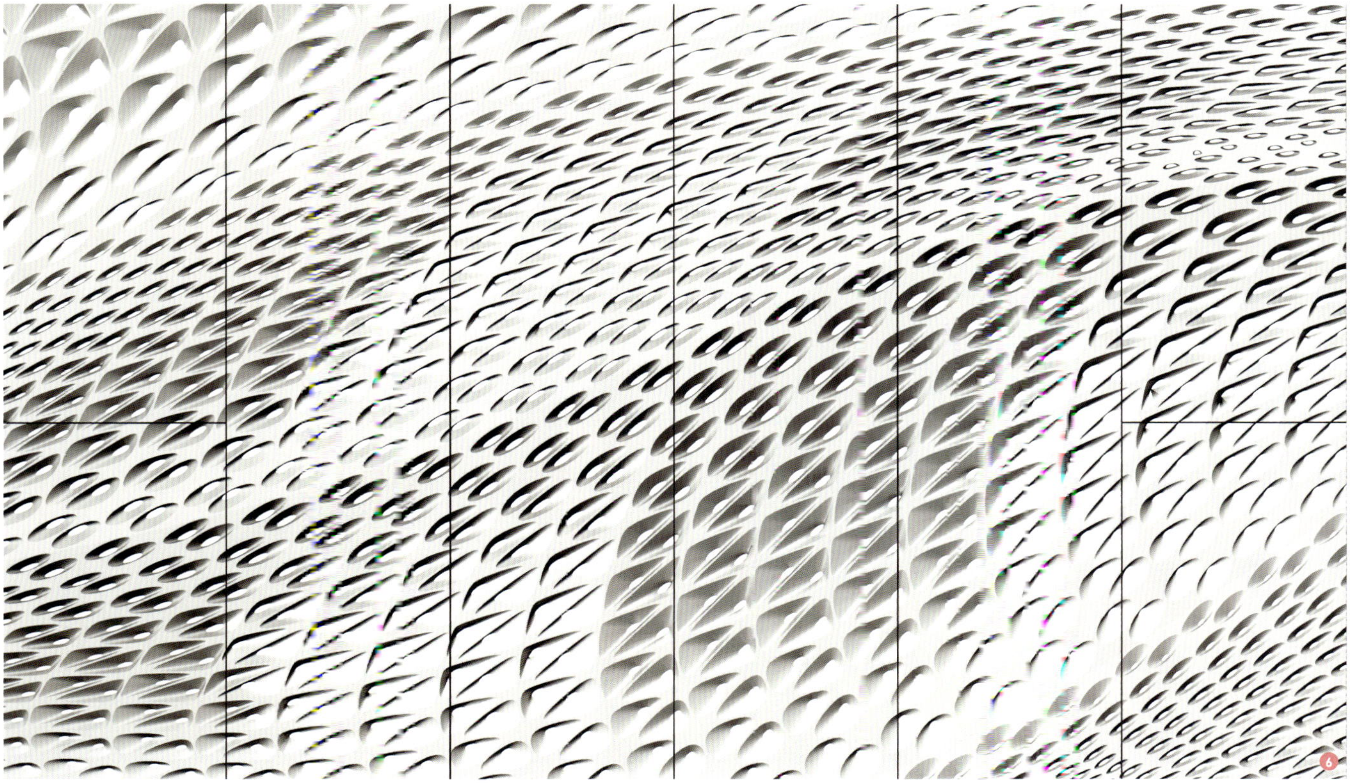

6

1

1-3 PERFORATION CNC mill details
4-5 PATTERN detail

1 VIEW perforated plywood surface
2 SKETCH twisting surface
3 PERFORATION plywood screen details
4-5 VIEW perforated plywood surface

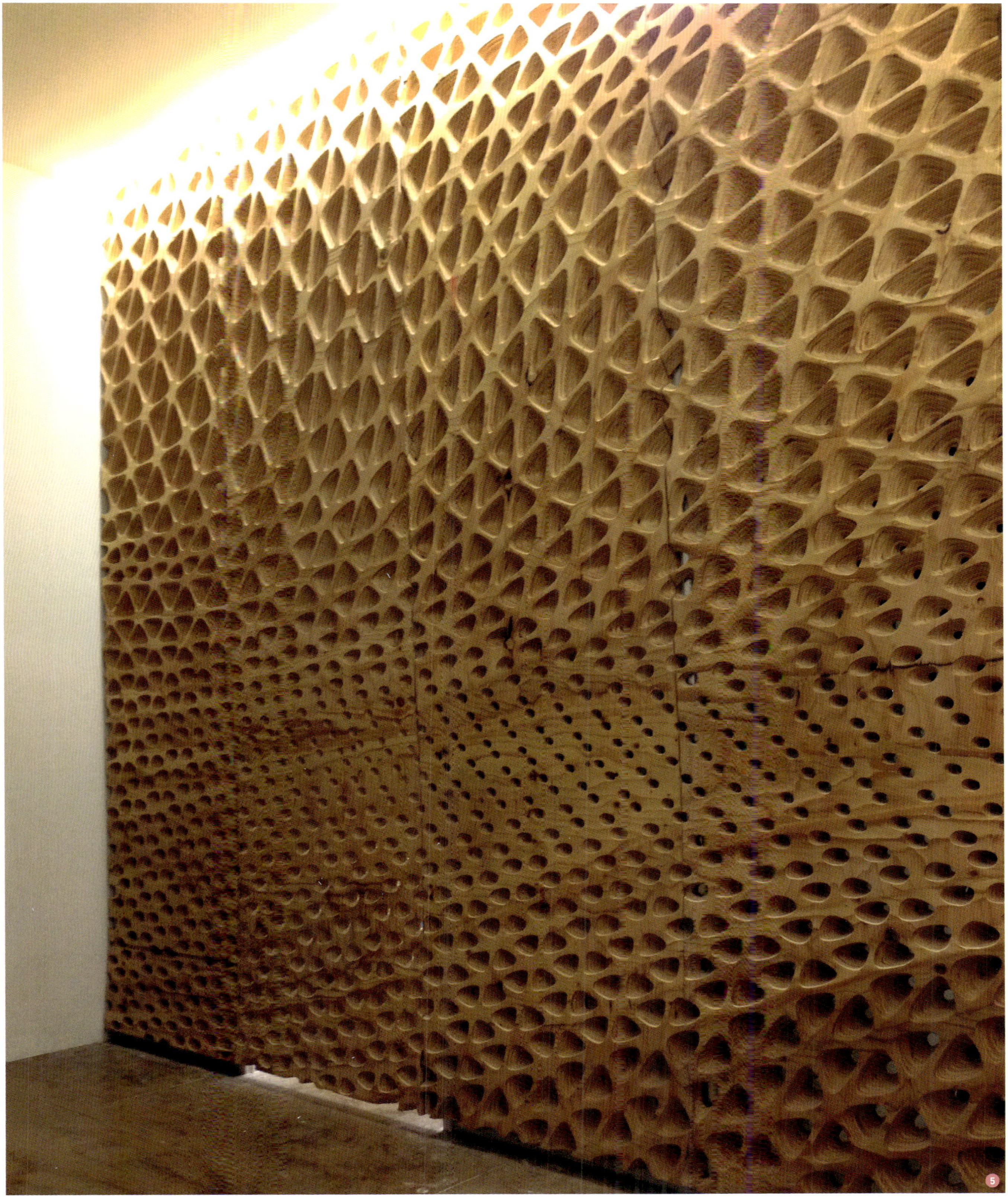

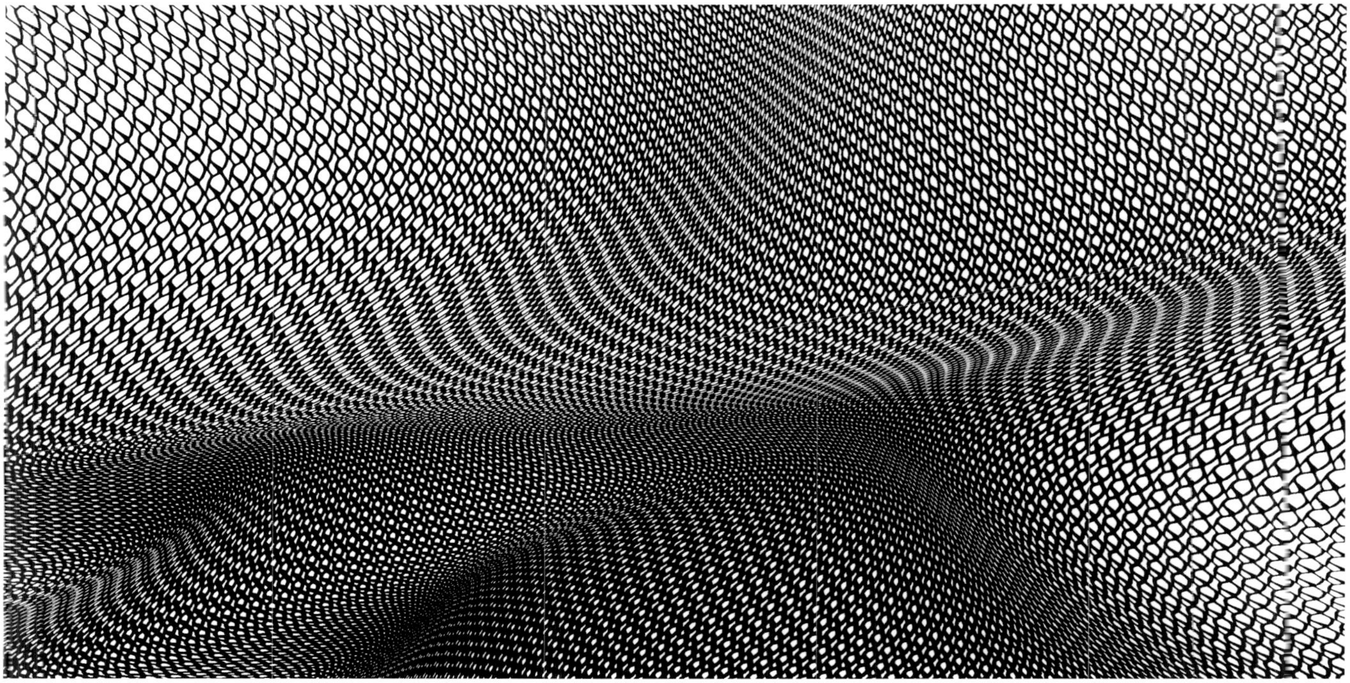

1

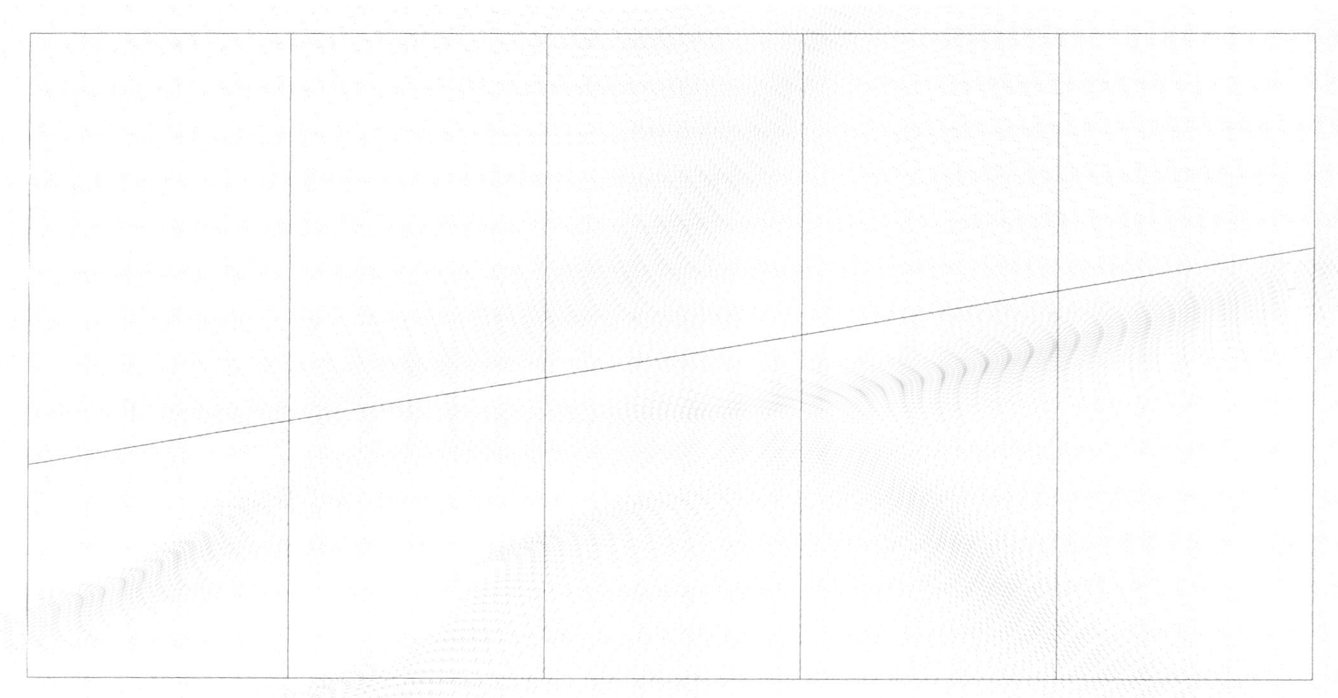

2

1 PERFORATION steel wall showing folds — option #03
2 PERFORATION steel wall with panel overlay
3 ELEVATION — steel wall
4-5 PERFOATED fabric steel screen wall

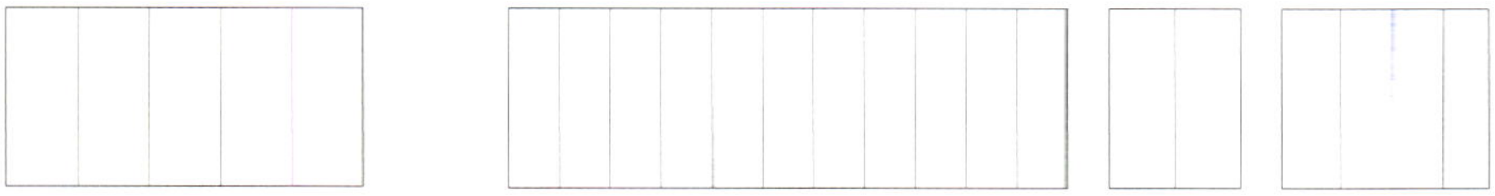

3

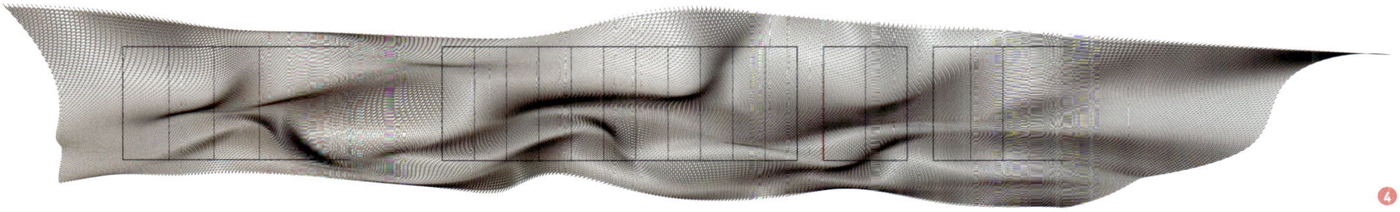

4

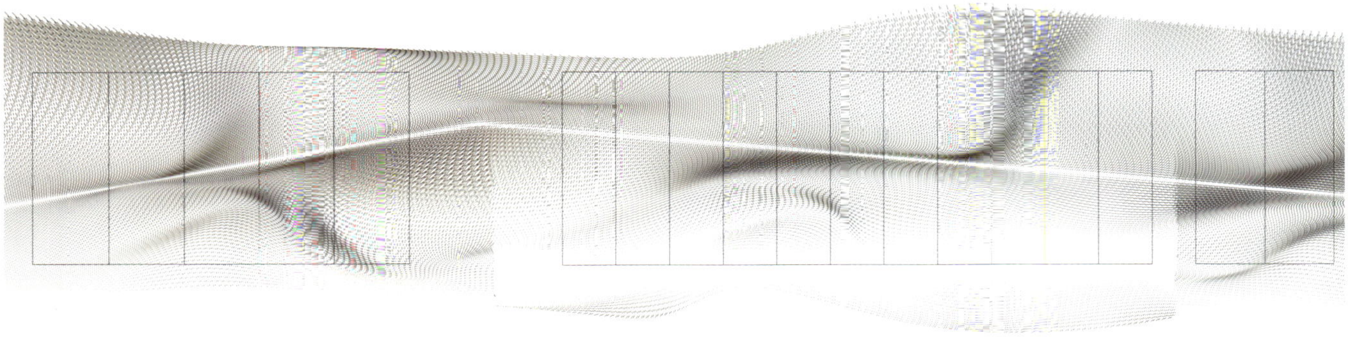

5

1 MIRROR looking back
2 CONSTRUCTION steel screen fitted to frame
3 VIEW metal screen, frame, and fin behind
4 VIEW metal fins supporting screen
5 ELEVATION folded screen

4

5

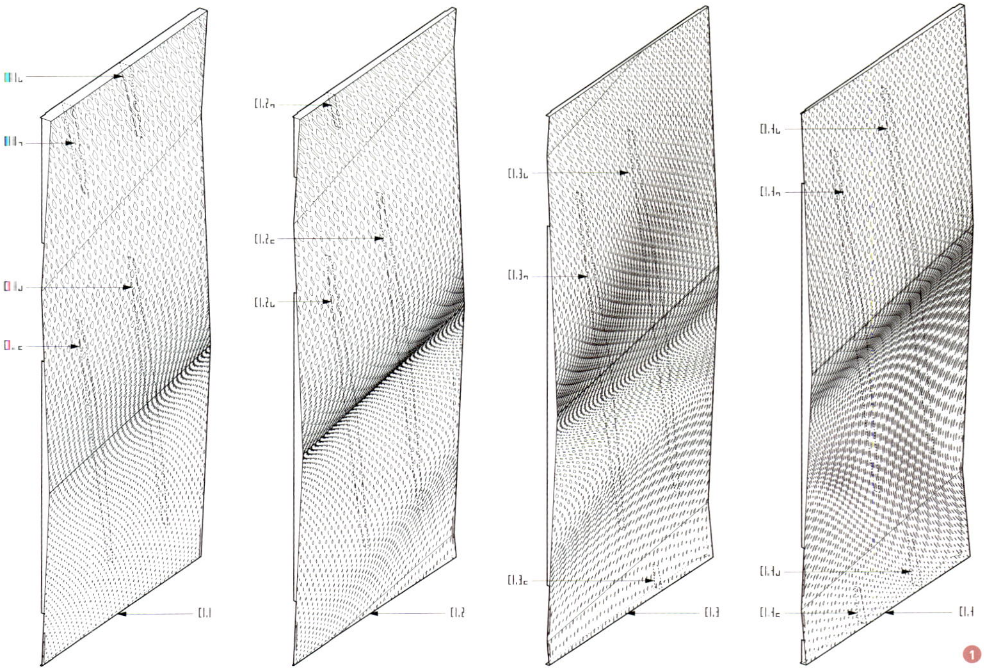

1

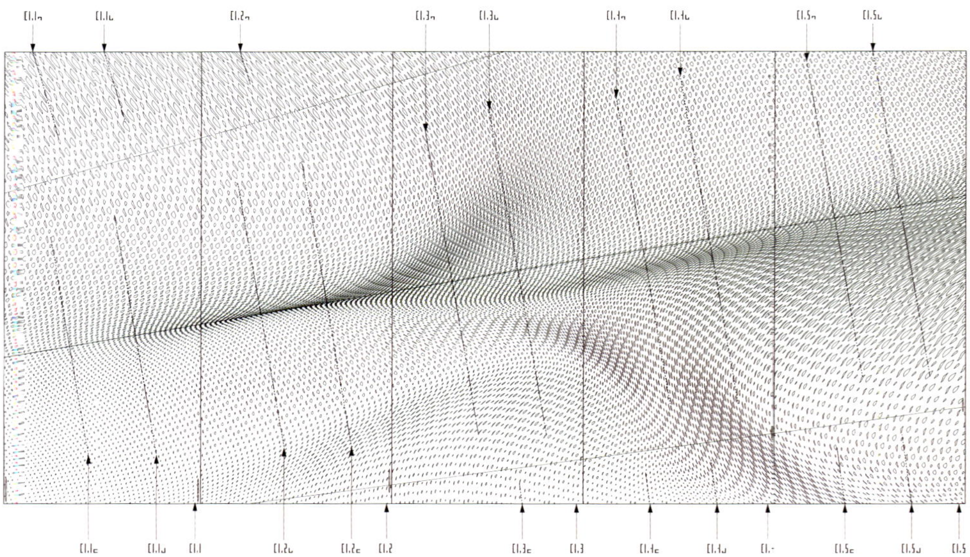

2

1 ASSEMBLY perforated panels
2 ELEVATION — steel screen geometry
3 PATTERN
4 VIEW folded screen surface

3

2

3

1 VIEW folded screens opening
2 PERFORATION backlit metal screens
3 ELEVATION metal screen panel geometry
4 VIEW metal screens in place

4

4

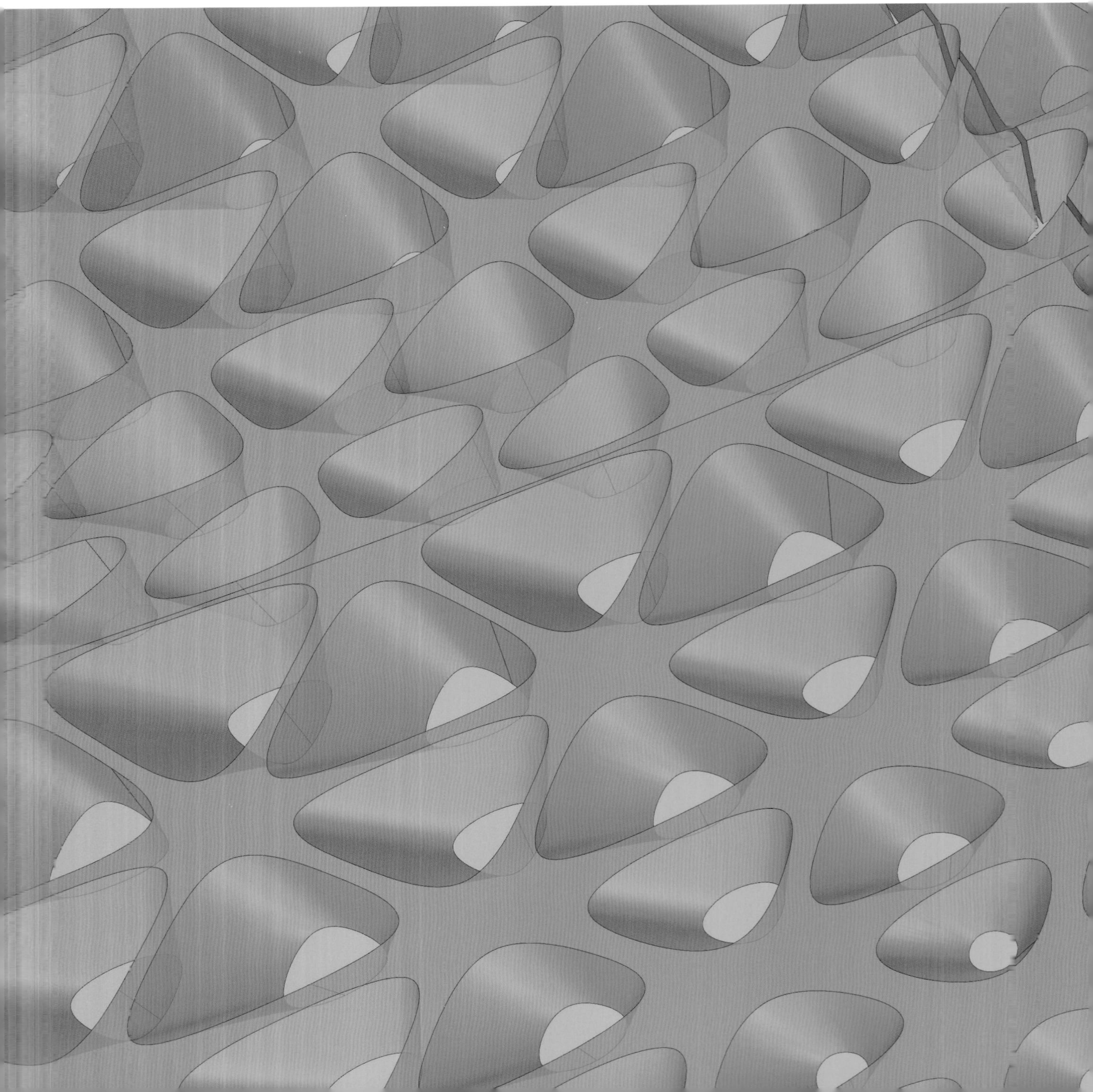

material + depth

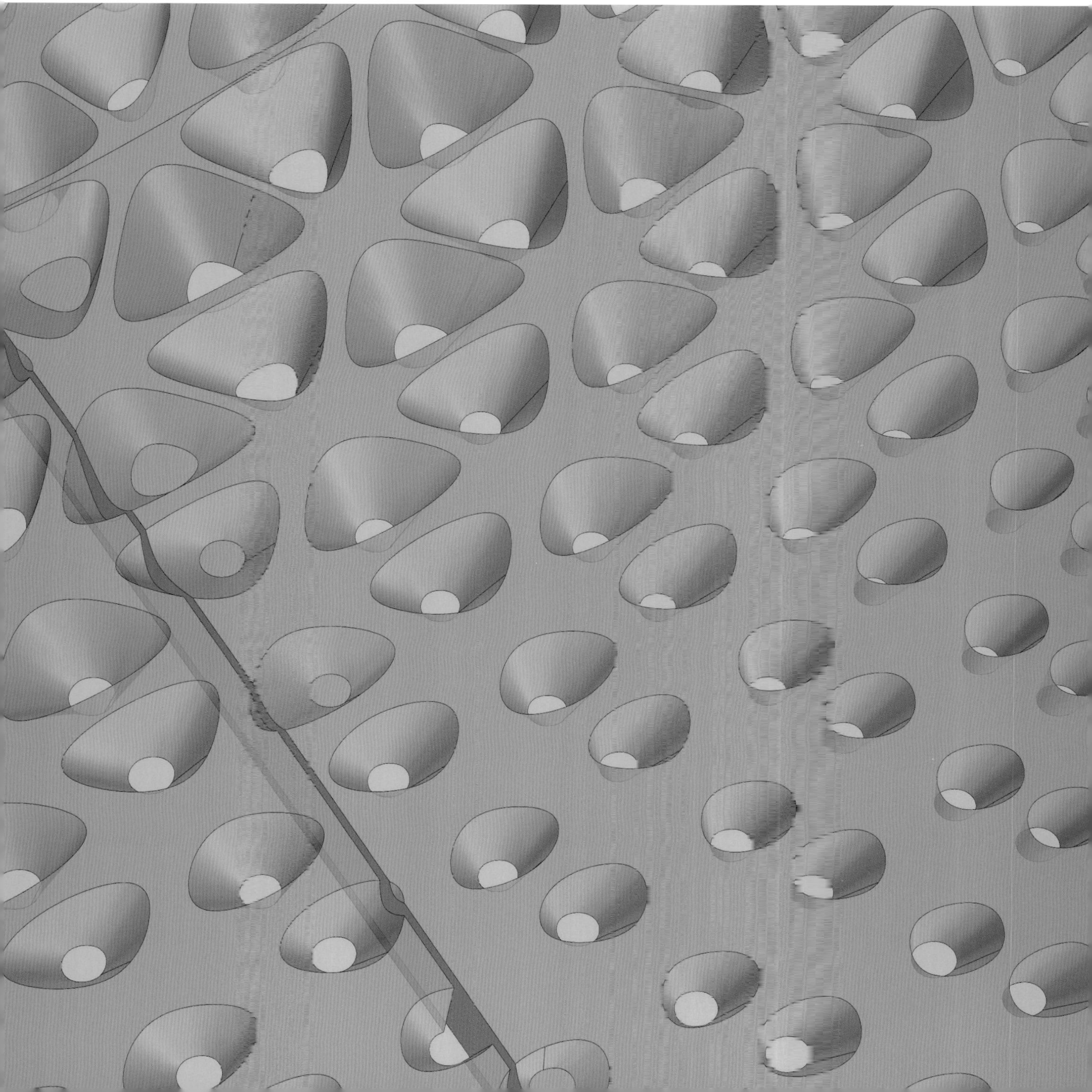

material + depth

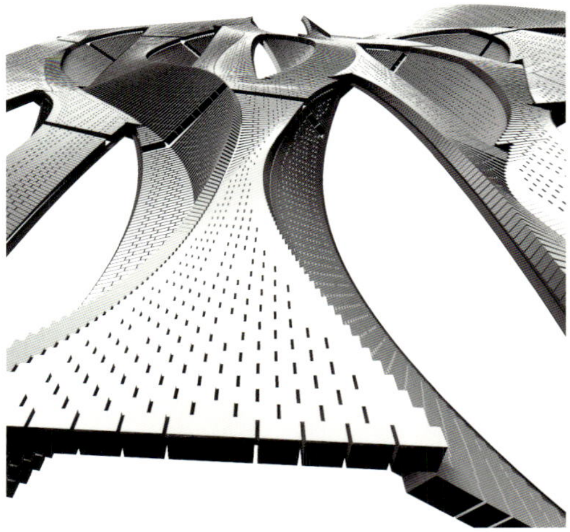

In the course of pursuing pattern as a design intervention, SYSTEM sought out materials that could add a layer of articulation, one that is less controlled. The materiality and depth of a project are the final development of the surface and form. Plywood, obviously, has been one of the materials we've used. The other, somewhat to our own surprise, is brick.

The evolution of the technology for producing building materials means that there are identifiable distinctions in the quality and aesthetics of those materials over time. In the 1910s, for example, some bricks were fired in a bee-hive kiln, a drum-shaped oven topped by a shallow dome. The idea is that the shape of the kiln promotes a small variation in the temperature throughout the kiln, rather than the very even heat of modern-day tunnel kilns. This allows the clay to exhibit a multitude of colour shades within a single brick according to the temperature range and air circulation unique to the kiln.

The success of this firing method is dependent on tradition and repeated experimentation to finely calibrate the results. Data about firing schedules, heat ranges, gas and oxygen mixes for the beehive kilns is crucial. But so is a kiln manager who has spent thousands of hours learning the characteristics of each kiln, who can interpret the data and make the real time adjustments learned from the kiln manager before him, and who has improved upon them.

Perhaps the key factor in our brick choice for UNhistoric townHOUSE (page 182) was that the beehive kilns in Sugarcreek, Ohio, were built in the 1920s and have been continuously used since then. This would connect our bricks to the material of the historic area we were building in and to the work of Ralph Walker, the architect of our favorite building in that neighborhood.

Another material with an intrinsic pattern, plywood, has always been favored among designers for experimentation with constructed ideas. Almost as soon as it became commercially available it was used to make curved and twisted forms that required structural rigidity as well as complex geometries curving in two directions.

Painted, unpainted, epoxied, clear coated, pigmented or varnished, plywood retains some of the qualities of the veneers that it is made from. But it engineers away the uncertainties of wood, reducing the need for structural redundancy. Thus plywood makes better use of the tree, one of our few renewable building materials.

The work in this book has not been displayed to highlight the environmental issues each project addresses. An understanding of ecosystems, however, is at the heart of each project SYSTEM undertakes. If there is to be a truly environmental architecture, it will not be an assemblage of greener solutions to the current programmes and ways of living, it will be the creation of spaces that change the way humans and natural systems interact.

Building has always been considered the antidote to wilderness: stones and trees are made square and parallel and civilised. But instead of erasing the organic, or regulating the uncultivated, architecture's role is to mediate between the two systems. SYSTEM's geometries and methods of building aim to move people away from the orthogonal and demonstrate a different kind of order, just as systemic, not unlike that found in the wilderness. Of course the architecture seeks to use less energy in the production and use of its buildings and employ renewable materials and build in a manner that is sustainable, but most importantly, it seeks to make a connection so that as humans engage with the built environment, they better understand the environment that lies beyond.

4.1 UNhistoric townHOUSE

With Robert Baker

1 DIAGRAM view lines
2-9 Tribeca neighbourhood

The Landmark Preservation Commission (LPC) was established in New York to preserve historic buildings after the McKim, Mead, and White-designed Penn Station was pulled down. The Commission has jurisdiction over the site of a townhouse that SYSTEM was commissioned to renovate and enlarge in 2010. An odd leftover, the lot is only 25- feet deep and has buildings on three sides, but has almost 40 feet of street frontage. The current house does not meet the basic standards of cross ventilation, light and open green space that are required for residential habitation, yet is in a very desirable Manhattan neighbourhood. Tribeca was originally built for manufacturing, trade and warehousing when that part of the Hudson River was a thriving shipping port. The 10-storey building across the narrow street is now used for offices and movie production. Our site had little or no privacy or sense of domesticity, particularly as the building is only one room deep.

The argument we made successfully to the LPC was that our building was to be made from materials characteristic of the historic neighbourhood—brick, steel, glass, and cast iron—but used in a revolutionary fashion.

The windows are carefully angled to increase the views up and down the street while decreasing the view into the house from the commercial building across the way. This has the effect of turning the brick façade into a continuous twisting surface as the windows face any direction except straight on to the street. The bricks become like drapery, corbelling from their cast iron base up to the overhanging cornice.

After construction experiments with robotic bricklayers and backup walls made of plywood or honeycombed plastic, we decided to build with brick hand-laid onsite against a permanent foam template that is CNC cut to form every brick course and position every brick. The foam insulates, helps with the waterproofing and prevents damage from condensation between the walls. The interior of the façade is also brick, creating a four wythe wall, in which one of the interior wythes is foam. This enhances insulation and eliminates street noise.

Balconies extend beyond the façade and provide small outdoor spaces nestled in and jutting out from the brick wall. They're conceived as a second fabric swelling out from the brick surface, extending the habitable space through the wall, their balustrades screening the interior even further.

In the interior, the twisting geometry of the façade brings an intimate domestic scale to the interior spaces. The curves and kinks create alcoves, cubbies, and nooks that can be personalised. One might be a window seat, another a place for a plant, another a spot to talk on the phone or look out the window. Thus an otherwise commercial and impersonal environment can be made more intimate and domestic without the necessity of drawn shades.

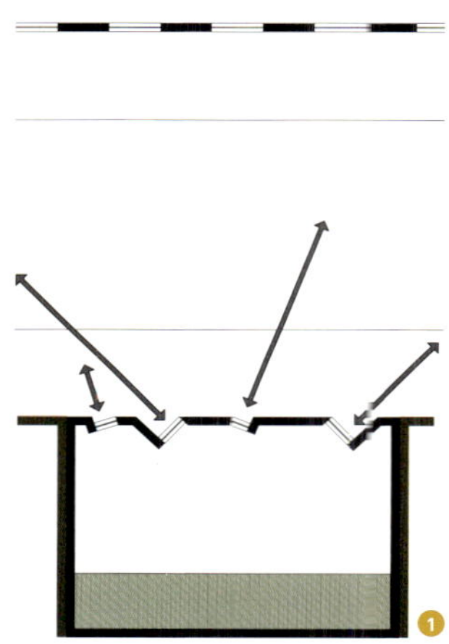

1

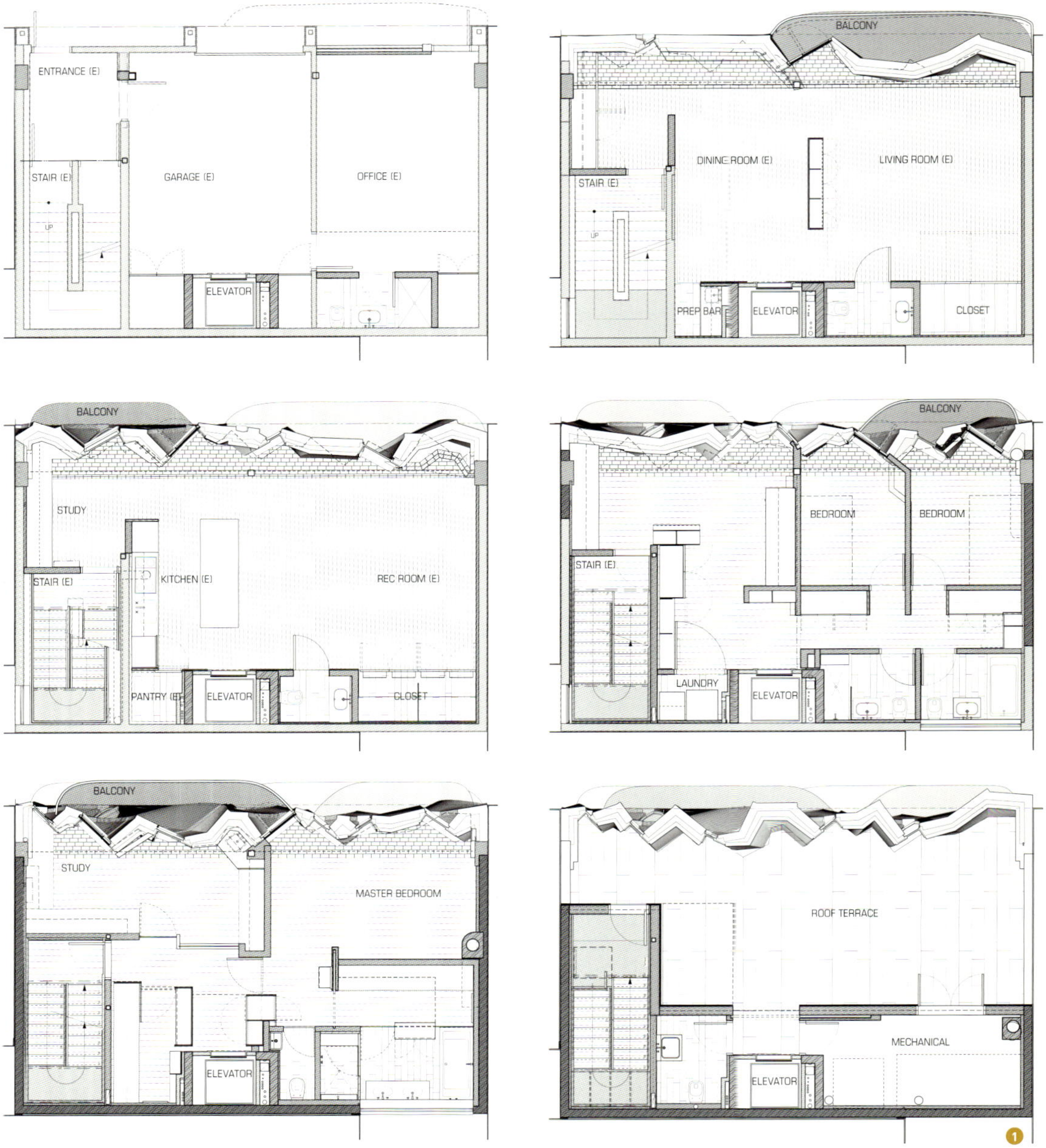

1

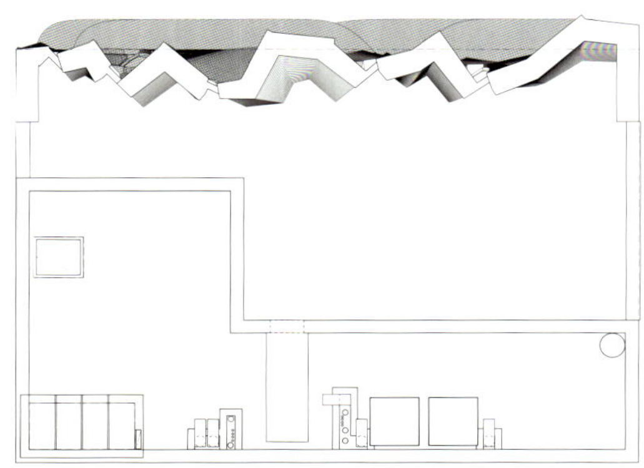

1 PLAN — ground level to roof level
2 ELEVATION — existing site conditions
3-5 TIMELINE 187 Franklin St. 1930-2014
6 CONSTRUCTION brick beehive kiln exterior
7 CONSTRUCTION brick beehive kiln interior
8 SKETCH — geometric setout
9 SKETCH — revolving arcs

2

3

4

5

6

7

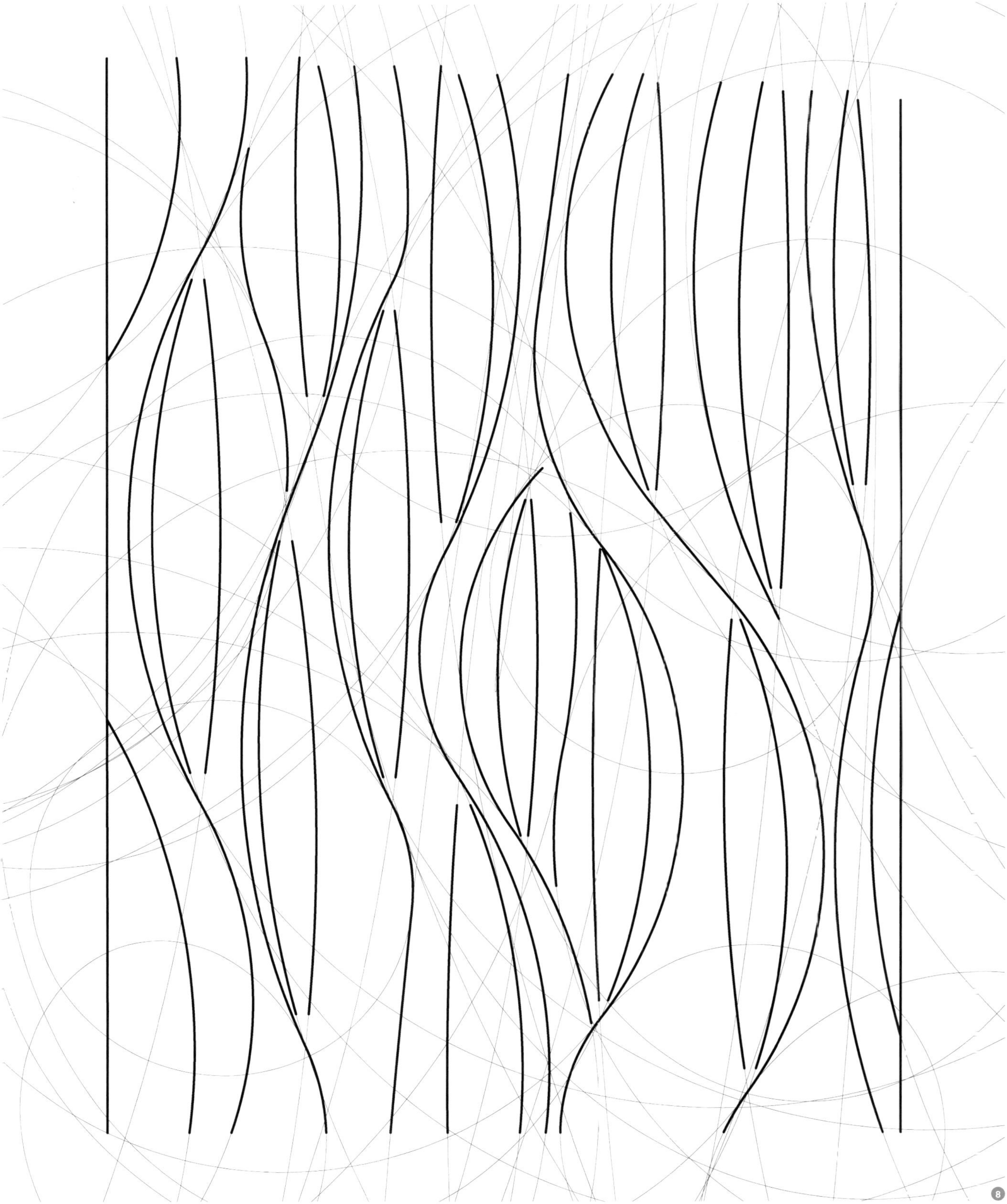

8

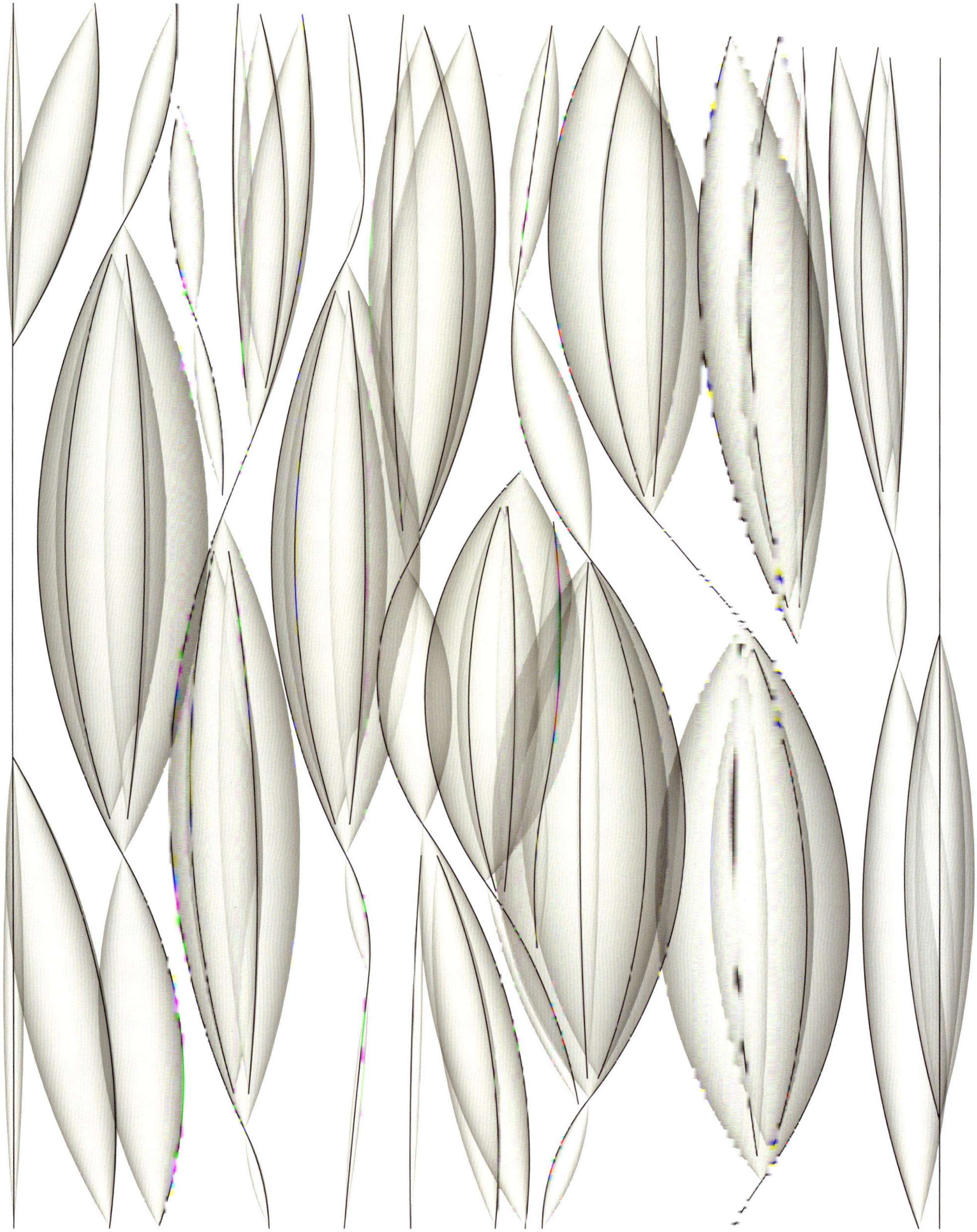

9

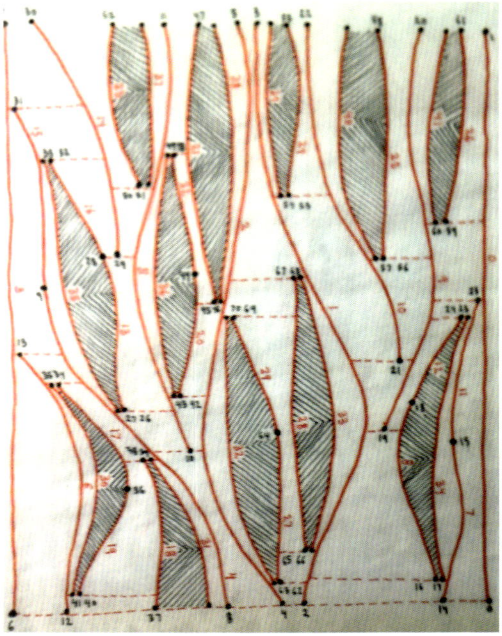

1

2

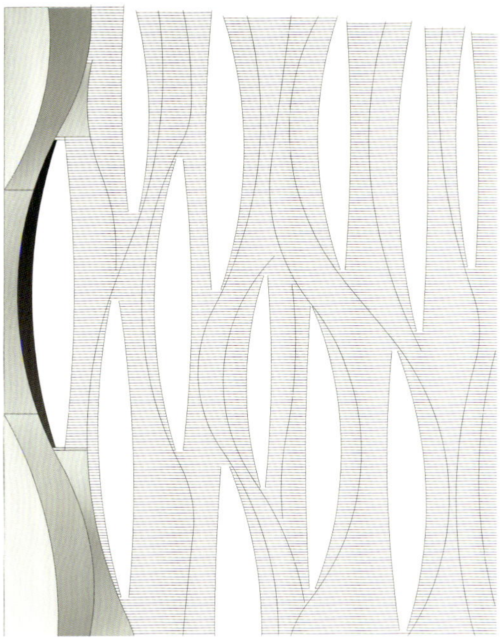

3

4

1 SKETCH parametric diagram
2 ELEVATION — exterior + interior folds
3 ELEVATION with brick courses
4 ELEVATION with brick pattern
5 DIAGRAM mapping rotating setout lines
6 DIAGRAM rotation setout lines

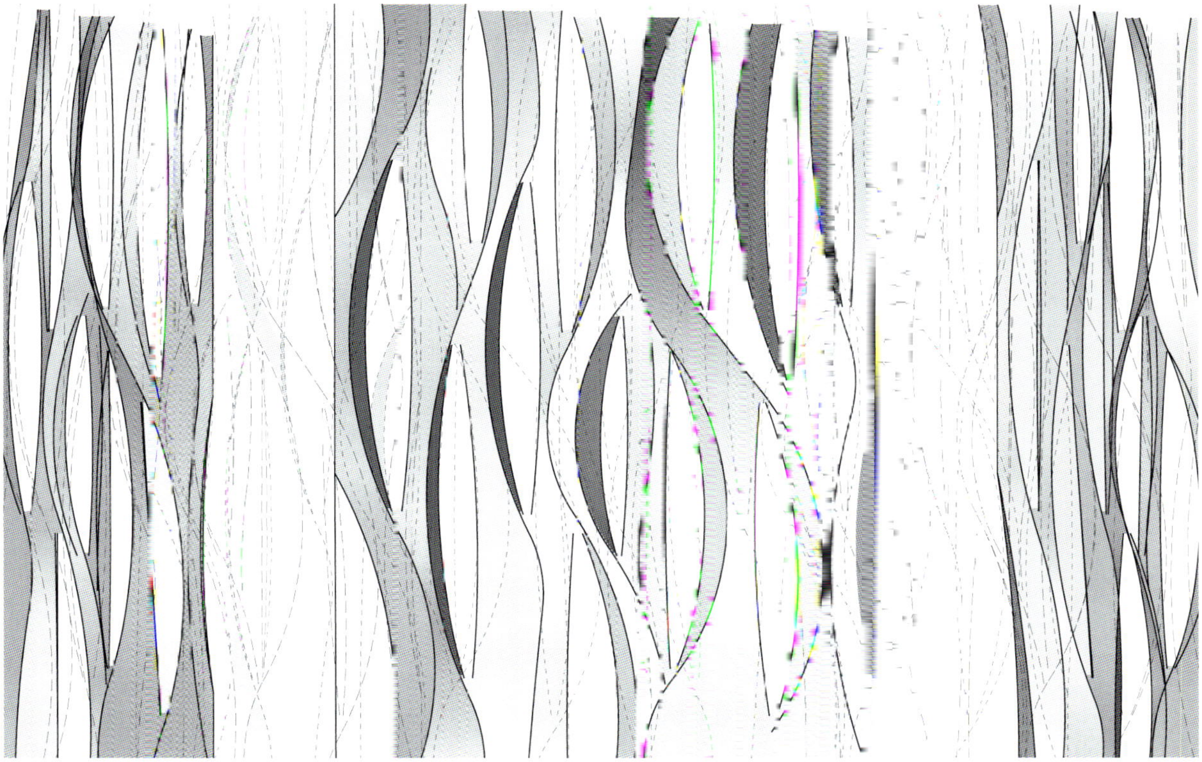

5

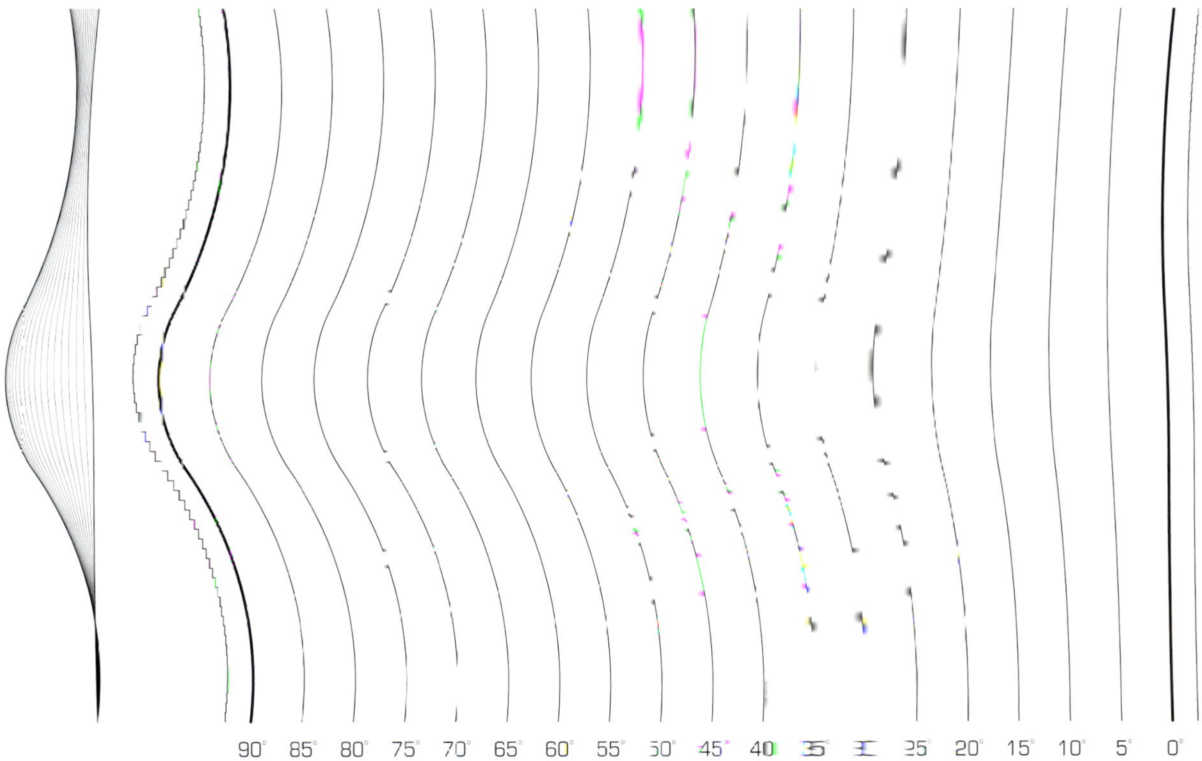

6

1

1 ELEVATION — perforated metal screen geometry
2-3 PRECENDENT study balconies
4 PERFORATED fabric
5 PERFORATED steel balcony detail
6-7 PATTERN

2

3

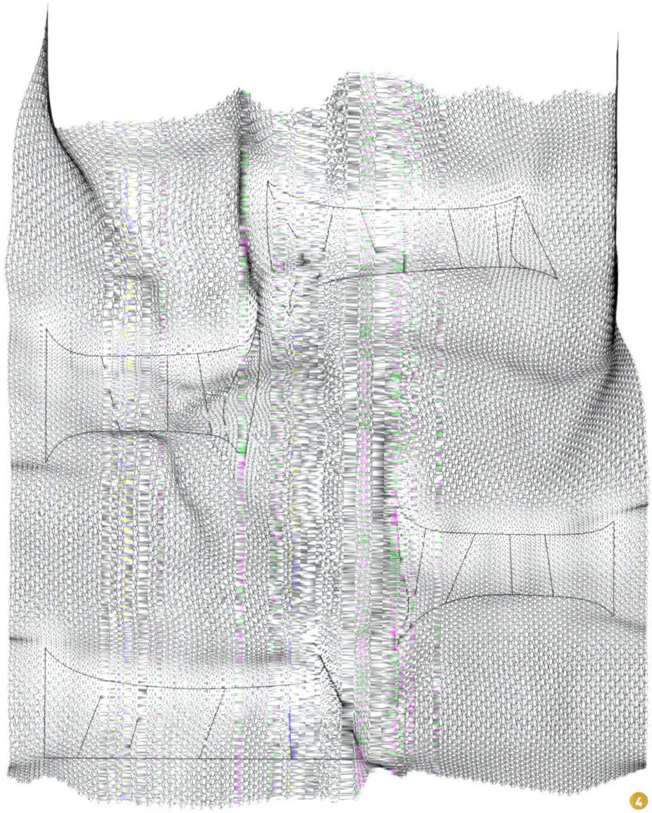
4

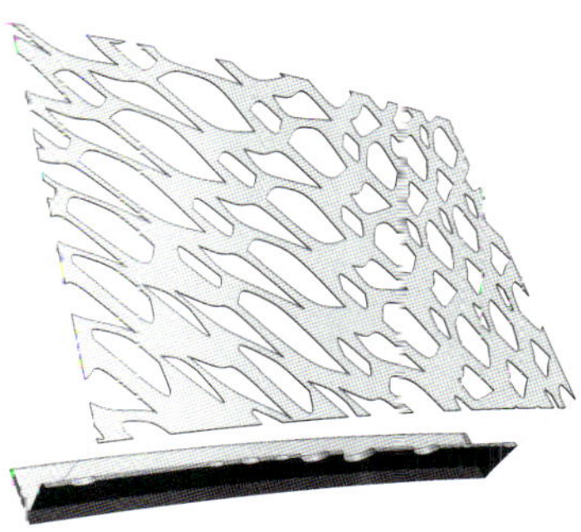
5

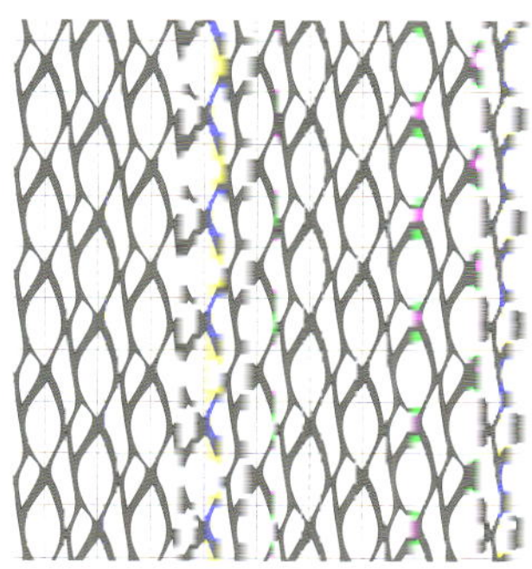
6

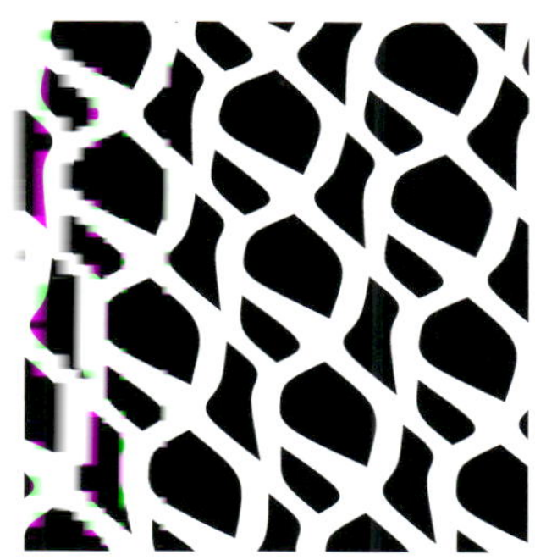
7

1

2

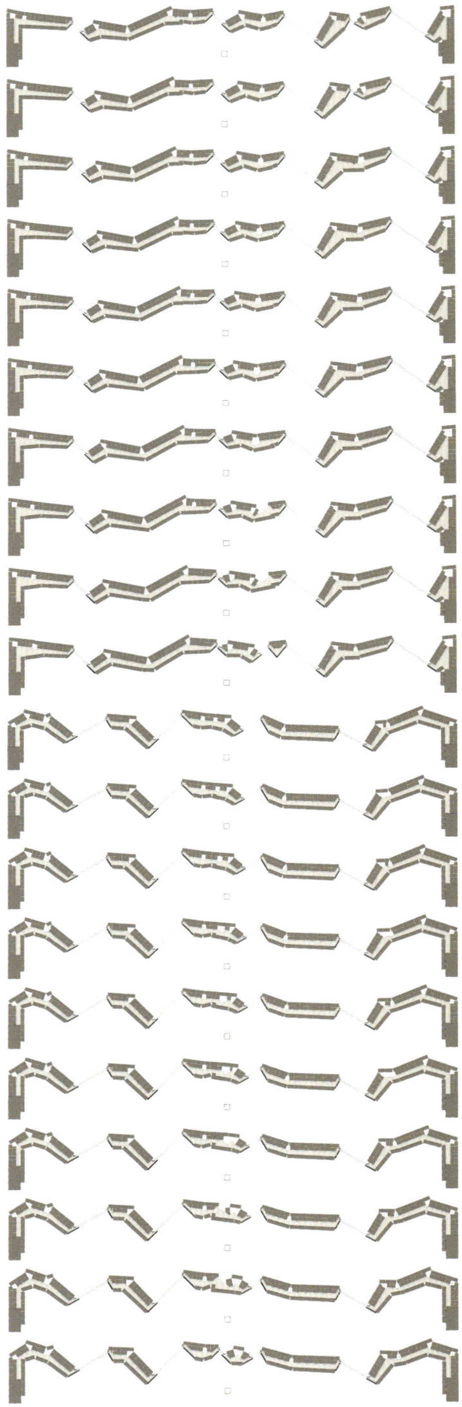

3

1 ELEVATION structural load path
2 SECTION diagram façade columns
3 PLAN — every course of brick in façade
4 KEY scripting rules
5-6 BRICK façade prototype
7 VIEW — beehive bricks pre-fired
8 VIEW — beehive bricks post-fired

length < 8": Cut brick

8" < length < 12": Cut Brick and Header Brick. Flip positions to minimize vertical grout alignment with the course below.

12" < length < 16": Header Brick aligned with center of Stretcher Brick below. One Cut Brick on left and one Cut Brick on right.

16" < length: Header Brick aligned with center of Stretcher Brick below. Alternate Stretcher Bricks and Header Bricks with Cut Bricks on both ends. If Left over cut length is less than 3-5/8", either replace previous Stretcher Brick with Header Brick and add a Cut Brick or eiliminate previous Header Brick and add Cut Brick.

ODD COURSES

length < 8": Cut brick

8" < length < 12": Cut Brick and Header Brick. Flip positions to minimize vertical grout alignment with the course below.

12" < length < 16": One Cut Brick on left and one Cut Brick on right.

16" < length: Header Brick aligned with center of Stretcher Brick below. Alternate Stretcher Bricks and Header Bricks with Cut Bricks on both ends. If Left over cut length is less than 3-5/8", either replace previous Stretcher Brick with Header Brick and add a Cut Brick or eiliminate previous Header Brick and add Cut Brick.

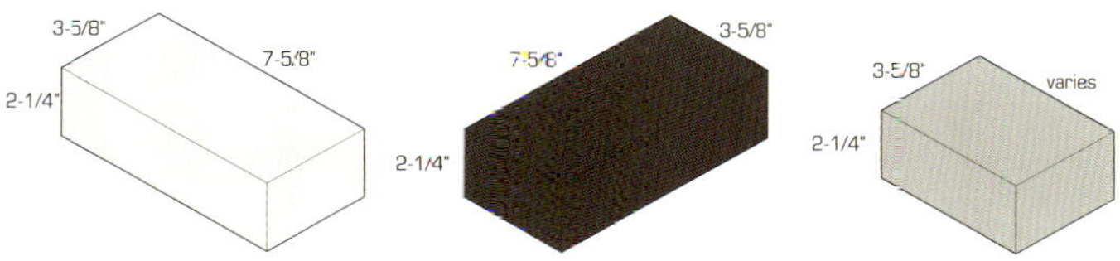

STRETCHER BRICK

Face Brick Count: 2,671

HEADER BRICK

Face Brick Count: 6,726

CUT BRICK

Face Brick Count: 6,825

Total Face Brick Count: ***16,226***

At course #200, refer to Brick Pattern Drawing 3/A701 for replacing Stretcher Bricks with two Header Bricks to achieve gradient from Flemish Bond brick pattern to English Bond brick pattern.

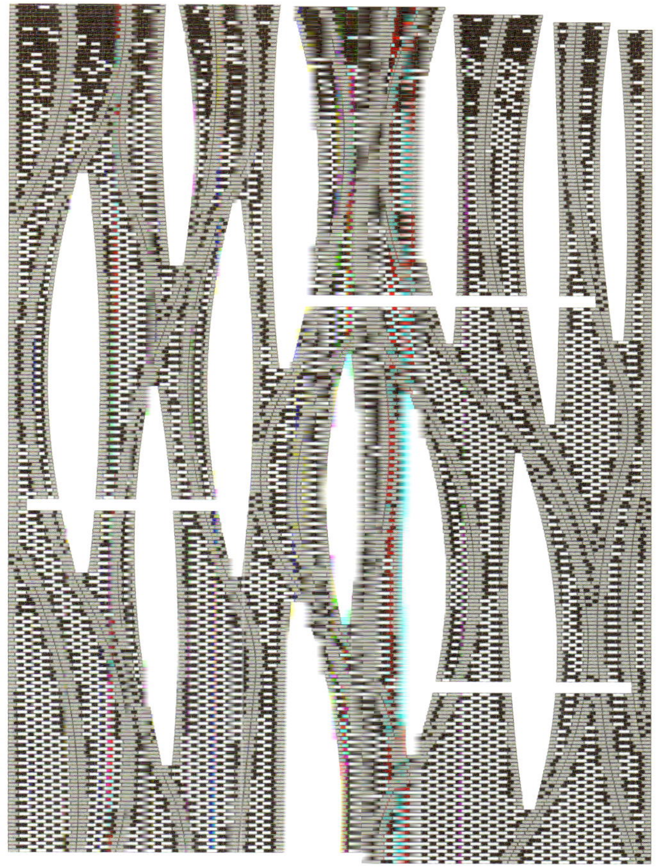

4

5

6

7

8

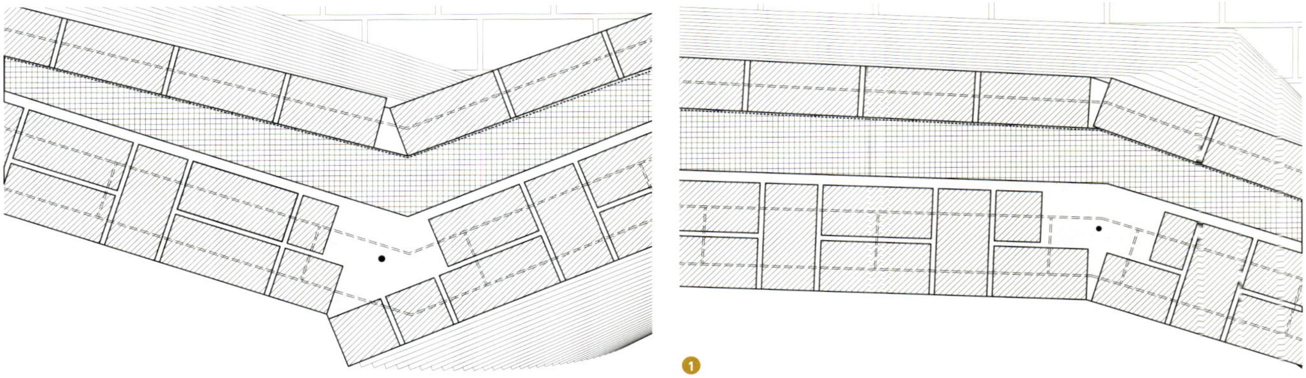

1

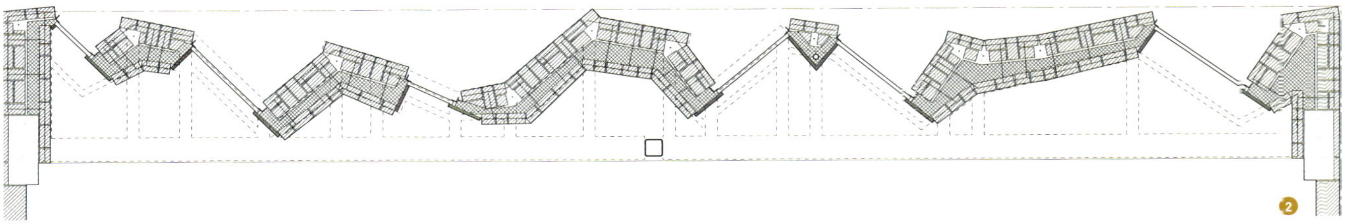

2

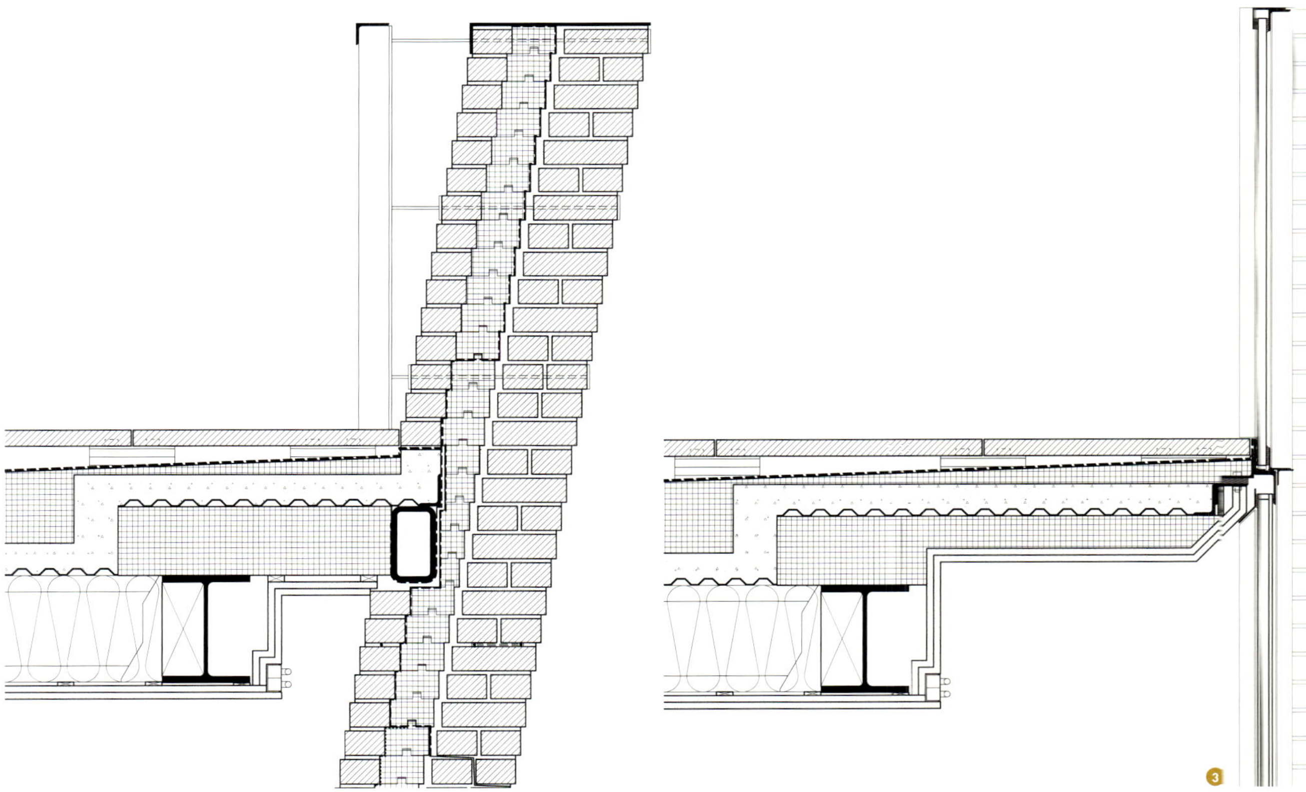

3

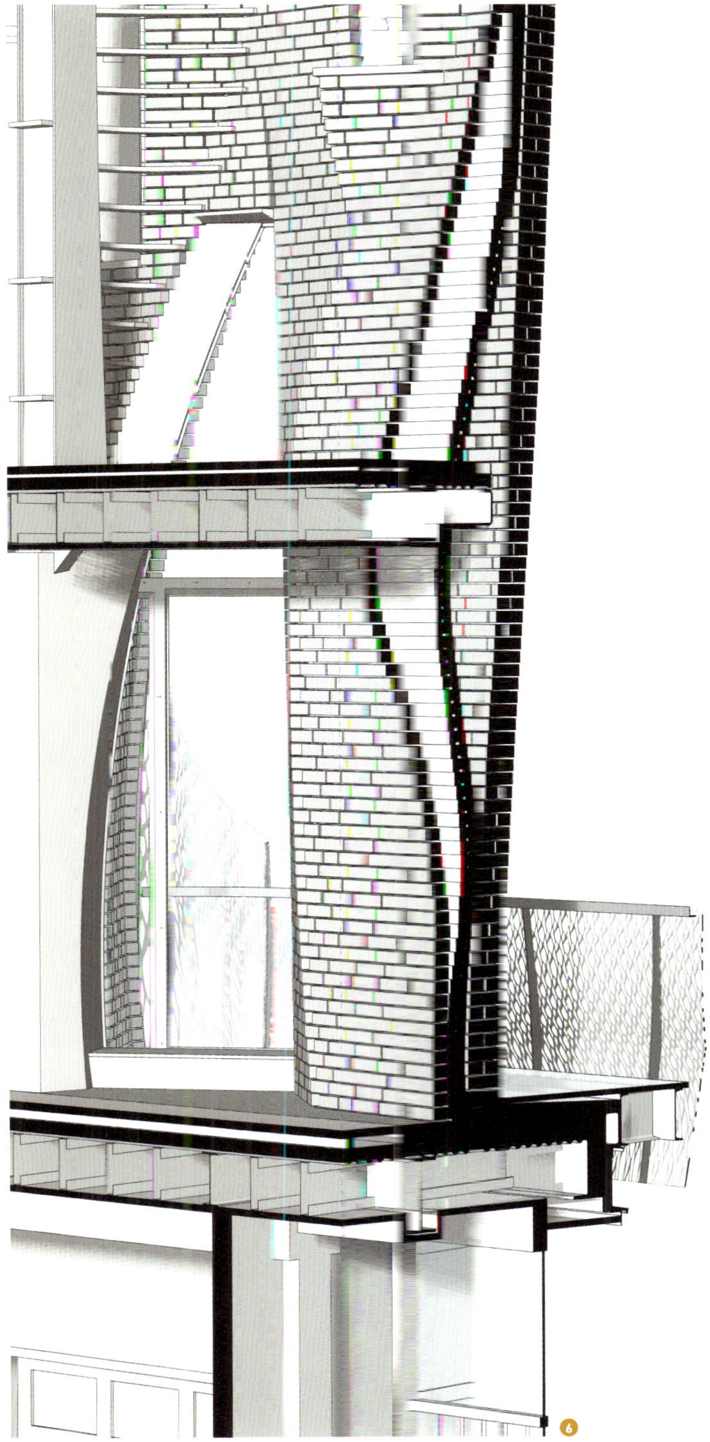

1 PLAN — façade brick wall detail
2 PLAN — façade brick + window detail
3 SECTION — façade brick details
4-6 BRICK samples
7 PERSPECTIVE section façade

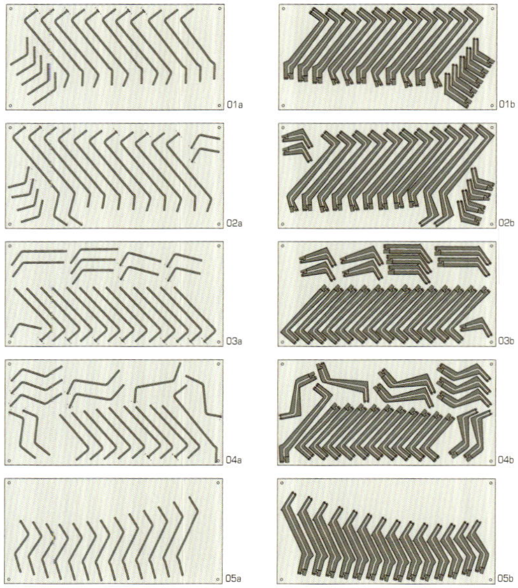

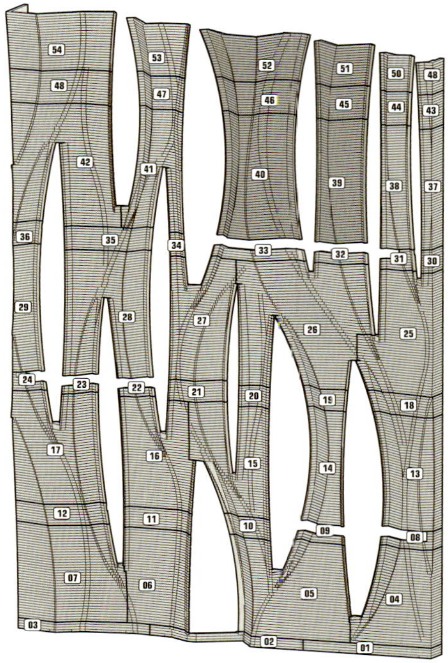

1

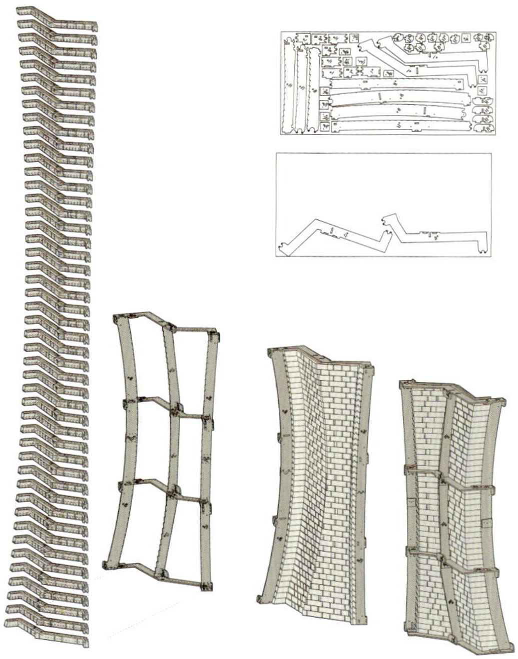

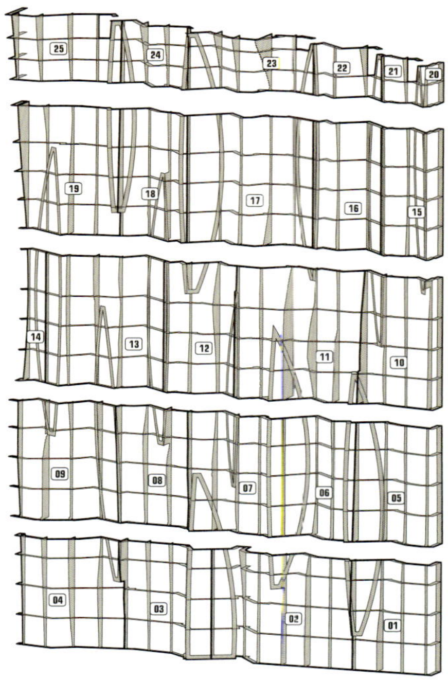

2

1 ASSEMBLY foam template
3 BRICKstudy laid with plywood framing prototype
4 ASSEMBLY foam template
5-7 CONSTRUCTION foam template insulation

3

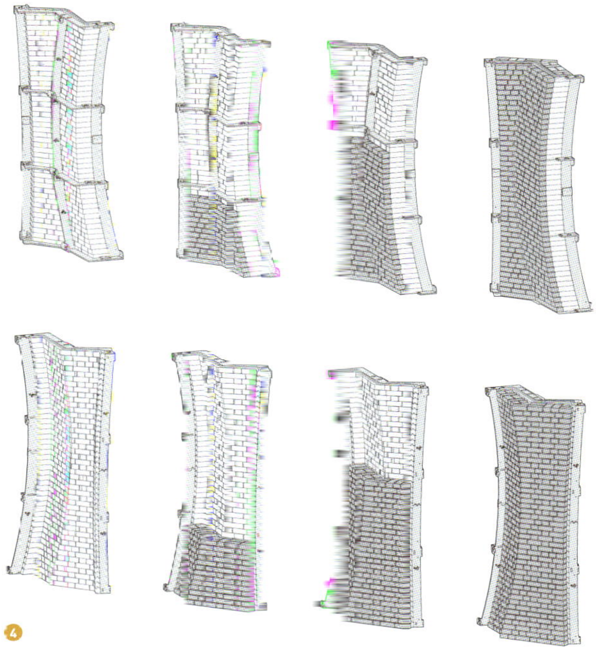

4

5

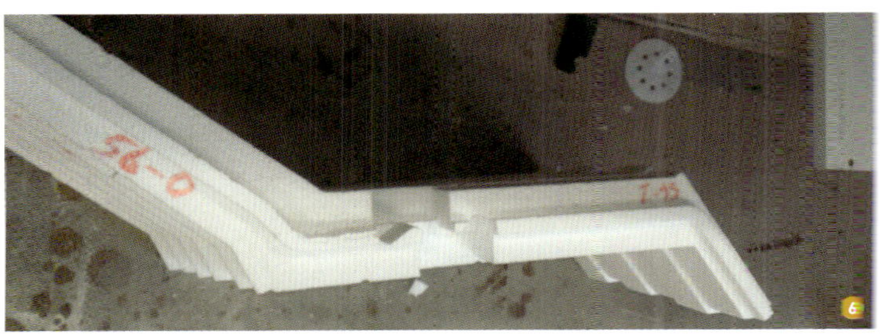

6

7

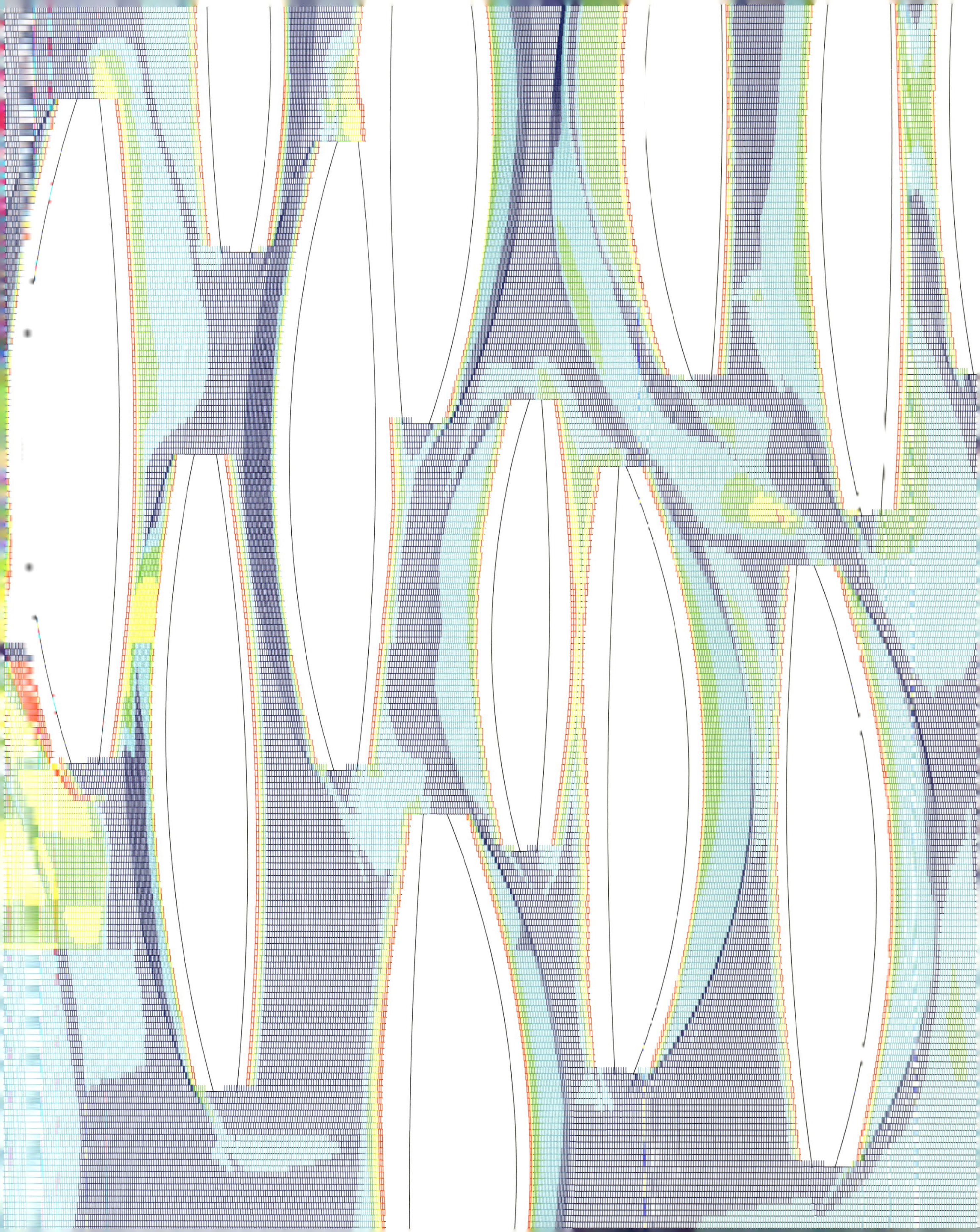

1

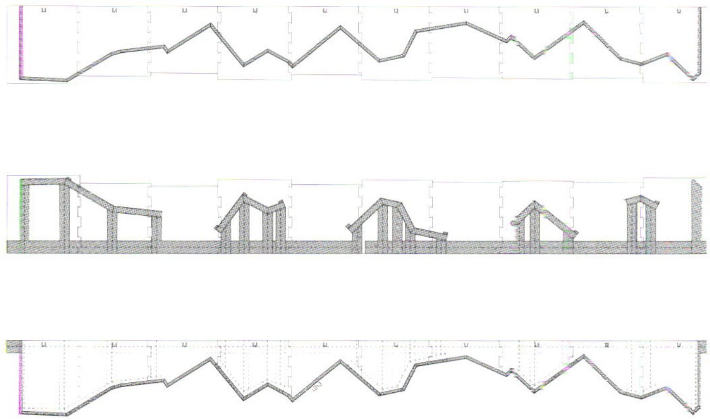

2

5

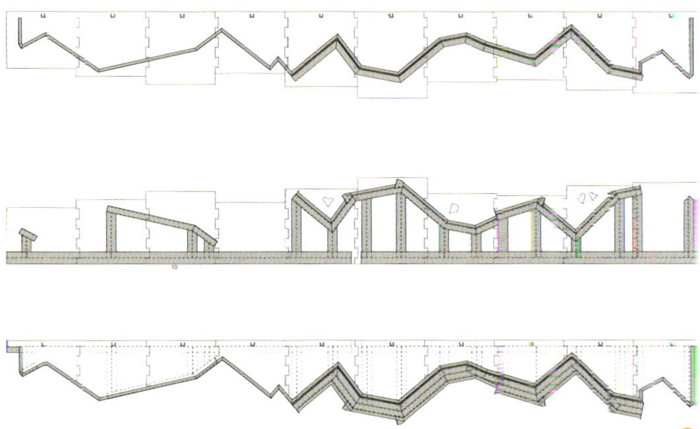

3

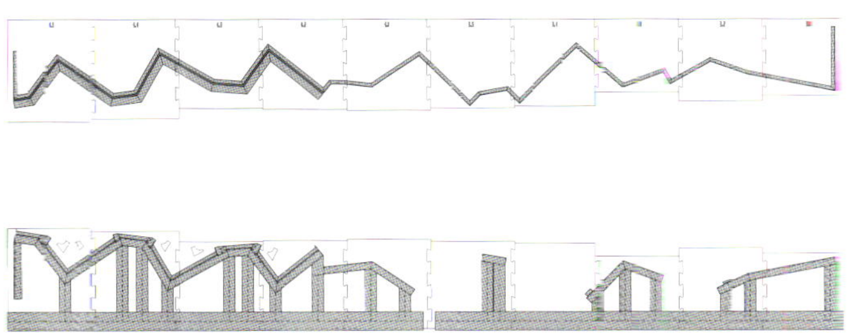

4

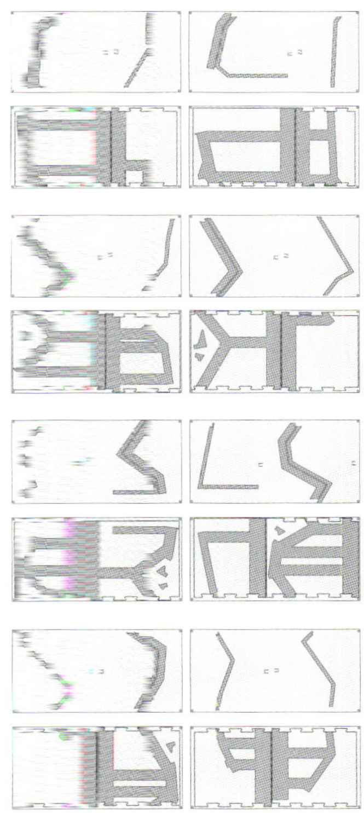

6

0" > 1"
1" > 2"
2" > 3"
3" > 4"
4" >

1 DIAGRAM foam insulation depth in inches
2-4 CONSTRUCTION structural steel template
5 CONSTRUCTION steel template
6 CONSTRUCTION fabrication

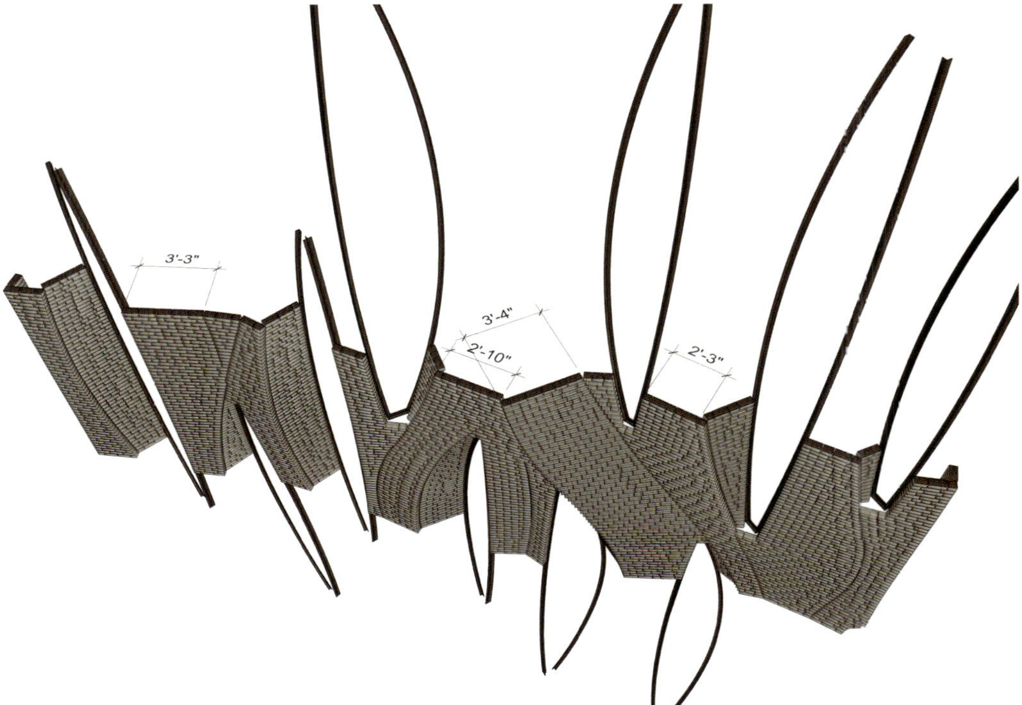

1

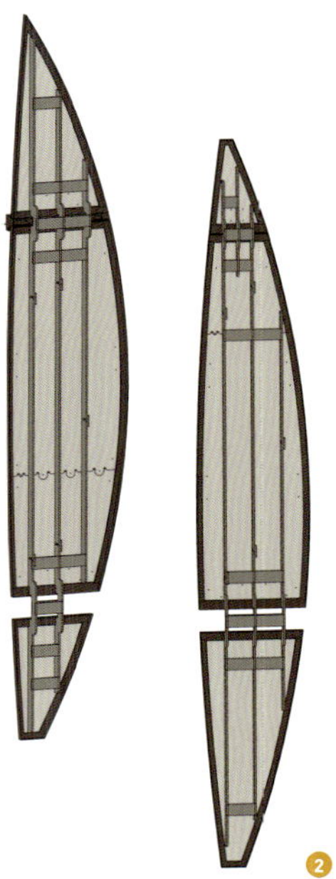

2

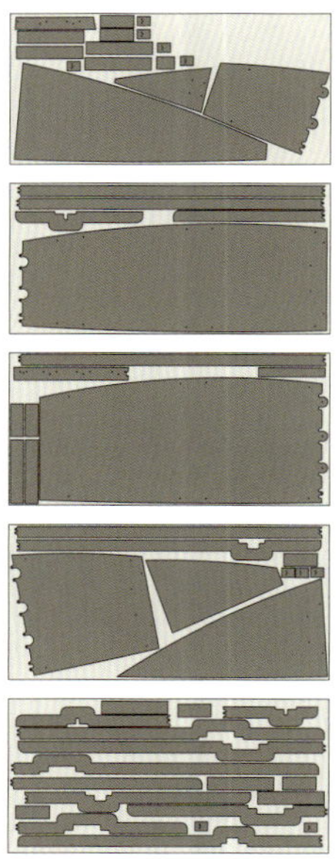

3

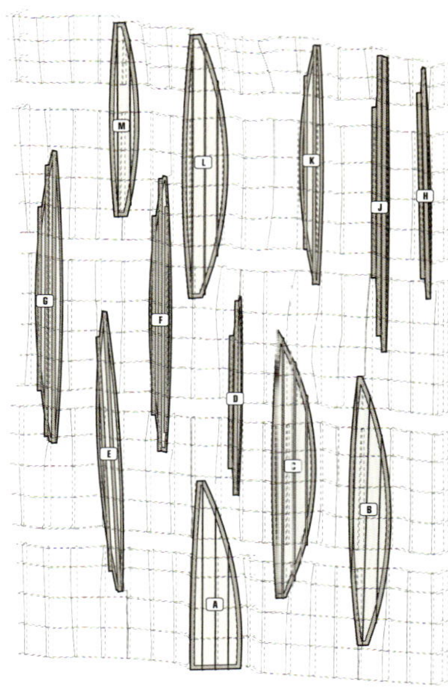

4

1 AERIAL perspective — window frames
2 ISOMETRIC — window frame template
3 CONSTRUCTION cut-file
4 ISOMETRIC — window fame assembly
5 exploded AXONOMETRIC window assembly

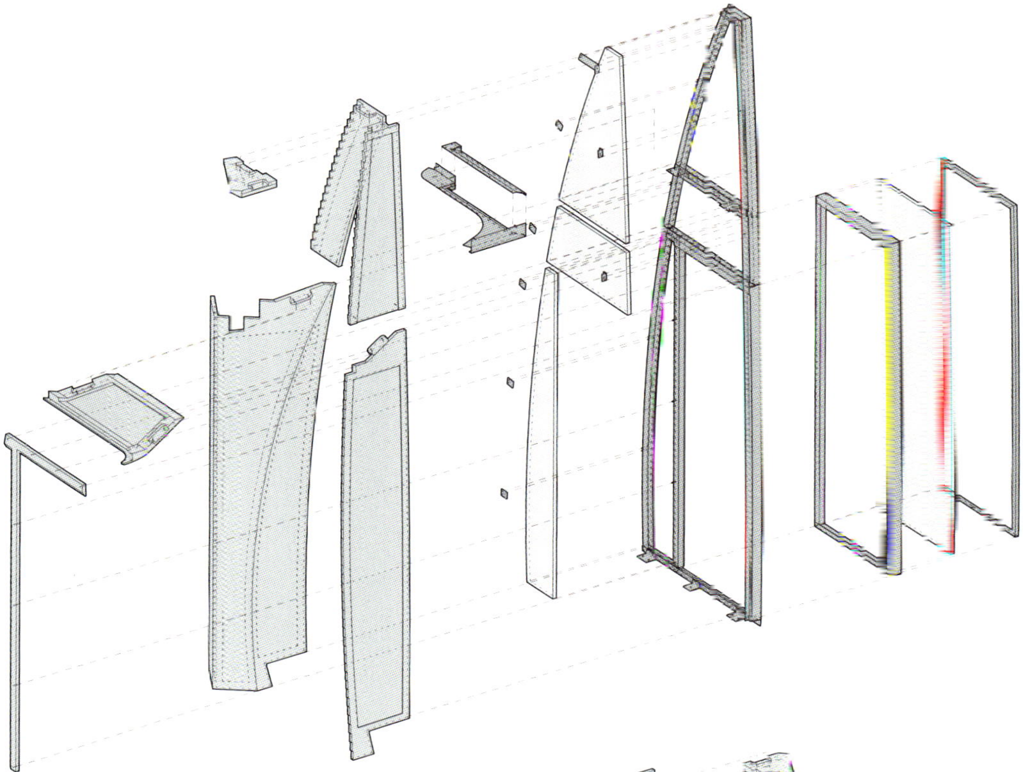

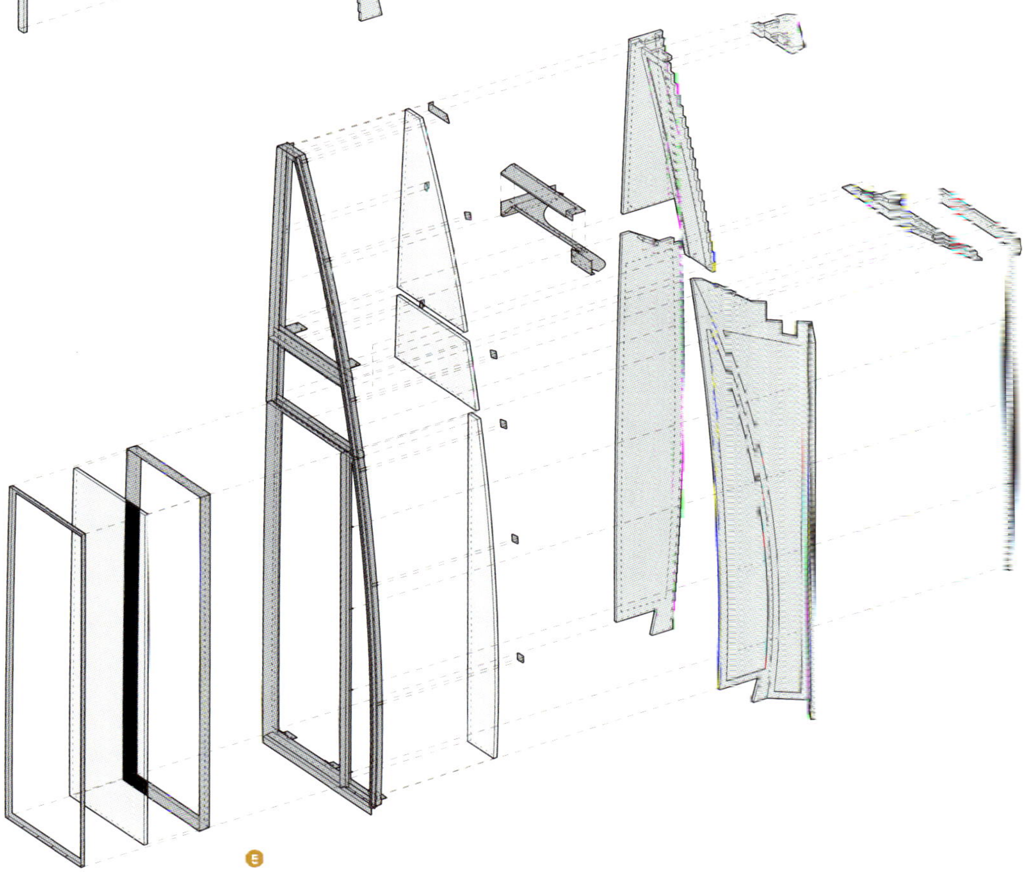

E

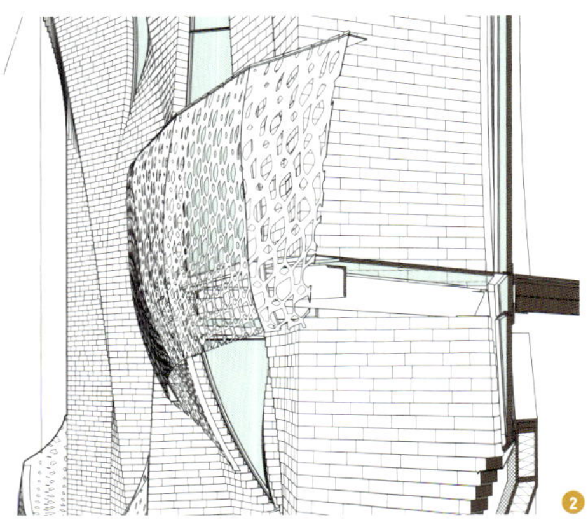

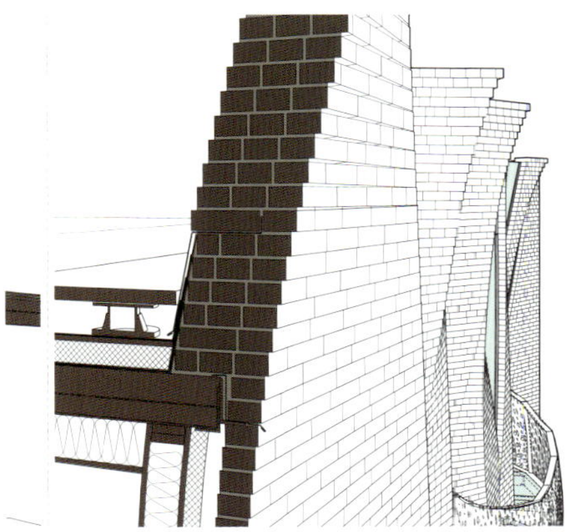

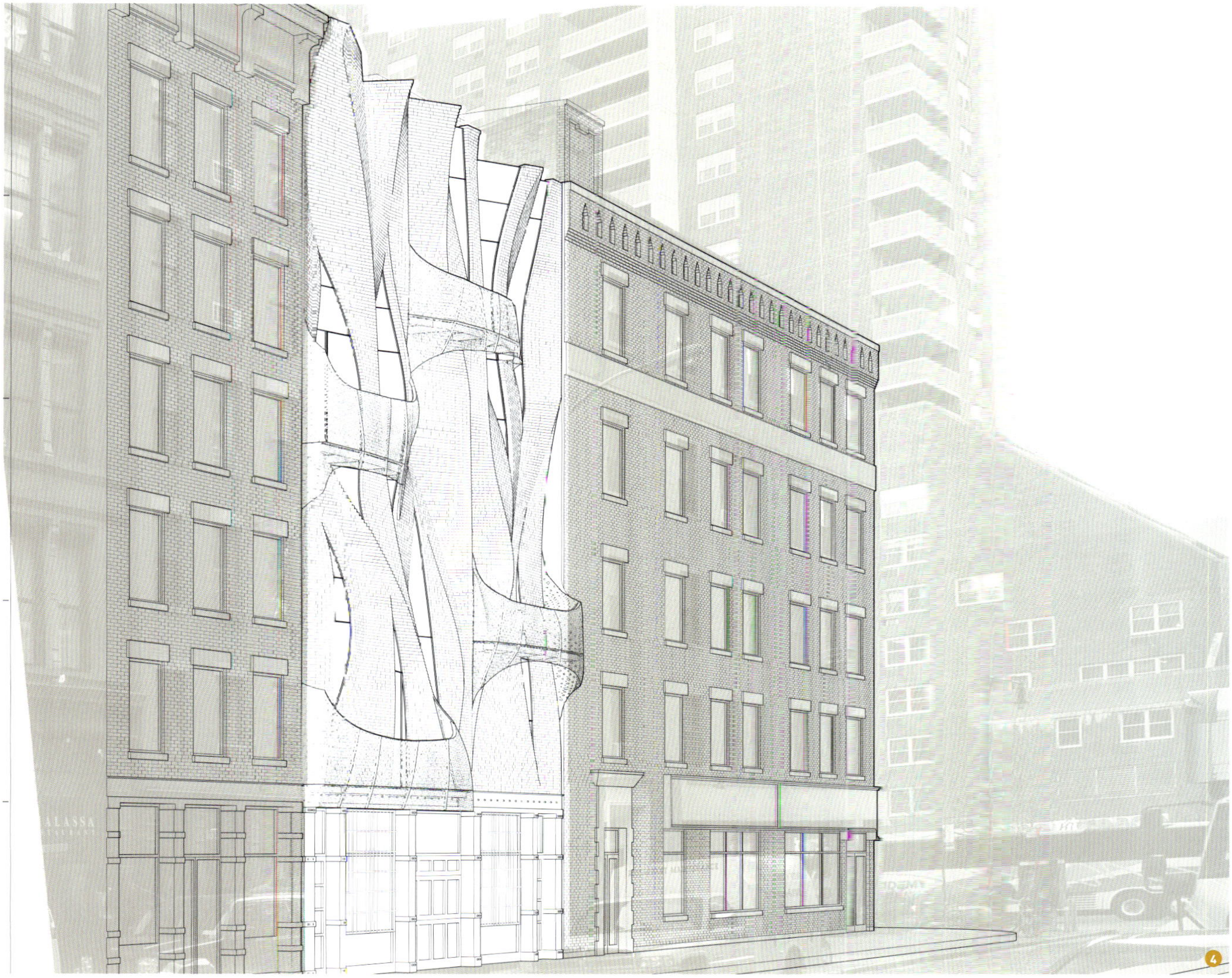

1 MODEL façade 137F
2-3 SECTION perspective — façace
4 PERSPECTIVE from street view
5-6 MODEL brick prototype

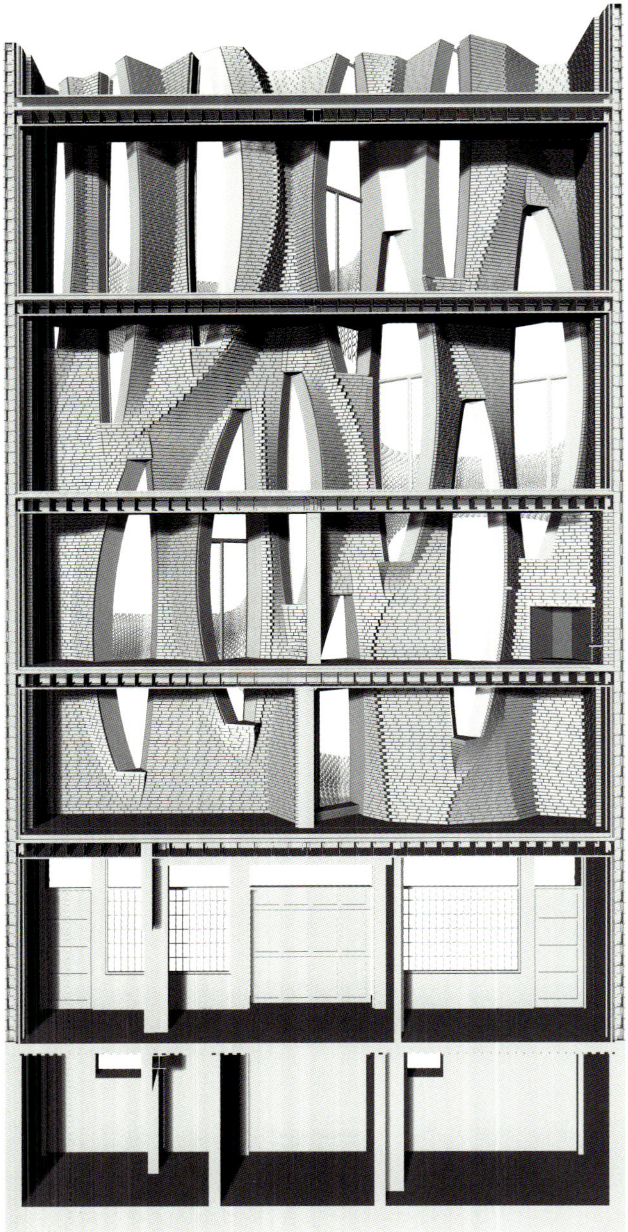

1

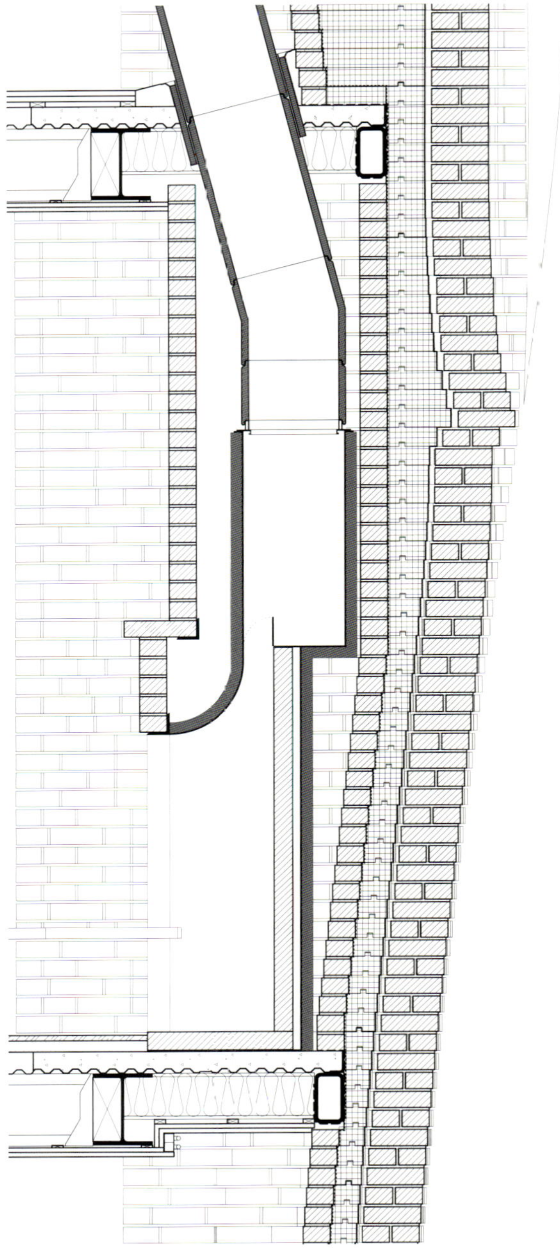

2

1 SECTION — interior brick wall
2 SECTION — fireplace construction details
3 PERSPECTIVE movement of exterior brick façade

4.2 ballast 2N

When seeking a material with depth, it's hard to go past lead. Just 1/16 inch thickness of lead over a wall of moving plywood panels is enough to weigh 600 pounds. Used in x-ray rooms and usually covered with plasterboard, lead sheet has a surface quality that seems alive in the way it changes as it absorbs and reflects the light.

While lead is rarely used in a domestic context, for ballast 2N, SYSTEM designed sliding lead panels to separate the private areas of a converted loft from the more public living areas. One long wall of the loft is floor to ceiling windows; the lead panels run perpendicular to them under a beam. The panels can be opened to allow free circulation between the two domains or closed off when more privacy is needed.

Each sliding wall panel is made up of several lead-clad pieces of plywood set at slightly different angles. This enabled the builders to more easily install the panels, but it also creates different sheens and shades of deep grey as the light plays across the differently tilted planes. Lead in this form is, of course, quite inert.

There is a kit to the construction of these walls—a steel frame structure, precise templates that position steel connections to the plywood tabs that attach the folded geometry of the lead to the orthogonal steel frames. The lead is laminated to plywood sheets that have been precut and prejointed. The joints provide the folds and make mortises for plywood fins that stiffen and position the panels. While this kit makes assembly easier, and prefabricates a complex millwork project, it also provides detail and texture.

1 VIEW sliding lead panels open
2 ASSEMBLY wall components
3 ELEVATION — construction elements
4 ELEVATION — forms + geometry

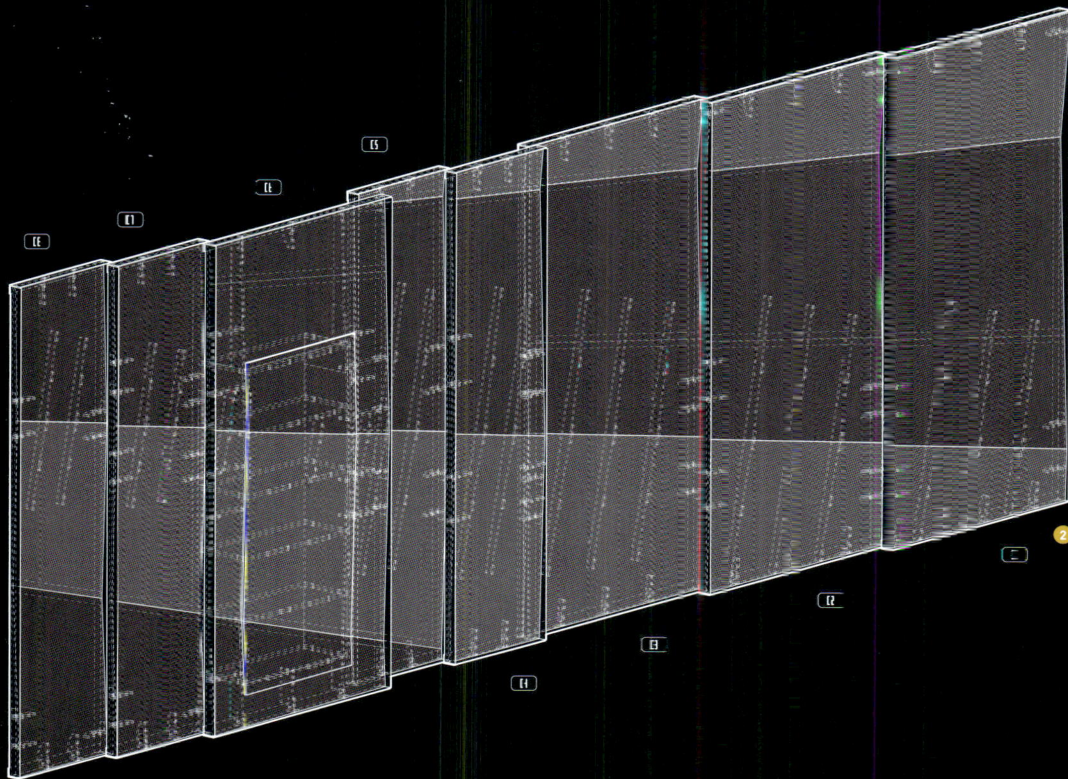

2

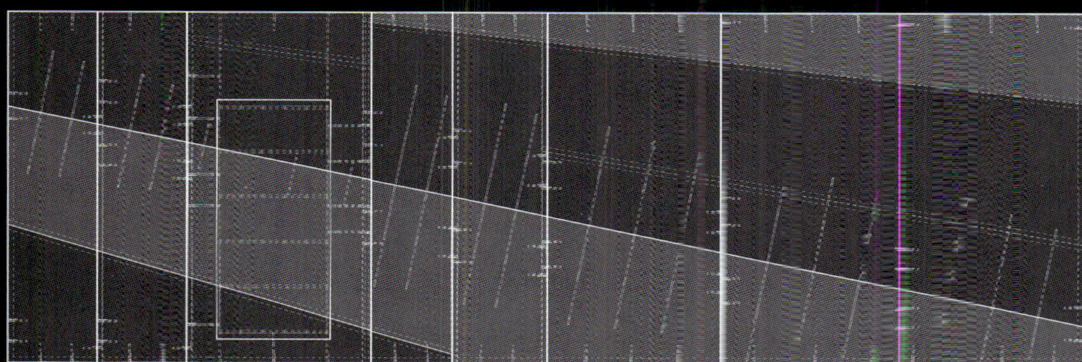

3

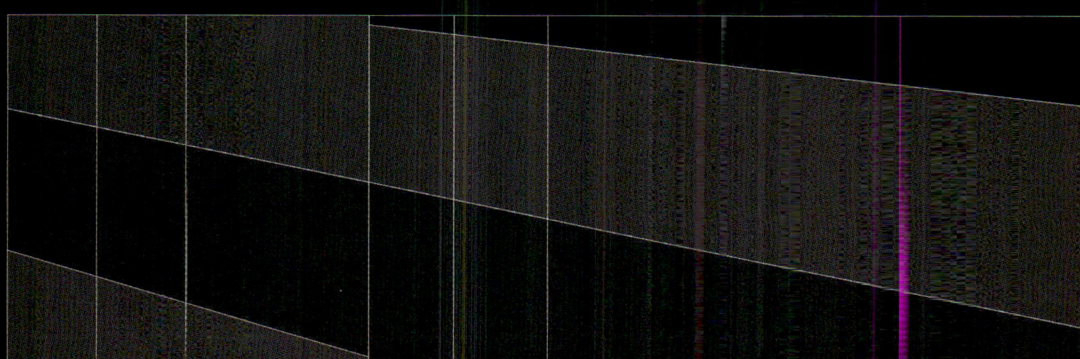

4

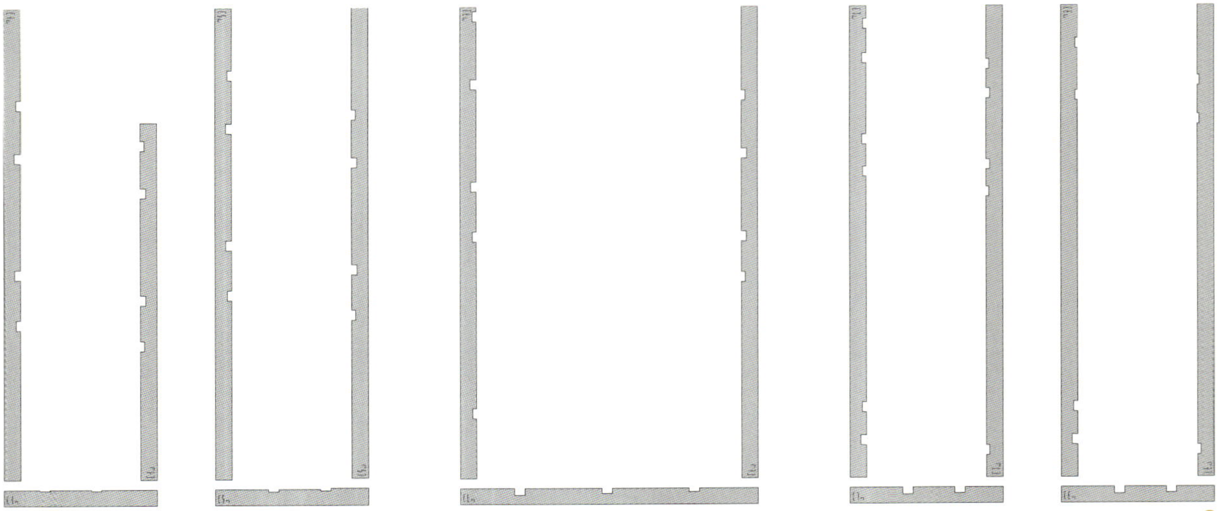

1

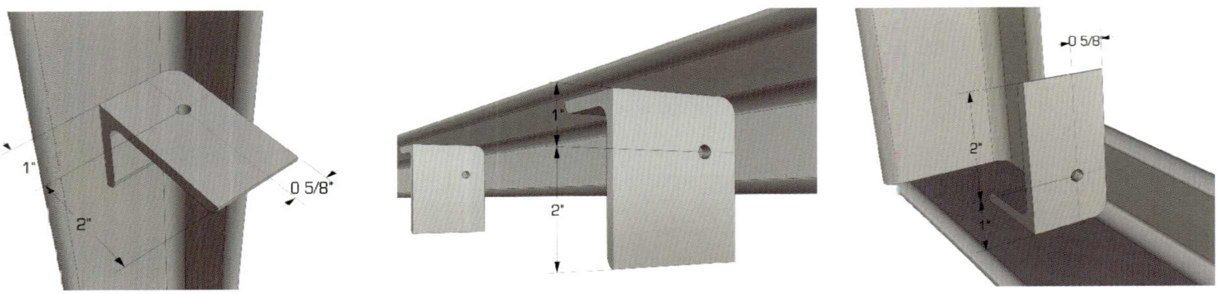

2

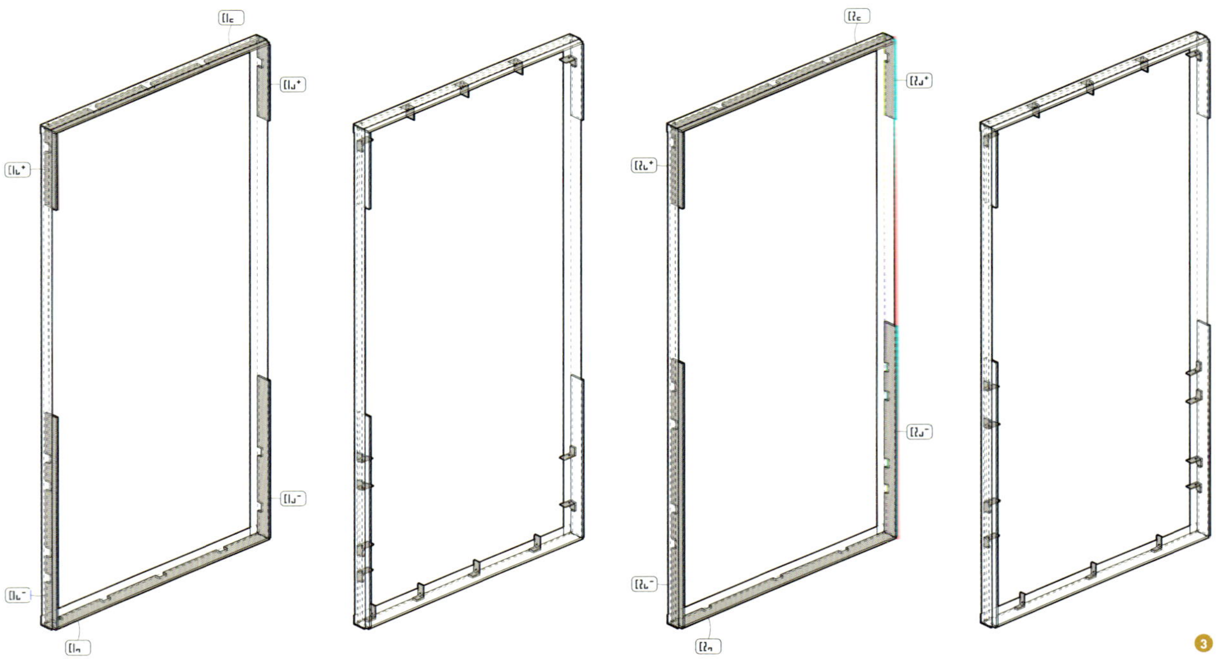

3

1 CONSTRUCTION steel frame template
2 ASSEMBLY steel angles
3 ASSEMBLY door bracket templates
4 VIEW interior lead panel closed
5 VIEW plywood fins
6 CONSTRUCTION plywood parts

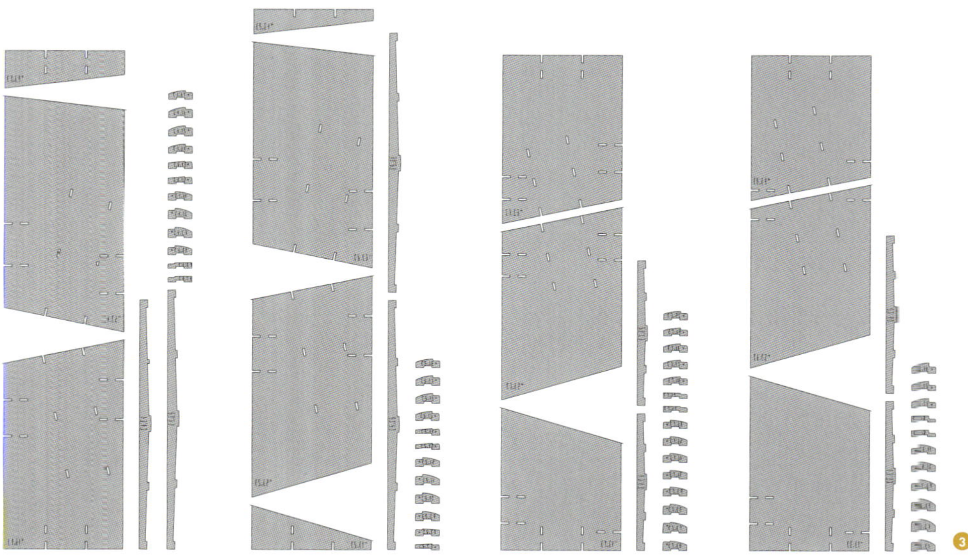

1 VIEW steel frame and lead surface
2 ASSEMBLY plywood/lead parts
3 ELEVATION plywood parts
4 VIEW door lock detail
5 AXONOMETRIC panel assembly parts

4

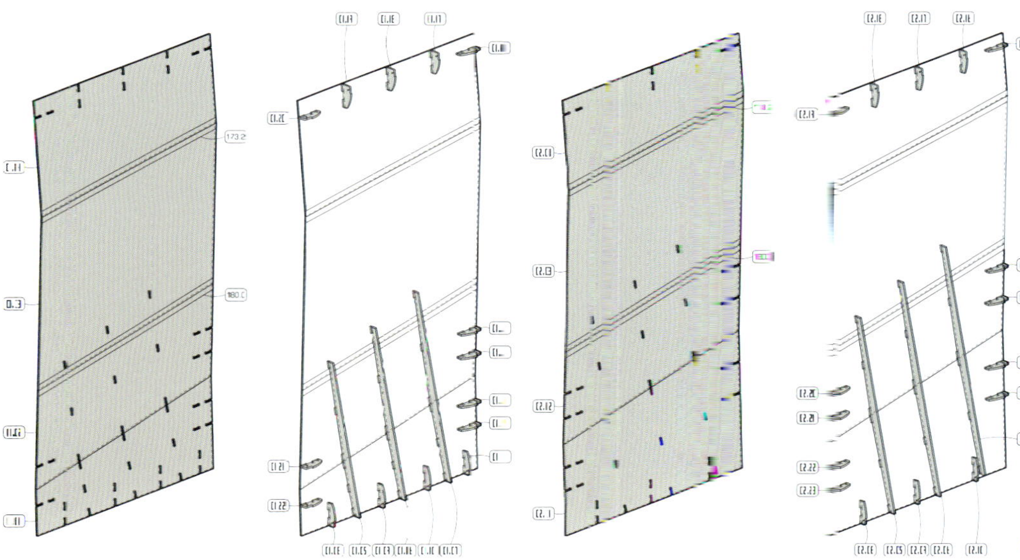

5

1 **VIEW** form
2 VIEW lead wall
3 VIEW entry twisted wall with shelves
4 VIEW pivoting wall panel open
5 PERSPECTIVE curved wall with perforated panel

3

4

5

4.3 Pied-á-Terre

A one bedroom apartment in a converted high-rise became the site for two twisting interventions. The first is a wall that defined the entrance and enclosed the kitchen, while also smoothing the transition from the intimate spaces of the apartment (bedroom and bathroom) to the main living space. The second is a perforated screen hung from the ceiling to impart a domestic feel to an otherwise raw loft space.

The wall is made from an inexpensively produced CNC milled kit of parts and the surface is a combination of plywood and plasterboard finished in painted plaster. It was executed quickly and simply but the form is among the most geometrically intricate that SYSTEM has made—the product of much experimenting with the execution of complex shapes. At one end the wall has several raised creases or darts, which balloon into a curve before becoming strictly vertical again, round the corner, a small cave starts to form. One ridge continues to stand out, turning into a shelf. The resulting lip-shaped shelving unit, right opposite the front door, becomes a dramatic point of entry into the apartment.

The two steel screens that hang from the ceiling also smooth out the transition between rooms. The panels warp and curve as they move from the lower ceiling height at the entrance to the taller living space. Their shape and colour alter the reflection of the outside light from the windows along the south side of the apartment. And the perforations manipulate the light emitted from the ceiling fixtures. As the screens move away from the windows, the perforations become larger and more frequent, allowing more light from above. The holes in the screen create subtle dappled shadow patterns through the space and onto the floor.

The flow of the shaped interventions and the light tell a story of discrete moments of more intense action that converge seamlessly into a unified whole because of smooth, continuous, and always changing surfaces.

1 PERSPECTIVE curved wall with perforated panel
2 PERSPECTIVE wall form
3 VIEW entry twisted wall with shelves
4 VIEW pivoting wall panel open
5 VIEW form

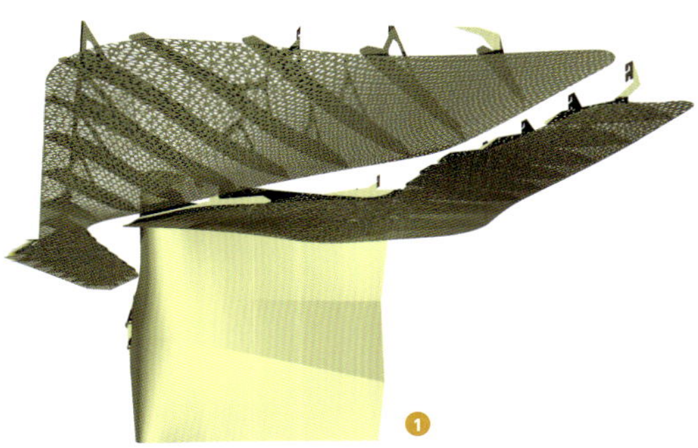

1

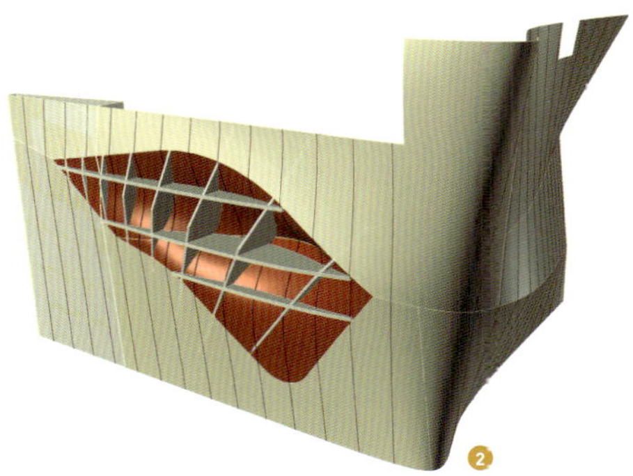

2

3

4

5

1

2

3

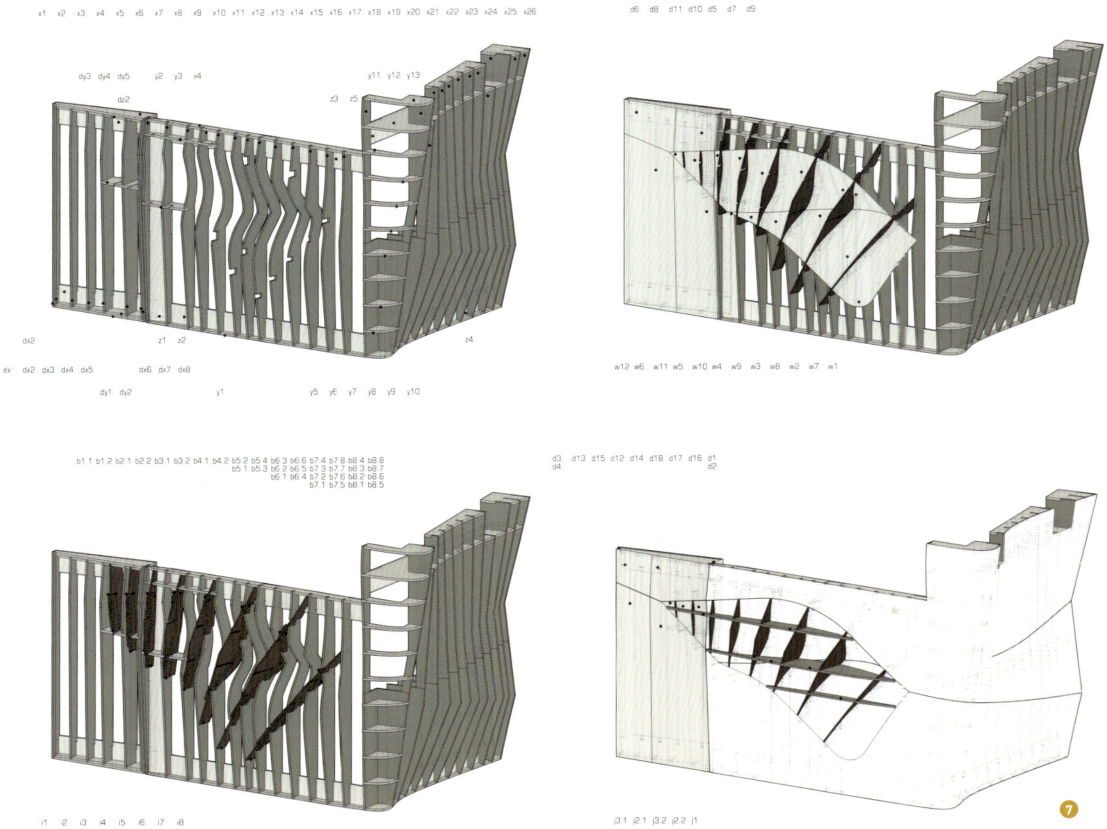

7

1-6 CONSTRUCTION structure of twisting wall
7 AXONOMETRIC — twisted wall showing construction sequence + geometry embedded in the structure
8 PLAN — twisting wall + kitchen
9 ASSEMBLY rib + wall pieces
10 SECTION — ceiling panels
11 SECTION — main living space sharing elevation of twisted wall and perforated ceiling panels

4

5

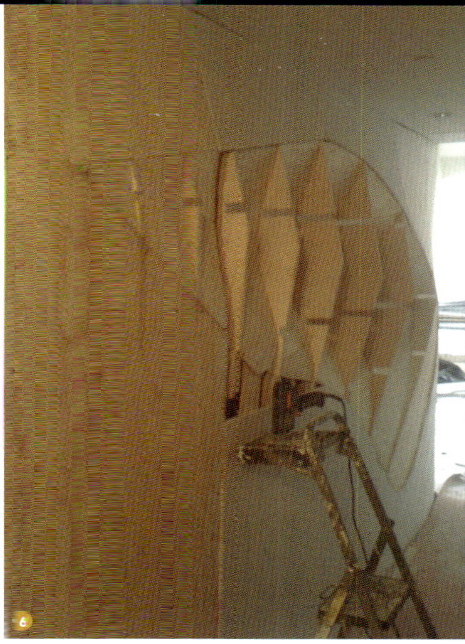

6

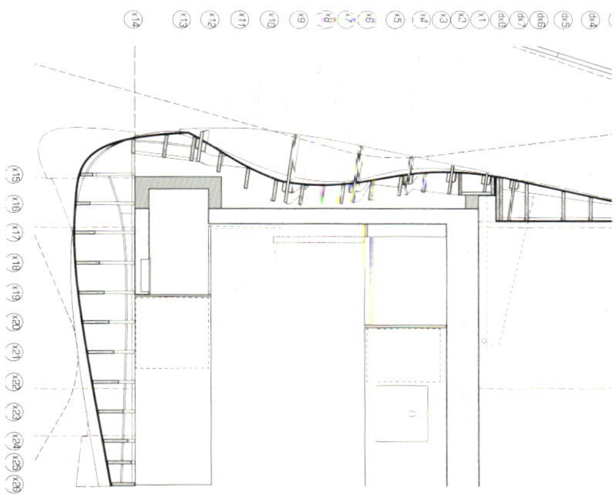

8

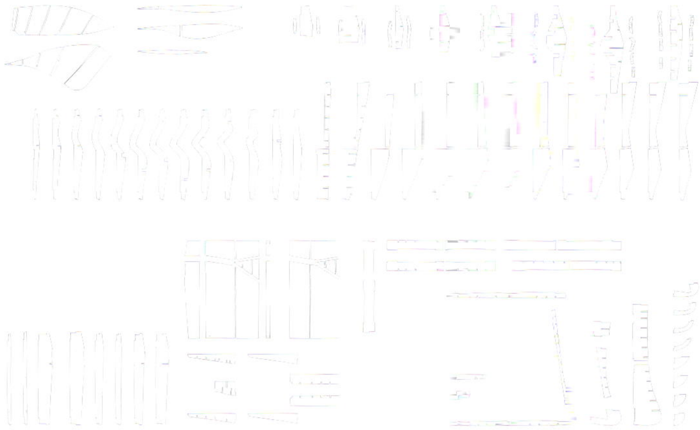

9

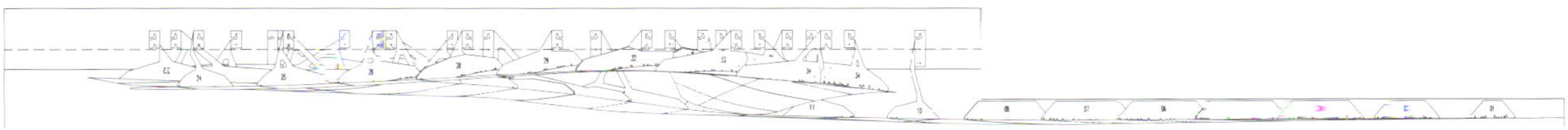

10

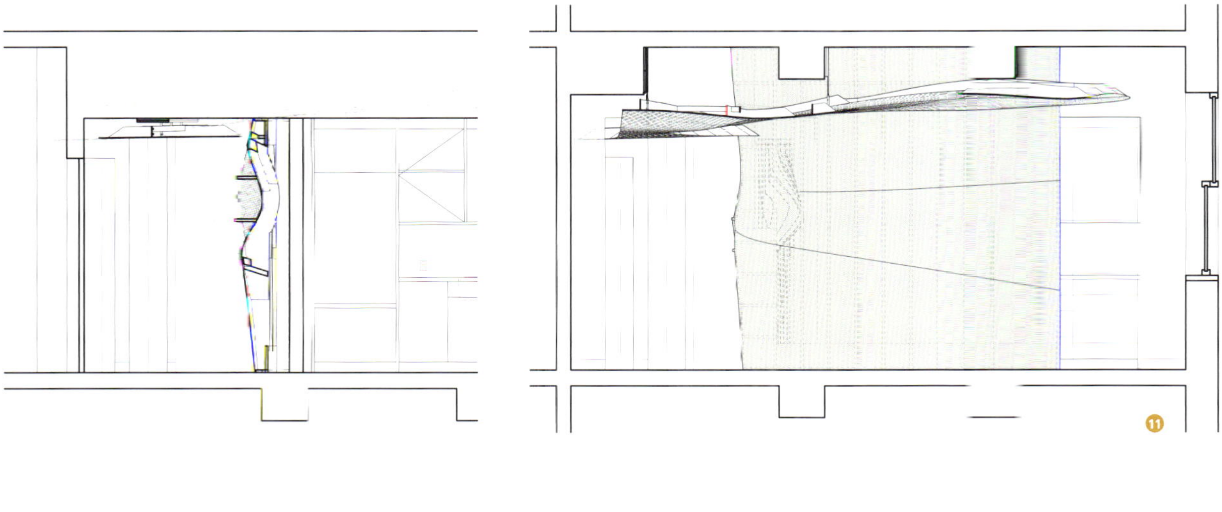

11

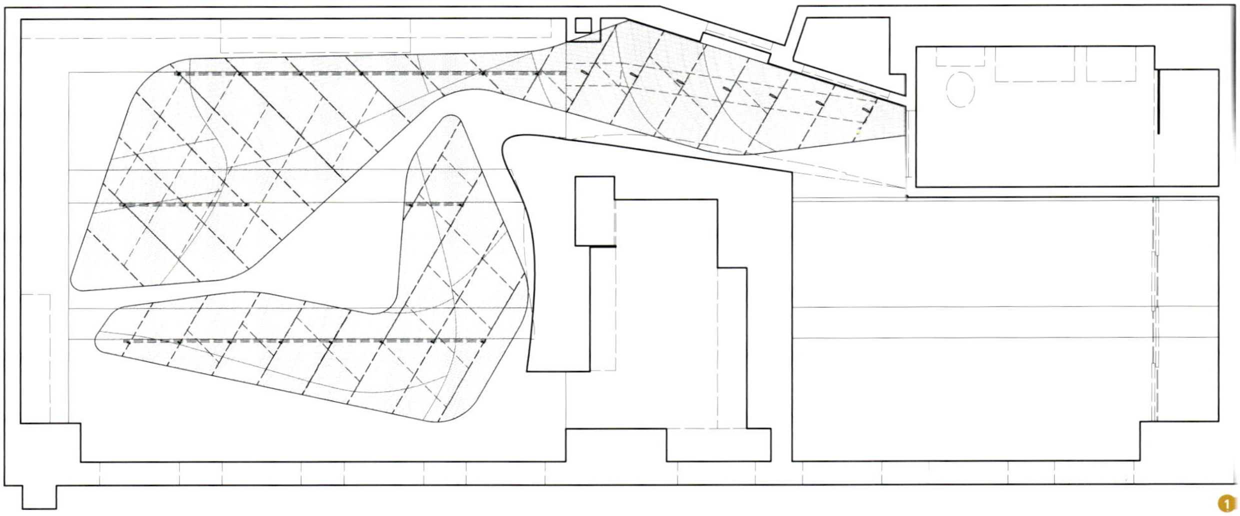

1

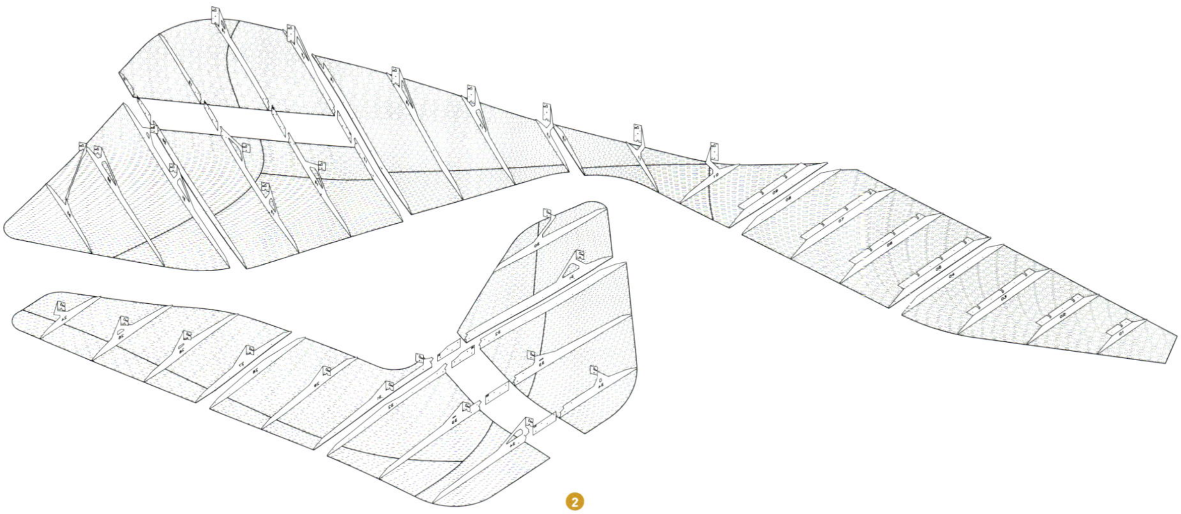

2

3

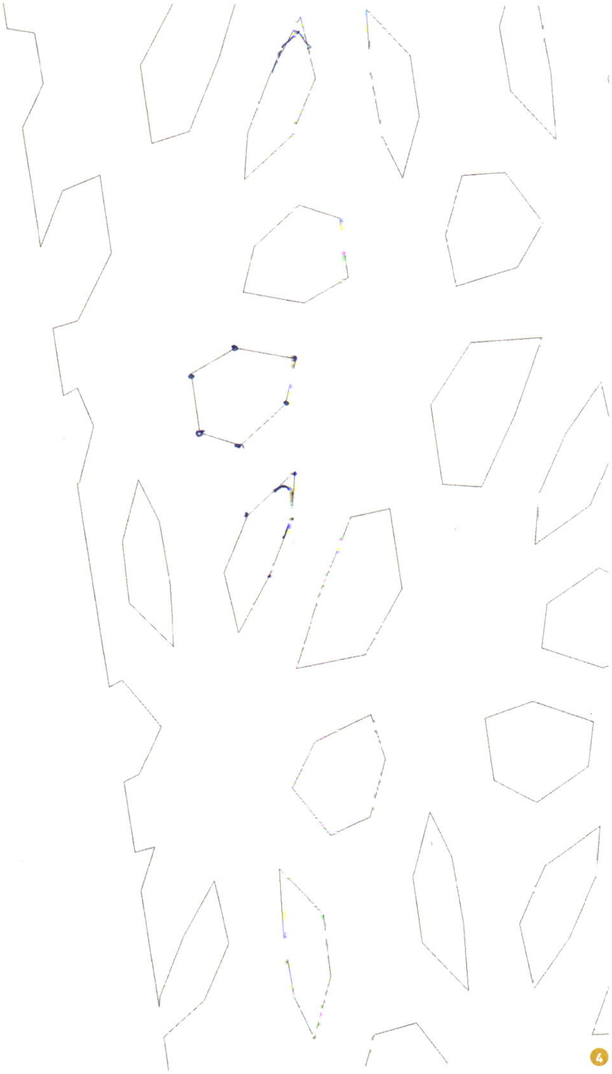

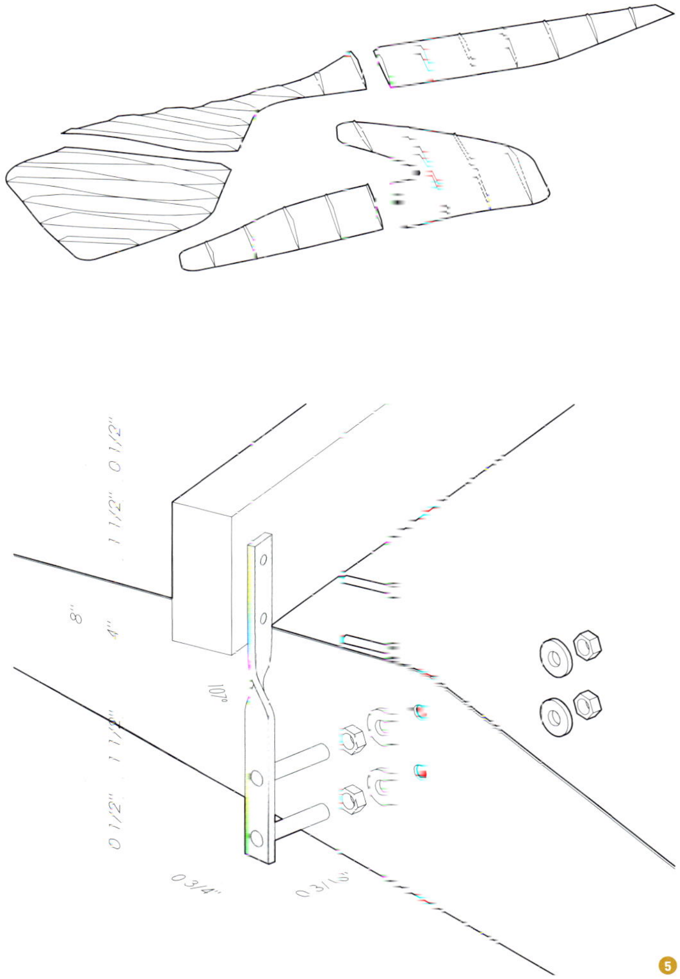

1 PLAN — ceiling perforated screen
2 ASSEMBLY perforated screen
3 PATTERN
4 PATTERN perforation control points
5 ASSEMBLY screen fabrication
6 PATTERN

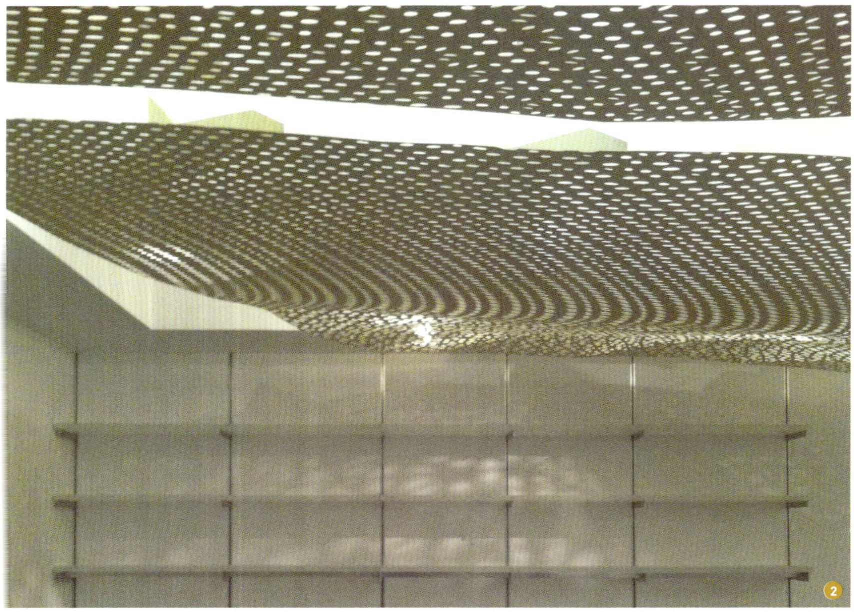

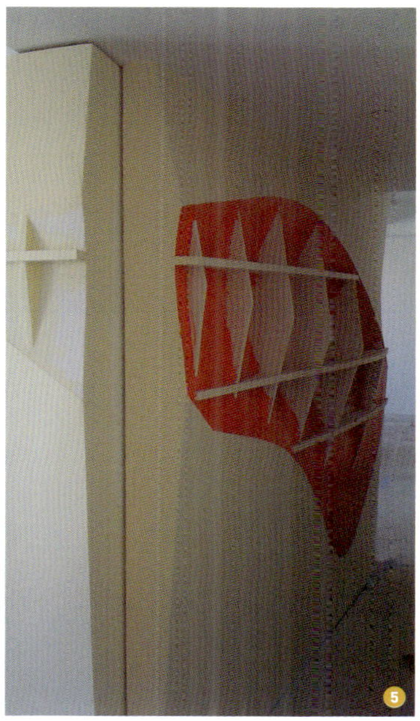

1 VIEW: sh[illegible]ows and wall contour
2 VIEW: perforated ceiling screen
3 VIEW: wall contour + perforated ceiling pattern
4 VIEW: of wall from entrance
5 VIEW: wall during conception

2

1

1 VIEW wall contour + perforated ceiling pattern
2 VIEW ceiling detail

appendix

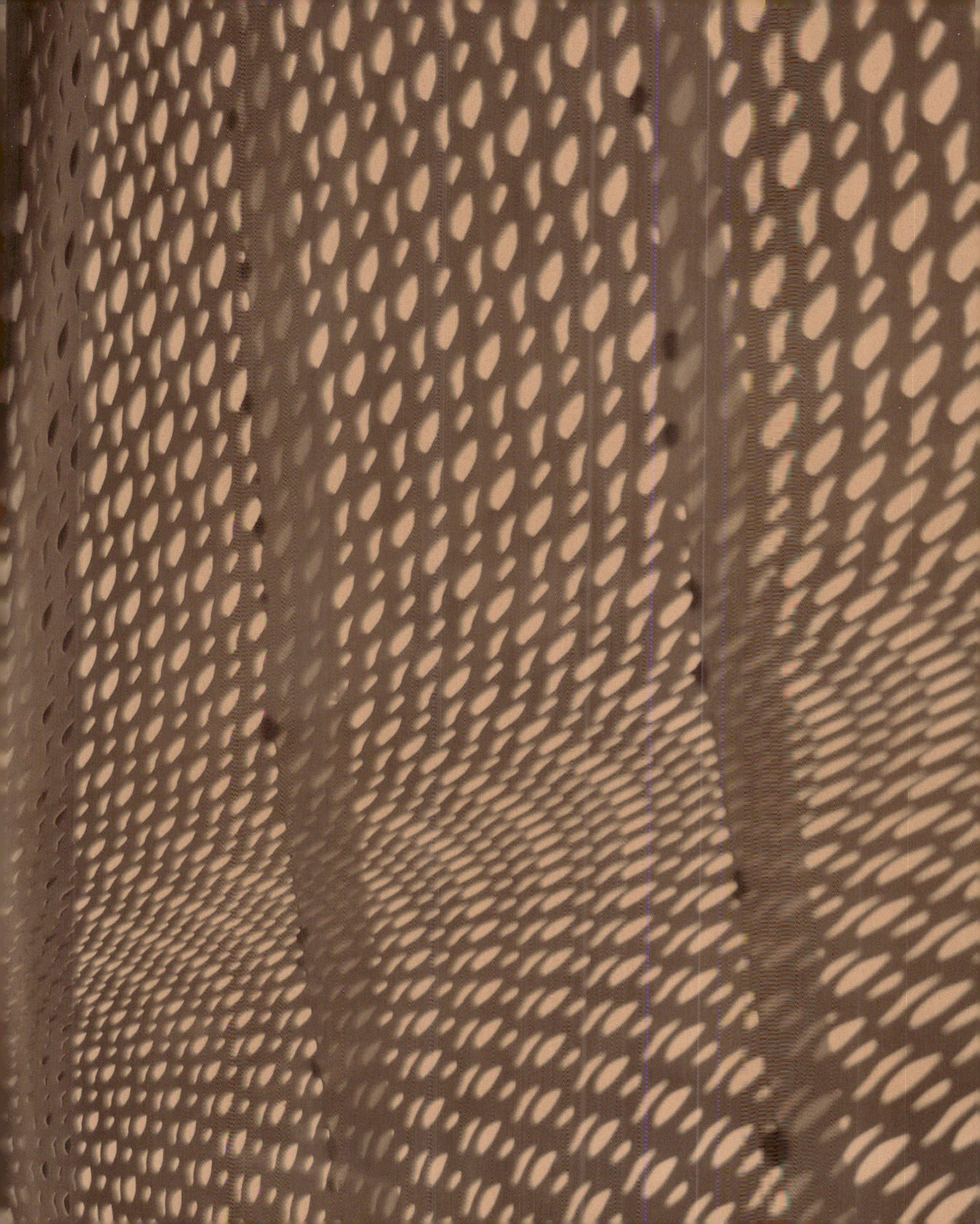

SYSTEMarchitects profile.

SYSTEM is an idea—to engage in contemporary culture with the practice of architecture.

SYSTEM's particular zone of enquiry is the overlap and interplay between the urban and natural; how the built environment and the organic environment might and do participate in each other's systems.

The pursuit of this practice has included exhibiting, publishing, writing, teaching, participating in competitions, and the daily studio discipline of making designs and building. Design is a practice and a discipline where scale and programme are only fields of operation, used as markers within a process that cycles through activities of invention and testing. Therefore, the projects at SYSTEM range from the design of a wood joint to the design of cities, and clients include private individuals, institutions, corporations, funding agencies, and government organisations.

SYSTEM started as a conversation between a group of recent graduates from the architecture programme at Columbia University eager to continue the ideas and discussions that were started in the school. The belief that architecture only becomes better through discussion has survived throughout the practice. There are too many people to name here that were and are a part of the conversation that is SYSTEM. Douglas Gauthier was a partner from the beginning until 2006 and his enormous contributions are a part of what SYSTEM is. The fintellectual and physical foundations that were made during those years continue to inform the activities of the studio. Natalie Jeremijenko is an inspiration and has collaborated on numerous projects that seek to provide a structure around the engagement with the natural world. Robert Baker has allowed the discussion of technology to continue and expand, changing not only the design and making of the work but the way we approach the work.

Recently the work has been published in *Bauwelt, Domus, the New York Times, The Wall Street Journal, The New York Review of Books, LeFigaro, The Financial Times, The Washington Post, the Huffington Post, and Womens Wear Daily.* Television segments include Bloomberg National and the ABC, radio segments include NPR and ABC Radio.

awards/ exhibitions.

SYSTEM's architecture encompasses built work, speculations, competitions, exhibitions, lectures, teaching, and publications. Built work includes residential, commercial, and institutional projects in New York City as well as the rest of North America, Europe, and Australia. The practice has received numerous awards and honours from the American Institute of Architects, Royal Australian Institute of Architects, *Architizer*, The Architectural League of New York, *Architectural Record*, and The Museum of Modern Art.

AWARDS

Winner – *Architizer* A+ Award in Architecture + Materials, Popular Choice Award – 187F UNhistoric townHOUSE, New York, NY, 2014;

AIA Design Award – Interiors Merit Award for aA SHELTER, New York, NY, 2011;

Award – McGraw Hill Construction Best of 2008, for MoMA exhibit Home Delivery: Fabricating the Modern Dwelling, with Douglas Gauthier, for construction of BURST*008;

Award – RAIA Wilkinson Award — for outstanding residential building, 2006,to BURST* housing prototype, with Douglas Gauthier;

US Department of Energy, Center of Excellence Research Fellow, Active Shafts, Principal Investigator, 2006-2007;

Invited Participation – (five teams selected from the US) History Channel, City of the Future: A Design and Engineering Challenge, with Douglas Gauthier, 2006;

Finalist – Syracuse Connective Corridor Urban Design Competition — with Douglas Gauthier and David Rockwell, 2006;

Finalist – Australian Design Review Idea Awards, BURST* with Douglas Gauthier, annual design competition, 2006;

Award – Australian Timber Design Award — BURST* Highly Commended, with Douglas Gauthier, biennial design competition, 2006;

Finalist – FERROUS PARK International Design Competition — with Douglas Gauthier, art pavilion installation design competition, 2006;

Invited Participation – TIME Magazine. Housing: Forcing the Future Innovators. BURST* with Douglas Gauthier, 2005;

Award – AIA New Housing New York Competition. Universal Housing — Third Prize, with Douglas Gauthier, 2004;

Invited Participation – Metropolis magazine Special Issue — City of the Near-Future, Universal House with Douglas Gauthier, 2003;

Award – Bank of America Design Award Winner: SECCA HOME House Competition, with Douglas Gauthier, 2003;

Nominated and finalist – P.S.1 Young Architects Program: Warm-Up Bridge — Finalist, with Douglas Gauthier 2003;

Lindbergh Grant Recipient – Research titled 'Nature and the City', 2002;

Award – Architectural Record: Design Vanguard, with Douglas Gauthier, 2001;

Nominated and finalist – P.S.1/MoMA Young Architects Program, Warm-Up: Dazzle Island — Finalist, with Douglas Gauthier, 2001;

Award – Young Architects Forum: 2ndNATURE — The Architectural League of New York, with Douglas Gauthier, 2000

Invited Participation – La Biennale di Venezia — The 7th Annual Exhibition of Architecture — kosovoKIT, with Douglas Gauthier, 1999;

Invited Participation – Techno-Fiction the 7th International Bauhaus Colloquium — International Panelist discussion and presentation of the Green Cyborg, 1996;

Invited Participation – Fifth World Congress-Council on Tall-Buildings and Urban Habitat — Invited Panelist discussion and presentation of the Green Cyborg, 1995;

EXHIBITIONS

A Civic Action: A Vision For Long Island City, Noguchi Museum, New York NY, 2011-2012 exhibited the USS (Urban Space Station);

Green House, Baltic Architecture Center Riga, Latvia, curated by Vladimir Belogolovsky Jan. – Feb. 2011;

(re)designing nature, Stadtische Galerie Bremen, Austria, curated by Susanne Witzgal 2011;

prefabs, 2009 shown at varies locations throughout the US; a film by Bongiorno Productions, MaryLou Tibaldo director;

AIA Awards Exhibition, Center for Architecture, New York NY, April 14-July 12, 2011;

BiodiverCITY, Washington DC, curated by Natalie Jeremijenko, October 06-November 26 2010;

KOKODAschool, University of Pennsylvania School of Architecture, May 06-14 2010;

Aspire, UTS Tower Building, Sydney, Australia, curated by Eric Ng, October 05-December 19, 2009;

Impact by Degrees, Washington D.C. 2009, exhibited the USS model and drawings a provisional rooftop urban farming facility;

YAP 10th Anniversary Exhibition, P.S.1. Long Island City, NY, June 28–September 14 2009;

Home Delivery: Fabricating the Modern Dwelling, Museum of Modern Art, New York NY, July 20–October 28 2008, curated by Barry Bergdoll, exhibited BURST*008;

University of British Columbia, Vancouver — Parametric Exhibition 2007;

SECCA HOME House Project Competition Exhibition New York Public Library 2007;

City of the Future: A Design and Engineering Challenge. Installation at Grand Central Station 2006;

Connective Corridor Urban Design Competition Exhibition. Syracuse School of Architecture 2006;

OOZ, Inc. (...for the birds) Exhibition, POSTMASTERS Gallery. Permanent Installation 2006;

RAIA Annual Exhibition — Sydney, Australia 2005;

New Housing New York Design Competition Exhibition, Center for Architecture 2004;

Barnard + Columbia Architecture Faculty Exhibition — elevenbyseventeen 2004;

Barnard College, School of Architecture Exhibition — SYSTEMsystems 2003;

SECCA HOME House Project Competition Exhibition, Winston Salem 2003;

P.S.1 Young Architects Program Exhibition MoMA QNS — Warm-Up 2003;

nny3 Multiples: Small Civic Works, Exhibition Design. The Architectural League of New York 2002;

seaFRONT — Selected Team for Arverne Housing Proposals Exhibition 2002;

The Architectural League of New York and Yale Graduate School of Architecture 2002;

Dazzle Island Exhibition, MoMA for P.S.1 Young Architects Program — Warm-Up 2001;

Shower Curtain Exhibition of SYSTEM projects and work, Roger Williams University 2001

Four Frames; Eighteen Panels Installation of SYSTEM projects — City College, CCNY 2001;

Four Frames: 2ndNATURE Young Architects Forum — Architectural League of New York 2001;

Yale Library, Studio Projects Exhibition at the Desmond Fish Library, Garrison New York 2001;

Housing the Next 10 Million Travelling Exhibition — Selected Competition Submission 2001.

glossary.

BLOCKS — planar plywood parts for connecting ribs to skins when tabs are not sufficient. These conditions often occur when skins drift from the outside surface of the rib form towards the interior, exposing the edges of the ribs. Blocks set out the location of the edges of the skins within grid cells of the structure. They are cut with a CNC cutter in order to precisely set out the curvature and positioning of the skins along the vertical sides of the ribs. Identification markings that correspond to their parent ribs are etched into the sides. Drill holes in the blocks that align with drill holes on the ribs allowing for the precise positioning and lamination of the blocks to the ribs.

CLIPS — steel connectors for joining plywood ribs in three types: the splice clip, the standard dimension clip and the standard angle clip. (1) The splice clip is an H-shaped piece of steel made by tack welding together two channels. Precut straight slots between two planar ribs accept the middle section of the steel, while four bolt holes precisely position and join the adjacent ribs. (2) The standard dimension clip is either an angle cut to a standard length or two dimensionally standard sheets of steel folded at a standard angle and welded together. The factory process includes the drilling of holes of standard dimensions and distances from the centre that correspond to holes on the ribs. Taping these holes eliminates the need for a nut and washer during onsite construction. (3) Standard angle clips are non-standard shapes folded at a standard angle. The profile of each clip follows the profile of its corresponding rib. The separation of the holes is maximised along this shape and match corresponding holes in the ribs. These clips are CNC laser cut as unique shapes and formed along set out markings cut into the profile of the shapes.

CNC LASER CUTTER — computer numerical controlled laser cutting machine used for cutting acrylic, plywood, and steel components. The CNC laser cutter is frequently used in the rapid production of scale models of inexpensive materials for testing forms and constructability. The CNC laser cutter is also used in the production of full scale construction parts. Indiscriminate of the size or complexity of the shapes the CNC laser cutter etches or cuts the profiles of the parts as trajectories in the x-y axis by following a set of instructions of machine code generated from computer drawings. Desk sized CNC laser cutters with limited power are used for small scale model production of thin sheets of acrylic, wood and chip board, while larger room sized CNC laser cutters with greater power settings are used for full scale construction parts of steel and plywood. The capacity of a CNC laser cutter to cut various materials at various thicknesses depends on the upper limits of its power settings.

CNC ROUTER — computer numerical controlled router used for cutting, milling, engraving, and etching wood components. The CNC router is numerically controlled in three directions and follows trajectories in three dimensions. Series of stepped planar profiles are programmed to cut fully through thick material like plywood with a straight edge router bit and a series of stepped pocket cuts are programmed for rough cutting complex shapes followed by profiling milling with a ball end router bit. SYSTEMarchitects have worked closely with Bill Young of ShopBot to utilise a set of machine code scripts he has written for cutting sophisticated joints with simple straight edge router bits. An example of this is his code that instructs the machine to cut dove tail joints at angled trajectories from simple set out lines and parameters, allowing for the rapid design and fabrication of robust connections between adjoining plywood parts.

CODE — the encoding of information for translating geometry into an ordered set of actions involved in machine cutting as wells as generating and assembling the kit of parts. Intermediate software translates digitally generated geometry into machine code, an ordered set of instructions for dictating the motions of individual mechanisms of a machine necessary for manipulating physical material to match the precise shapes and sizes of the designed parts. The parts have coded markings that are generated as a result of a systematic scripting process of mapping relationships of connected elements that translate into a construction sequence for the kit of parts.

JOINTS — the adoption of historical carpentry joints with the use of a CNC router. Prior to wide adoption of glues and mechanical fasteners, rigid wood joints relied primarily on friction and locking shapes. These techniques have been abandoned in favor of less labor intensive adhesives and screws. The ability to program details such as mortise and tenon, dovetail and butterfly joints seamlessly within the design and machine cutting process allows for not only the reintroduction of these joining techniques but also the scaling up of their use from finish carpentry into building construction. In addition to increasing the rigidity of connections between parts, these details help to eliminate any ambiguity in how parts are meant to fit together.

KIT OF PARTS — a building system for the precise construction of complex building forms from an ordered set of unique CNC machined parts and steel connectors. When assembled, the kit becomes a tightly knit and rigid network of structural elements capable of withstanding a greater range of loads and forces than conventional wood structures of comparable weight. The kit of parts is a kind of pre-fab architecture where modularity is in the process of generating parts and construction by an ordered sequence of repetitive actions. Because the modularity is in a procedural generation of non-standard parts rather than an aggregation of standard components, the generation of each unique part can be achieved through the encoding of this process in the form of scripts. The drawing of each part in three dimensions as well as the drawing of its flattened representation as digital files to be read by a CNC machine are automated processes. The scripts are able to automatically generate each skin, rib, tab, block, clip, and seam part including all the part identification markings and cuts for aligning connections between parts from the mere input of an abstract design form and a short list of parameters pertaining to the thickness of material and spar lengths.

PERFORATIONS — patterns of openings in the surface of skins. These are typically created as fields of parametrically controlled curves with the scaling of the parameters that control the shapes and sizes of the openings locally tuned in response to light, air, and privacy. A CNC laser cutter is used to cut the perforations out of sheets of steel while a CNC router is used for cutting perforations out of sheets of plywood as either straight cuts or compound milling cuts when the holes have deep sloped edges. Because of the use of the CNC laser cutter, steel perforations can have very sharp edges and very small openings that come very close to approaching zero. Perforations with plywood will have rounded edges and openings that are constrained by the radius of the bit used in cutting them. More complex shapes however may be achieved by adjusting the shapes and sizes of each opening as the bit cuts through the thickness of the material, exposing the grain and layers of material as sloped surfaces.

PROFILES — deliberately drawn edges of surfaces as lines and curves constrained by the dimensions and proportions of programme and site. They set out the initial ideas of form within a three-dimensional coordinate system and eventually become the rails for the digital construction of three-dimensional surfaces. They are not merely slices of moments in plan or section, rather they are representative of a larger network of three-dimensional profiles that define the limits and shape of a complete building form.

RIBS — primary structural elements that frame spanning surfaces and programmatic forms. Together they are a continuous structural network of non-standard shapes that tie together geometrically independent internal and external surfaces. They can be either the support structure for skins or be expressed as implied surfaces of exposed edges. Ribs are planar elements mathematically generated through the projection of either orthogonal or rotated grids of planes though a continuous closed form with either a single global projection direction or varying directions derived from localised readings of surface orientation. Because each rib is a unique shape and occupies a very specific location within in the overall structure and construction sequence, identification markings are created by pocket cutting plywood with a CNC router or full depth cutting of steel or etching of plywood with a CNC laser cutter. Other cuts, etchings, and engravings are embedded within the machining of each part in order to facilitate the precise joining with other parts such as tabs, skins and blocks through a rapid onsite construction process of minimal measurement and no onsite cutting.

SCRIPTS — sets of instructions written in a programming language within a computer-aid design software. Scripts are utilised to take advantage of computational principles for finding relational symmetries of design within variable ranges as well as identifying and designing for moments where relational symmetries break. Automation, variability and logical gates are properties of a computational design process entirely dependent on precise geometric definitions of connected design elements. This precision enables the embedding of physical parameters of material and tolerances within digital form - making while allowing the process of design to focus more directly on networks of relationships and the digital and physical ordering of form.

SEAMS — connections between adjoining plywood skins. They are strategies for strengthening and sharpening edges between adjoining surfaces. Skins that meet along folded curve edges can be stitched together with light gauge steel strips precut to fit the compound curves. Planar skins that meet as outside folds along straight lines are joined with light gauge steel with three parallel folds. The second fold extends a line off the faces of the plywood providing a finishing edge. Extending edges beyond the thickness of finishing creates a toughened corner and a sharp shadow line. When thicker skins meet at a tangent, edges are milled with the CNC router to provide a lap joint between adjoining parts.

SIPS — structural insulated panels. They are [illegible] panels of rigid foam insulation and plywood and can be cut with a [illegible] as a single unit, limiting the number of pre-fabricated units [illegible] parts delivered to site. SIPS with two layers of plywood reduce [illegible] of connections since they encapsulate both the interior and exterior [illegible] as well as the building insulation all within one unit.

SKINS — plywood or steel surfaces that act [illegible] diaphragm when connected to ribs. While machined as planar [illegible] like the ribs, they are thinner in material thickness allowing them [illegible] twist, and fold into more geometrically complex shapes. The behavio[illegible] material is a critical constraint in the initial design of form. Pattern[illegible]ings and cuts with a CNC router or a CNC laser cutter are utilise[illegible] stresses within the sheet of material in order to extend the range [illegible]sical manipulation. Etchings and cuts also help the contractor i[illegible] skin part and its position relative to the underlying rib struct[illegible]kin is a subdivision of a design surface sized to fit on a sheet of stan[illegible]struction material and the bed of a CNC router or CNC laser cutter. [illegible] layered to create more rigid composite surfaces with greater [illegible]etting the subdivision pattern between layers strengthens weak e[illegible]een skins of a single layer.

TABS — planar plywood shapes with notches [illegible]tion and connect the skins to the rib structure. When the surfaces [illegible]ns are bending in one direction and perpendicular to the plane of the [illegible] tabs are simply short extensions from the face of the rib that corres[illegible] holes or pocket cuts in the surface of the skins. The skins are ro[illegible] edges of the ribs and locked into position with the tabs. When ski[illegible]aces curving in two directions or planar surfaces not perpendicular [illegible] plane of the ribs, the tab are calculated planar surfaces that are [illegible]ular to both the ribs and instantaneous points on the skins. In th[illegible], the tabs notch into the ribs at 90 degrees and are glued and sc[illegible] skins bend along the edges of the ribs and are locked into notches [illegible]er end of the tabs. The skins can then be glued and screwed a[illegible] angels to the tabs, completing the connection between the ski[illegible] ribs.

TEMPLATES — machine cut parts for simp[illegible]cons ruction of complex forms with conventional building meth[illegible] can serve as either temporary or permanent digitally generated [illegible] when measurement is difficult and the tolerances must be mini[illegible]mples of temporary templates include full size drawing printou[illegible]cut sheet material of setout shapes for factory assembly as well as [illegible]back up frames or plates for accurately positioning geometrically com[illegible]abricated parts in space. A machine cut foam wall that serves as a [illegible] for the construction of an interior and exterior hand-laid brick wa[illegible]aining in place as the building insulation is an example of a perm[illegible]plate.

project/photo credits.

BURST*003:

SYSTEMarchitects — Jeremy Edmiston, Douglas Gauthier principals

Project Team
Sarkis Arakelyan, Amber Lynn Bard, Ayat Fadaifard, Sara Goldsmith, Henry Grosman, Kobi Jakov, Joseph Jelinek, Ginny Hyo-jin Kang, Gen Kato, Yarek Karawczyk, Ioanna Karagiannakou, Tony Su

Buro Happold — Consulting Engineers, Cristobal Correa, Project Engineer

Client
Andrew Katay and Catriona Grant

Local Consultants
Site Architect
Robin Edmiston & Associates

Site Engineer
Peter Marcus

Site Architect for
SYSTEMarchitects, Chris Knapp

Construction Team
KATAY/SYSTEMarchitects, Project Manager: Chris Knapp

Suppliers and Fabricators
Laser Cutting, Grifco International Inc., John Fuller, Gunnersen Plywood Supply, Mitchell Badelles, X-Clip Fabrication, P.C. Steck , Sue Wantz, File Optimization, Cutweb from STRING Nesting Solutions

Frame Assembly Team
Sarkis Arakelyan, Newcastle University Architecture Students: David Arnott, Andrew Cavill, Justice Chengeta, Louisa Gee, Ned Haughton, Simon Hayward, John Jones, Jonathon Mentink, Shaun Purcell, Jo Redden, Justin Spraull, Ksenia Totoeva

Construction sub-contractors
Waterproofing Manufacturing, Equus , Brian Greenall, Waterproofing Distributor, Tremco, John Medland, Waterproofing Installation, Midcoast Liquid Rubber, Wayne Halder, Floor finish Installation, Mr. Seal-It, Trevor Hill, Steel Fabrication, All-Structural Steel, Greg Bullock, Industrial Painting, Hastings Panel and Paint, Glazier, All Glass Constructions, Gary Hughes, Greg Turner, Electrician, Duane Bligh, Millwork, Laurieton Kitchens, Neil Whalley

Photo Shoot
Completed photography, floto+warner studio, Jeremy Floto + Cassandra Warner, DOMO Collections, Daniel Mercer, Dinosaur Designs, Louise Olsen, - Stephen Ormandy, - Liane Rossler, Sandy Feet Longboards, Glenn 'Blackie', Dikkie Andrews.

Wellfleet

SYSTEMarchitects — Jeremy Edmiston, Douglas Gauthier principals

Project Team
Ian Baldwin, Henry Grosman, Joe Jelinek, Ginny Hyo-jin Kang, Ioanna Karagiannakou, Maciej Kusmierski, Megumi Mieno.

Structural Engineers
Buro Happold, Craig Schwitter, Cristobal Correa.

USS (Urban Space Station)

SYSTEMarchitects — Jeremy Edmiston, principal, with Natalie Jeremijenko

Project Team
Robert Baker, Charles Kwan, Haruka Black, Hyunsoo Ki, Tony Jin, Helen Levin

---

Bulkhead 2E

SYSTEMarchitects — Jeremy Edmiston, principal
Robert Baker

Structural Engineering
MacIntosh Engineering, James Baker
CNC Milling, Woodwright Inc.
Robert Bridges

---

teminalPOPup

SYSTEMarchitects — Jeremy Edmiston, principal
Robert Baker

Structural Engineer
Arup, New York, Marcus Shulte

KOKODAschool

SYSTEMarchitects — Jeremy Edmiston, principal
Robert Baker, Charles Kwan

Project Team
Julia Watson, Steven Addington, Bretaigne Walliser

UPenn research design lab
Emaan Farhoud, Jake Chandler, Chris Allen, Florina Dutt, Jae-Hun Hur, Hyunsoo Kim, Johanna Lofstrom, Crista McDonald, Becky Shoemaker, Yu-Han Su, Jessica Yubas.

CNC Milling, Robert Bridges

Boats 2E + 2N

SYSTEMarchitects — Jeremy Edmiston, principal
Robert Baker, Charles Kwan
CNC Milling, Woodwright Inc., Robert Bridges
Laser Cutting, Laserfab

BURST*008

Architects
Jeremy Edmiston and Douglas Gauthier

Project Team
Rob Baker, Michela Chiavi, Franz Daniel, Kevin Field, Maryana Grinshpun, Henry Grosman, Glen Ho, Rebecca Hora, Malvin Hwee, Kristina Kesler, Jung Min Kim, Edward Kim-Yujoong, Charles Kwan, Philip Lee, Scott Nicholl, Brian Osborne, Christian Prasch, Megan Pryor, Vicente Quiroga, Seth Roye, Troy Thierrer, William Tucker

Structural Engineers
Buro Happold — Consulting Engineers
Craig Schwitter, Cristobal Correa, Alex Marin

Mechanical Engineers
Buro Happold — Consulting Engineers
Craig Schwitter, Byron Stigge, Matthew Herman

Lighting Designer
Johnson Lighting Studios, Clark Johnson

Construction Managers
Ryan Construction, Jim Friedman, Ashley Simone

Assembly Team
Ryan Associates — Vincent Flegar, Greg Koch, Paul Moore, Craig Nadeau, Kyle Reed, Mike Schweitzberger, Ashley Simone, Molly Thorkelson
Tania Amodio, Matthew Besser, Kevin Field, Lourd Galvez, Paul Hasty, Fidelma Hawrey, Glen Ho, Howard Jones, Mathew Kalivris, Alfie Koetter, Margaret Mackbee, Scott Nicholl, Christian Prasch, Megan Pryor, Perry Randazzo, Craig Rosman, Brian Manning-Spindt, William Tucker, Bretaigne Walliser

Suppliers and Fabricators
AF Supply Corp. Bennett, Aluma Craft Products, Aspen Supply Corp. Maureen Heaer, Associated Fabrication LLC, Benjamin Moore Paint, Blaine Window Hardware Inc., Budco Enterprises, Inc., Chilewich/Sultan LLC, Designer Epoxy Flooring, Luke Palladino, Euclid Roofing & Siding Inc, F. W. Honerkamp Co. Inc., Jeff Honerkamp, LED Waves, Inc., Leviton, Lightolier, McMaster-Carr, Millenium Steel, The Murus Company, Inc., NJIT FabLAB, Tremco Inc.
P.C. Steck Inc., Sue Wanz, Emily Steck, Zero International, Inc.

Sponsorship provided by
AF Supply Corp., All-Boro Building Supply, Aluma Craft Products Architectural League of New York, Aspen Supply Corp., The Athena Group, LLC, Anthony Rossello and Certain Pictures, Benjamin Moore Paint, Buro Happold Engineering, Chilewich/Sultan LLC, City College of New York School of Architecture, Crate and Barrel, Carla Emil and Rich Silverstein, Designer Epoxy Finishes Inc., Euclid Roofing & Siding Inc., F. W. Honerkamp Co. Inc., Johnson Light Studio, LLC, LED Waves, Inc., Lightolier, Leviton, New Jersey Institute of Technology School of Architecture FABLAB, Ross and Daisy Newman, Qantas Airways, Rotasa Foundation on behalf of Susan Cummins, Ryan Associates, Stern Tannenbaum & Bell, LLP, Stewart Title Insurance Company
Tremco Inc., Asher Waldfogel and Helyn MacLean, Carla Emil and Rich Silverstein, Designer Epoxy Finishes Inc, Euclid Roofing & Siding Inc., Johnson Light Studio, LLC, Ryan Associates, 3M.

---

fulcrumSTAIR

SYSTEMarchitects — Jeremy Edmiston, Douglas Gauthier principals

Structural Engineer
Buro Happold Engineering
Cristobal Correa

---

aA SHELTER

SYSTEMarchitects — Jeremy Edmiston, principal
Robert Baker, Charles Kwan

Project Team
Holly McCurdy, Bretaigne Walliser, Steven Addington, Frantz Daniel, Maryana Grinshpun, Tony Jin, Anya Kouzminova, Helen Levin, Becky Shoemaker

Construction
Dan Keeport, Jesee Lee Wilson

Donations
CNC Milling: Bill Young & Robert Bridges, Metal work: P.C. Steck, Sue Wanz, Epoxy Supply: Aspen Supply Corp. Maureen Heaer, Laser Cutting and Forming: Precision Shape Solutions, Corey Akers, Lights: Lightolier, Maggie Smith, Construction: Tom Kozlowski, Anton Berisaj.

---

cMcF

SYSTEMarchitects — Jeremy Edmiston principal, Brian Osborn

Painting
Nicholas von Bujdoss

Lattice 3N

SYSTEMarchitects — Jeremy Edmiston principal
Rob Baker, Helen Levin,
Laser Cutting, Precision Shape Solutions,
Corey Akers
CNC Milling
Jorge Plazas, Sebastian Caro

UNhistoric townHOUSE

SYSTEMarchitects — Jeremy Edmiston principal with Rob Baker

Project Team
Alex Baranovich, Haruka Black, Johnathon Calderon, Jamie Edindjiklian, Tony Jin, Charles Kwan, Helen Levin

Structural Engineer
MacIntosh Engineering,
James Baker

Consultants
Seodyal Singh
Masonry Consultants, Craig Tooman, Chris Allen, John Murray, Bill Merritt
CNC Milling, Robert Bridges,
Laser Cutting, Corey Akers
Construction, Richard Wilson,
Andreas Froech, Perry Rardazzo,
Art Kozyr.

Ballast 2N

SYSTEMarchitects — Jeremy Edmiston principal
Rob Baker

CNC Milling, Robert Bridges
Steel Fabrication, Armando Saca

Pied-à-Terre

SYSTEMarchitects — Jeremy Edmiston principal
Rob Baker

CNC Milling, Robert Bridges
Laser Cutting, Precision Shape Solutions, Corey Akers
Steel Fabrication, Armando Saca
Painting, Kate Taylor

PHOTO CREDITS

All drawings and images by SYSTEMarchitects Llc unless otherwise noted below.

Page	
0[illegible]	[illegible] + Warner
0[illegible]	[illegible] + Warner
0[illegible]	[illegible] images Floto + Warner
0[illegible]	[illegible] + Warner
0[illegible]	[illegible] oto + Warner
0[illegible]	fig [illegible] Chris Knapp
052	fig [illegible]5, Chris Knapp
053	[illegible] Knapp
054-[illegible]	[illegible] + Warner
0[illegible]2	fig [illegible] Hyunsoo Kim
0[illegible]5	fig [illegible] David McIntyre
[illegible]	fig [illegible] David McIntyre, fig [illegible] Alanna Lauter
[illegible]7	fig [illegible] David McIntyre
[illegible]	fig [illegible] David McIntyre
[illegible]	fig [illegible]3 David McIntyre
[illegible]	David McIntyre
[illegible]	fig [illegible] Alanna Lauter, fig [illegible] David McIntyre
[illegible]	fig [illegible]5, David McIntyre, fig [illegible], Alanna Lauter
0[illegible]7	fig [illegible], Howard Jones
0[illegible]8	fig [illegible], Howard Jones
0[illegible]9	fig [illegible], lower 2 images, Howard Jones
0[illegible]1	fig [illegible], Howard Jones
0[illegible]5	fig [illegible], Howard Jones
[illegible]3	fig [illegible], David McIntyre
[illegible]6	fig [illegible], David McIntyre
1[illegible]4	fig [illegible], Richard Barnes
1[illegible]7-[illegible]	[illegible]in Robinson
1[illegible]5	fig [illegible], Tony Jin
1[illegible]8	fig [illegible], Albert Padulla
1[illegible]2	fig [illegible], Tony Jin
1[illegible]	Tony Jin
[illegible]2-3	fig [illegible],3, Tony Jin
[illegible]4-5	[illegible]rt Vecerka
[illegible]-9	[illegible]d McIntyre
[illegible]	fig [illegible], Robert Bridges, fig [illegible], Spike Edmiston
[illegible]	fig [illegible], David McIntyre
[illegible]4	fig [illegible], David McIntyre
[illegible]	fig [illegible], David McIntyre
[illegible]	[illegible]d McIntyre
[illegible]	Tony Jin
[illegible]	fig [illegible],7, Robert Bridges
[illegible]	fig [illegible], Robert Bridges
[illegible]	fig 1, Tony Jin
[illegible]	fig [illegible], Andreas Froelich
[illegible]	fig 4, David McIntyre
[illegible]	[illegible]c McIntyre

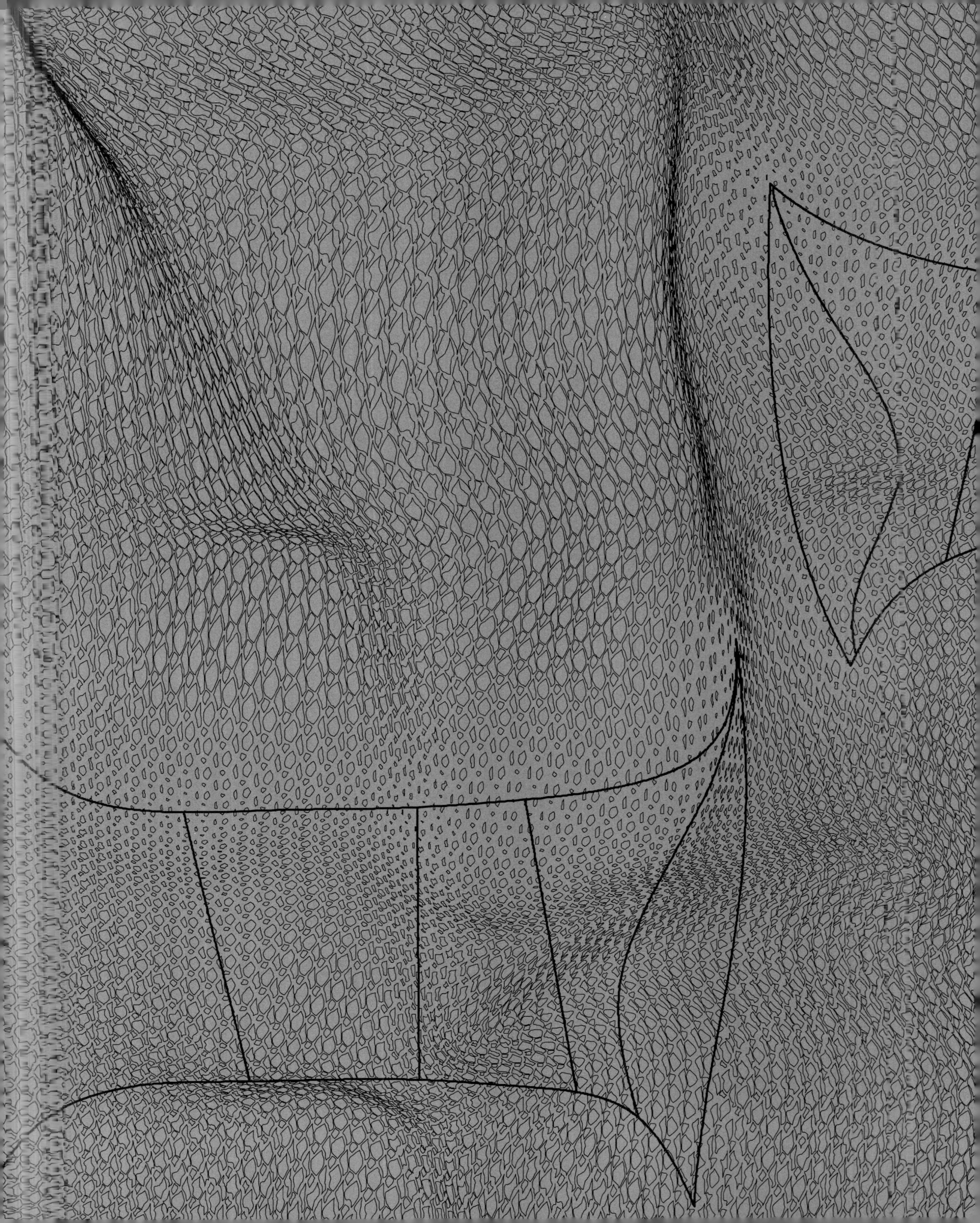

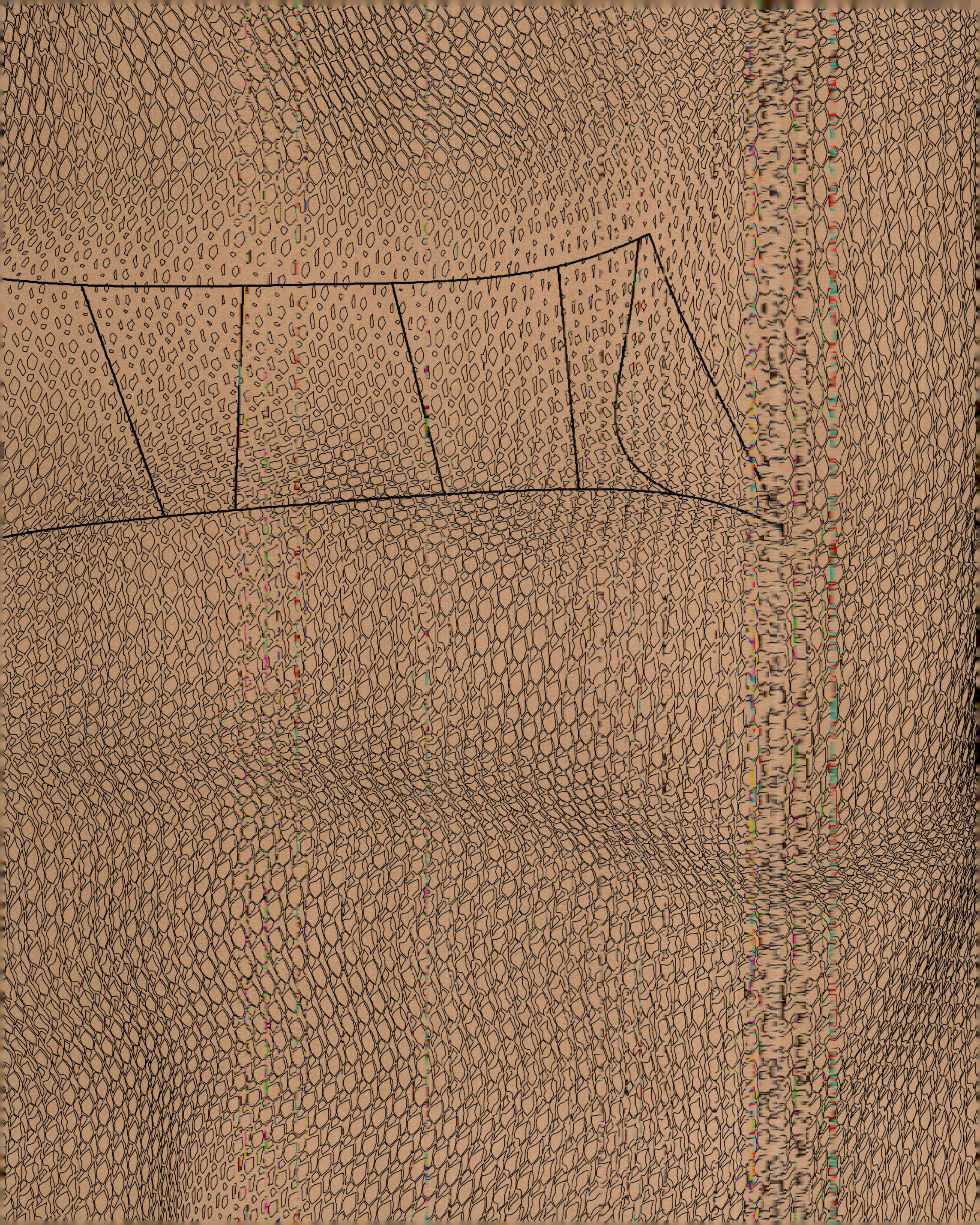

book credits.

Creative direction by Leo Malinow
Copy editing by Brigette Brown

OSCAR RIERA OJEDA
PUBLISHERS

ISBN 978-988-12252-3-8
Published by Oscar Riera Ojeda Publishers Limited
Printed in China by Artron Art Center

Oscar Riera Ojeda Publishers Limited
Unit 6, 22/F.,
Far East Consortium Building,
121 Des Voeux Road Central, Hong Kong
T: +852-5311-1625

Production Offices | China
Suit 19, Shenyun Road,
Nanshan District, Shenzhen 518055
T:+86-182-0098-3774

www.oropublishers.com | www.oscarrieraojeda.com
oscar@oscarrieraojeda.com
